Conceiving a Nation

The New History of Scotland
Series Editor: Jenny Wormald

Original titles in the New History of Scotland series were published in the 1980s and reissued in the 1990s. This popular and enduring series is now being updated with the following published and forthcoming titles:

Vol. 1 *Conceiving a Nation: Scotland to AD 900* by Gilbert Márkus (new volume to replace *Warlords and Holy Men* by Alfred Smyth)

Vol. 2 *The Beginning of Scotland 900–1304* by Dauvit Broun (new volume to replace *Kingship and Unity* by G. W. S. Barrow)

Vol. 3 *Power and Propaganda: Scotland 1306–1488* by Katie Stevenson (new volume to replace *Independence and Nationhood* by Alexander Grant)

Vol. 4 *Court, Kirk, and Community: Scotland 1470–1625* by Jenny Wormald (reissued with new foreword by Keith M. Brown)

Vol. 5 *Union, Revolution and War: Scotland 1625–1745* by Laura Stewart (new volume to replace *Lordship to Patronage* by Rosalind Mitchison)

Vol. 6 *Enlightenment and Change: Scotland 1746–1832* by Bruce P. Lenman (second revised and updated edition of *Integration and Enlightenment*)

Vol. 7 *Ourselves and Others: Scotland 1832–1914* by Graeme Morton (new volume to replace *Industry and Ethos* by Olive and Sydney Checkland)

Vol. 8 *No Gods and Precious Few Heroes: Scotland 1900–2015* by Christopher Harvie (fourth revised and updated edition)

www.edinburghuniversitypress.com/series/nhs

Conceiving a Nation
Scotland to AD 900

Gilbert Márkus

EDINBURGH
University Press

Edinburgh University Press is one of the leading university presses in the UK. We publish academic books and journals in our selected subject areas across the humanities and social sciences, combining cutting-edge scholarship with high editorial and production values to produce academic works of lasting importance. For more information visit our website: edinburghuniversitypress.com

Edinburgh University Press Ltd
The Tun – Holyrood Road
12 (2f) Jackson's Entry
Edinburgh EH8 8PJ

Typeset in 10.5/13 Sabon by
Servis Filmsetting Ltd, Stockport, Cheshire,
and printed and bound in Great Britain by
CPI Group (UK) Ltd, Croydon CR0 4YY

A CIP record for this book is available from the British Library

ISBN 978 0 7486 7898 3 (hardback)
ISBN 978 0 7486 7899 0 (paperback)
ISBN 978 0 7486 7900 3 (webready PDF)
ISBN 978 0 7486 7901 0 (epub)

Contents

Figures

Preface

This book purports to be a 'history of Scotland' until AD 900. It is therefore the history of a country that did not exist. No one living in the territory we now call Scotland during this period would have identified the territory by that name, nor as any single nation. It was an area occupied by many different tribes and nations, all changing constantly. Throughout these centuries, such groups came into existence and disappeared, sometimes independent of each other, sometimes subject to one another, sometimes at war and sometimes in alliance.

For these reasons the word 'Scotland' will not be used in this volume to refer to an early medieval kingdom. It will be used to refer to the territory – the mainland, the islands and the bodies of water – which is called by that name today. The polities that occupied this territory during the centuries covered by this book will be referred to in these pages by their proper names: Damnonii, Gododdin, Dál Riata, Northumbria, Innsi Gall, Pictland, Fortriu, Scotia and so on. None of these can be identified with what we now call 'Scotland'.

APPROACHING THE SOURCES

Our understanding of this period has been transformed in the last twenty or thirty years. This is partly due to increasing archaeological evidence. Aerial photography, for example, has identified large numbers of Iron Age and early medieval Pictish settlements in eastern Scotland, while doubts once expressed about early Christianity in northern Pictland have been decisively laid to rest by Martin Carver's excavation at Portmahomack, which has provided carbon-dating for a monastery there in the sixth century.

Other advances in our understanding have been made because people have begun to read the historical sources in new ways. Scholars are less inclined to trust later medieval sources as evidence for earlier periods. A tenth-century text is certainly historical evidence, but it is evidence for the world view of its tenth-century writer, not for events that took place two or four centuries earlier. We cannot appeal to the idea, once popular, that information was accurately preserved for generations in oral traditions to be faithfully written down by later scribes.

We might add a further reminder: contemporary written records, even those produced by eyewitnesses to the events, were not written with some kind of even-handed objectivity, as a 'view from nowhere'. Their writers had a particular point of view as members of particular communities, with their own interests and enthusiasms. Some were commissioned by secular lords or ecclesiastical authorities who intended these works to offer ideological support for their own purposes. We must therefore be careful in drawing conclusions based on these writers' works, approaching every text in terms of the perceptions and concerns of the author and with an eye to the literary genre in which it was composed. Conversely, this approach opens up to us a new opportunity for study: not the events that the author was writing about, but the world view and mentality of the author himself (or perhaps, very rarely, herself).

As a constant reminder of this approach, each chapter of this book has a title that is a phrase from the Psalms. Following the fall of the Roman Empire in Scotland, almost anyone who could read and write had gone through a course of study whose first stage was to learn the Psalms in Latin by heart. By learning and copying the Psalms, by performing them and meditating on them in a daily round of prayer, almost every literate person passed through a process not only of memorisation, but also of a deeper internalisation. As George Steiner wrote in his essay

Real Presences, 'What we know by heart becomes an agency in our consciousness, a pace-maker in the growth and vital complication of our identity.' If this is true of an individual, how much more for a whole community where one text is known by heart by all its members. The Psalms provided the language, sound and imagery which was the 'pace-maker' for all medieval writers.

THE 'ETHNIC FALLACY'

In the pages that follow we will be exploring processes that take place in a multi-ethnic environment. Romans will conquer, or fail to conquer, Caledonians; Gaels will fight with Norsemen; Picts and Britons will live alongside Angles, and so on. Historians have sometimes oversimplified these stories, as if these were more or less fixed and homogeneous communities engaging with each other. The 'ethnic fallacy' is the view that:

(a) such clear-cut ethnic communities existed as stable and well-defined entities;
(b) a person inherited a single ethnic identity as a given, and lived with it for the rest of his or her life;
(c) people saw their own interests as corresponding to those of others in their own ethnic group and, by implication, as in conflict with those of other ethnic groups.

The ethnic fallacy may seduce the historian into general statements about 'Romans versus Celts' or 'Anglo-Saxons versus Britons' in a vision of the past in which clearly identifiable ethnic groups confront each other. While there are times when it is useful – at least as a kind of shorthand – to refer in these ways to ethnic groups and their interactions, our reading of the past must recognise that reality was rather more complicated.

(a) Ethnicity is a slippery concept, and most people have multiple identities: one can be a Roman and a Caledonian, for example, or a Pict and a Gael. And you may define yourself with one identity in one circumstance, and with another identity in different circumstances.

(b) Ethnic identity is not something you simply inherit. It is constantly created and re-created by individuals and communities. They adopt other languages, burial practices, religious customs and sartorial habits – all of which are ethnic markers. They transfer their loyalties from one overlord to another, and their enemies become their friends.

(c) Very often 'a man's enemies will be those of his own household'. That is to say, shared ethnic identity need not make people allies. Two Anglo-Saxon over-kings going to war against each other, for example, will deploy their own Anglo-Saxon troops, but will also use British warriors from their respective under-kingdoms.

In the light of these aspects of ethnicity and identity our title, *Conceiving a Nation*, becomes a useful *double entendre*. 'Conceiving' works as a metaphor for the origins of what would become Scotland: a process in which separate elements come together to form a new organism. But we are also concerned with 'conceiving' in the sense of forming a mental image. A 'nation' is a concept, an imagined community. A thread running through the following chapters is the question of how people imagined and re-imagined their communities, and how we might try to imagine them now.

THIN ICE

This book seeks to introduce the reader to the stories of different communities that co-existed over several centuries, but there are dangers in trying to create a narrative history. Our evidence is fragmentary and sparse, and though we may be tempted to magnify the significance of one piece of evidence to fill in the gaps in our narrative, we must bear in mind that each piece represents only one moment in a complex history of change, inconsistencies and paradox. It might reflect local conditions in one place which were quite different from those fifty miles away, or from those in the same place fifty years later. I will suggest that there were long-standing cultural traditions that shaped these societies over centuries, but there are limits to the permissibility of such generalisations. I may often be skating on thin ice, evidentially speaking, but such are the risks of writing a history using the limited evidence that we have.

In spite of the fragmentary nature of the evidence, James Fraser and Alex Woolf have written two splendid volumes offering a narrative history of Scotland in the period up to AD 1070. In this book we will therefore seek to complement their work by exploring themes of cultural and social history. The evidence for these is no less problematic – in short supply or difficult to interpret – but it is an approach that is capable of enriching our understanding of Scotland's past.

LANGUAGES

I will refer to various languages spoken by the inhabitants of Scotland. The P-Celtic language of the inhabitants of southern Scotland, is sometimes called Welsh, Old Welsh, Cumbrian or Brythonic. All these names have their advantages, but I will call the language, both in Scotland and further south, in all its different dialects, British – the language spoken by Britons.

The language spoken by the Picts has been the subject of much discussion by historians and philologists. I will call it Pictish, and will discuss in Chapter 2 what kind of language it was.

Throughout our period we see the growth through most of Scotland of the Q-Celtic language, which is ancestral to modern Gaelic. This language is usually referred to by scholars as Old Irish, but that name associates the language with Ireland at the expense of Scotland and lends itself to the idea that Scottish Gaelic was imported from Ireland, which is not necessarily true. I will therefore refer to this language as Gaelic, or Old Gaelic, connecting it to the modern languages that are its descendants in both Ireland and Scotland.

The Germanic language that first had an impact on Scotland in our period may be called Old English, Anglo-Saxon or Northumbrian. I will simply refer to all Germanic languages (other than the Scandinavian speech brought by the Vikings) as Anglo-Saxon. The Germanic language spoken by Scandinavian raiders and settlers, wherever they came from, I will refer to as Old Norse.

All these broad language names disguise a variety of dialects actually spoken at different times and in different areas, but this is not the place to explore the finer distinctions between such dialects.

Non-English words like Latin *limes*, Gaelic *tellach* and Old Norse *setr* will be italicised, as will place names when they are cited in their early forms (e.g., *Catraeth* for Catterick).

When events are assigned a particular date in this book, they will usually be allocated a BC or AD date, often preceded by 'around' or 'circa' (*c.*) to reflect the general elusiveness of precision in our period. Sometimes a date will be preceded by AU (for *Annals of Ulster*) or AT (for *Annals of Tigernach*), reflecting the record of an event in a particular year in a medieval source, or placed in that year by a modern edition of that source. For further discussion of source materials, see p. 279.

Translations of Latin and Gaelic texts are generally my own, but poetry in translation is taken from *The Triumph Tree*, a collection of early medieval Scottish poetry in which the editor, Thomas Owen Clancy, translated the Gaelic material, Joseph Clancy translated the British, I translated the Latin, and Paul Bibere and Judith Jesch translated the Old Norse.

My warm thanks are due to Rachel Butter, Alex Woolf, Thomas Owen Clancy, Dauvit Broun and Simon Taylor, all of whom read parts of – or in some cases all of – an earlier draft of the book; and to Nick Evans, Katherine Forsyth, James Fraser and Guto Rhys for their help in other ways. Finally, I am indebted to Jenny Wormald, the series editor of this New History of Scotland. Over the six years since she asked me to write my volume I have benefited from her bracing and entertaining conversation, her acceptance of my idiosyncratic approach and her sharp insights. I am very sorry not to have finished before she died in December 2015. *Requiescat in pace.*

Places and peoples in Roman Scotland

1

'I will give you nations as your heritage' (Psalm 2:8)

Trade, Culture and Empire in the Early Centuries

Scotland first appears over the horizon of history not in its own records, but in writings from the Mediterranean world. As early as the sixth century BC, traders from Marseilles (*Massilia*) were describing trade routes in a *periplus*, a merchant's guide to coastal ports and trading routes. The original text of the *Massilian Periplus* is lost, but parts of it survive in a Latin poem written in the fourth century AD. It is the earliest surviving record of a network of trade and cultural exchange embracing the Mediterranean and north Atlantic coasts of Europe.

Archaeological evidence shows that by the time the *periplus* was written such networks were already a long-standing feature of life on these coasts, where goods, people and ideas moved freely. The discovery of numerous bronze weapons, as well as tools, buttons and other more mundane objects, has demonstrated trading connections between Scotland and the Continent, as well as with southern parts of Britain and Ireland. A bronze sword found in the River Clyde is a ninth-century BC import from the Continent. Along the southern shores of the Moray Firth and in Aberdeenshire, several finds of bronze goods indicate connections with northwest Germany about 700 BC. In Corrymuckloch in Perthshire, a hoard of bronze objects dated to around 800 BC includes a sword of continental type. In the same hoard a 'ladle' points to a tradition in which food and drink were not merely for the satisfaction of bodily needs, nor even an expression of community cohesion, but provided an opportunity for the display of status. Feasting and drinking were ceremonies of power, and bronze swords are the material remains of a social order that probably pervaded most of Europe: a warrior elite in a hierarchical society exercised power by the exploitation of the labour of peasant farmers, expressing their power by their mastery of bronze weaponry, flaunting it by conspicuous consumption and by the use of luxury goods in social rituals and symbols associated with food and dress. The widespread use of bronze points to a society in which distant communities were connected by trade. Bronze is an alloy of two metals, copper and tin, which do not often occur close to each other in the earth. This means that mines in more or less distant locations must extract their ores and transport their produce to a single place in order to create the alloy. The very existence of bronze, therefore, requires a network of trade, exchange, transport and management. The tin used in Scottish bronze probably came from Cornwall, or perhaps from continental Europe.

Whoever acquired bronze by trade must also have had some form of wealth to give in exchange. The elite swordsmen and feasters of Perthshire must have been able to extract sufficient tribute from their underlings to pay for this metal – though words like 'trade' and 'pay' may be slightly misleading, and exchanges may have included a range of social interactions such as gift exchange, marriage gifts and symbols of political alliances. All these interactions could provide the impetus for the movement of goods around Europe.

Later Classical writers occasionally quote another Massilian called Pytheas, who wrote in the fourth century BC, referring to the island as *Bretannikē*, though some manuscripts represent the name with initial P- suggesting that he may originally have known the island as *Pretania*. Pytheas seems to have recorded Orkney (*Orkas*) in a passage cited by Diodorus (*c.* 30 BC) in which this is one of the three corners of Britain, the other two being *Kantion* (Kent) and *Belerion*, which must refer to Cornwall, where he says that the inhabitants mine and smelt tin, manufacturing ingots which were then transported to the coast of Gaul and from there to the mouth of the River Rhone. These

Cornish tin miners and traders were perhaps among the contacts with whom the Veneti in southern Brittany are recorded
as trading in about 56 BC, when Julius Caesar dealt with these
people. Caesar was impressed by their sea-faring skills and the
quality of their ships, and noted that the Veneti were a maritime
empire, 'holding as tributaries almost all those who are accus-
tomed to traffic in that sea'. Their skill and marine power could
not save them from his army, however, which, after a siege,
slaughtered their leaders and sold the rest of the population
into slavery. In sum, long before the Roman Empire showed
any interest in the island as a target for colonisation, Britain
(including Scotland) was part of a European culture of trade and
exchange. The 'insular' geographical position of Britain did not
make it culturally insular. The island was not separated from the
Continent by water; it was connected to it by water. Seaways
and rivers were, throughout the period discussed in this book,
the most efficient ways of transporting goods, people and ideas.

It was in this period of trade and cultural exchange that the
family of languages that we now call 'Celtic' evolved across a
wide swathe of European territory. It may, indeed, have developed and spread as a language of trading partners along the
coastlines and the great rivers that provided the trade routes
around the Continent. Here, where people brought goods to
exchange, the necessary spoken exchanges were perhaps conducted in a variety of Indo-European dialects out of which grew
the earliest stratum of the Celtic language. The conventional
view is that Celtic developed out of Proto-Indo-European in
west-central Europe, around the headwaters of the Danube, but
some recent scholarship proposes that it first appeared in the
Atlantic zone, the far west of Europe, and spread eastwards.

But this picture represents only a process of language formation. There is also a material culture that is often referred
to as 'Celtic'. Over the last few years scholars have become
more circumspect about the use of this word: if it is used primarily to represent a family of languages (both lost languages
like Lepontic, Gaulish and Pictish, and modern languages
such as Gaelic, Welsh and Breton), we must be careful about

applying it to ancient artefacts. There is a broad correspondence between places where Celtic languages have been spoken and the appearance of 'La Tène' artworks in the archaeological record (a term derived from the name of a place in Switzerland where finds of this style have been found and where Celtic languages were spoken). But the correspondence of language and archaeology is not absolute, and there are places where one is present while the other is absent.

Similarly, there is no precise correspondence between the peoples referred to as *Keltoi* or *Celti* by Classical authors and the groups that we now identify linguistically (from place names and personal names, for example) as Celtic-speaking peoples. Pytheas makes a clear distinction between Celtica and Britain, which he says is several days' sail away. Strabo makes a similar contrast in the first century BC, where he states that 'the whole island of Britain is parallel to and lies over against the whole of Celtica'. We know that the people of Britain spoke a Celtic language, but contemporary geographers did not always regard them as Celts or their lands as part of Celtica. It seems that Roman and Greek writers used the words *Celti* or *Keltoi* in rather vague ways to refer to various peoples with whom they might have had fairly minimal contact. It must also be said that it is unlikely that the Celtic-speaking people of Iron Age Britain and Ireland had any sense of themselves as being 'Celts'. This insight arose much later from a modern understanding of language and its development.

If the extensive trading routes of the European late Bronze Age and Iron Age helped to forge the Proto-Celtic language, and as languages convey not only grammar and vocabulary but also ideas, it would be surprising if the spread of the Celtic language across Europe did not also carry some cultural baggage with it. We might think of the widespread cult of the god Lugus, for example, which appears in Spain in a dedication (in dative case) to *Lvgvei*, and in stories of the god Lugh in Ireland, in the place name *Luguvalium* (Carlisle in Cumbria), and in Lyons, or *Lugdunum*, in France.

The evidence for Celtic language in Scotland and the rest of

Britain during the Iron Age is clear in the place names and personal names recorded by early geographers and Roman chroniclers. We have already encountered the name *Orkas* (Orkney) used by Pytheas (Proto-Celtic *orkos* (related to Latin *porcus*) 'pig, boar', but possibly here referring to 'sea-pigs' or whales. *Pretania* (Britain) has an underlying Proto-Celtic word *kwritu* 'form', the origin of Welsh *pryd* and Gaelic *cruth*, 'form, figure, shape'. It is possible that the Britons or *Pretani* saw themselves as 'the shapely people', or 'the people of shapes', referring to the practice of tattooing their bodies, or perhaps even as 'the shaped ones', that is, those who had been made, distinguished from the gods who shaped them.

As a brief aside here, it is worth pointing out that the derivation of both Welsh *pryd* and Gaelic *cruth* from an original *k^writu* is an instance of an important linguistic development in Insular Celtic (i.e., the Celtic spoken in Ireland and Britain). Very briefly, and at the risk of oversimplifying a more complex process, Insular Celtic subdivided into two families of languages usually referred to as P-Celtic and Q-Celtic. The P-Celtic family includes the ancient British and Pictish languages, and modern Welsh, Cornish and Breton, while Q-Celtic includes Irish and Scottish Gaelic and Manx. The terms Q-Celtic and P-Celtic refer to the fact that an original /k^w/ sound became a /k/ in some areas, and in other areas a /p/. Thus, an original *kwritu*, meaning 'form, shape', gives Gaelic *cruth* and Welsh *pryd*. The same alternation of /k/ and /p/ can be seen in Gaelic *ceann* and Welsh *pen*, both meaning 'head'; Gaelic *mac* and Welsh *map* or *mab*, 'son'.

A Greek-speaking Egyptian, Ptolemy, recorded many place names from Scotland in the mid-second century AD using earlier sources of information, and these also show a strongly Celtic character. He records the name of the Orkneys (*Orcades*), which we have already discussed, and also gives the names of various population groups such as *Selgovae* (proto-Celtic *selg-*, 'hunt'), *Caledonii* (*kaleto-* 'hard'), *Cornavii* (*korno*, 'horn', referring to the horn or promontory of Caithness), *Decantae* (*deko-*, 'good'), and in Kintyre the *Epidii* (*ekwo-*, 'horse'). This last

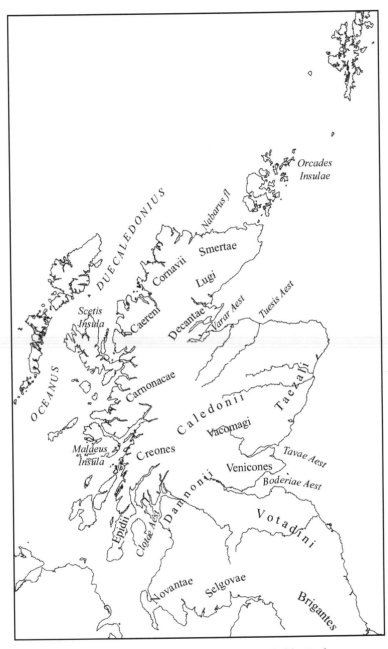

Tribal names and select topographical names recorded by Ptolemy

name looks like a good P-Celtic one, containing *ep(os)*, while a Q-Celtic form would have given *Ekidii* (compare modern Gaelic *each* 'horse'). However, since Ptolemy's name-forms may have been acquired through informants who spoke a P-Celtic language, it is possible that that Kintyre was already an area of Q-Celtic speech, but that Ptolemy recorded it in the form which his informant gave.

ROMANS IN FORCE

This picture of a Celtic-speaking population in Britain, connected to continental trading networks, long precedes the Roman Empire's first military contact with the island. The first confrontations between British warriors and the Roman army took place not in Britain itself but in Gaul, according to Caesar writing on the Gallic War. As Caesar was seeking to impose Roman rule in northern Gaul he found that his opponents, the Veneti, had called on military support from Britain. He adds that 'he sought to advance into Britain, because in almost all the wars with the Gauls he understood that assistance had been given from there to our enemies'. According to Caesar, it was merchants plying between Gaul and Britain who alerted the Britons to the planned Roman advance, whereupon southern British rulers sent ambassadors offering submission to Roman rule and offering hostages to guarantee their compliance. Caesar appointed a certain Commius, whose kingship of the Belgic tribe of the Atrebates he had supported, to go to Britain as an ambassador to persuade the British rulers to accept Roman rule.

Recording his expeditions to Britain in 55 and 54 BC, Caesar noted the constantly shifting responses of the British rulers: sometimes they surrendered, offering hostages and suing for peace, agreeing to pay tribute to Rome as determined by Caesar; at other times, they offered armed resistance and attacked Roman troops. Three sons of Commius appear to have ruled the British Atrebates after him: Tincomarus, Epillus and Verica. These men probably enjoyed some kind of alliance with Rome, even though there were no Roman troops in Britain during their rule.

Two British kings appeared as suppliants before the Emperor Augustus in about AD 7, and are named in his *Res Gestae*, the record of his reign, as 'Dumnobellaunus et Tincommius'. The first of these is probably Dubnovellaunus, who appears elsewhere as ruler of Kent. The second is Tincomarus, son of Commius, ruler of the Atrebates. It is also notable that some of the coins of Tincomarus' brother Eppilus bore the Latin title REX, 'king'. His brother, Verica (AD 15–40) also minted coins in the Roman style: a fine gold stater declares him to be *Commi[i] F[ilius]*, 'son of Commius' on one side, and REX on the other. The style of the coins and the use of the Latin title REX might be understood to reflect the status of these kings as Roman clients, though this is not certain; in any case, they were certainly adopting the symbols of Roman culture and power.

In favour of the view that Verica was a client of Rome – as was his father, Commius, before him – is the story recounted by Cassius Dio (d. AD 235) that a British king by the name of Berikos had been driven out of his kingdom and came to Rome seeking military help to recover it. It is likely that Dio's Berikos is Verica, who had been ousted by Caratacus and Togodumnus, two brothers of the neighbouring Catuvellauni. The fact that Verica was seeking Roman military support in this way suggests that there was a treaty between Rome and the Atrebates. In any case, Verica's request for support is what prompted the Emperor Claudius to send an invasion force to Britain in AD 43.

It might seem strange in a history of Scotland to rehearse such details of the Romanisation of one tribe in southeast England, but this story illustrates some of the subtlety and complexity of Roman expansion. Military confrontation would often be preceded by mercantile or other contacts, and these could be used for gathering intelligence about a new territory and also as a means of forging diplomatic links with local leaders. It shows that native Celtic rulers might be allies of Rome or opponents. They may have acquired their power over their own people by virtue of their resistance to Rome, or by collaboration and subsequent Roman support or by both at different times. Rome formed alliances well beyond the frontiers of her imperial territory, making and unmaking kings, entering into treaties, and thereby extending her influence into areas which were not formally part of the Empire.

The story of the Atrebates shows how the appearance of the Roman army in a new territory generated both fear and desire. On the one hand, there was fear of Rome's overwhelming military and economic power, and fear of the burdens of taxation or tribute, enslavement and of the recruitment of young men into the army which might ensue; there may also have been fear of the corrosive effect of this overwhelming political force on the complex networks of kinship and mutual obligation which were the foundation of native political life. On the other hand, there was desire for the advantage that Roman political support might bring to its clients and allies, and desire for the prestige goods (silver, gold, wine) which came in its wake and which were becoming essential elements of a ruler's expression of his own status and power. Each native ruler, with the elite decision-makers of his people, had to negotiate between these fears and desires, making choices which seemed most likely to minimise the threats and maximise the opportunities created by Rome.

There is no reliable account in any source, Roman, Greek or native, which gives any such detail of the Roman advent in Scotland, but we should keep this pattern in mind when we consider the Roman impact on Scotland in later years. The image of a blindly aggressive Roman Empire advancing by sheer military force and swallowing up universally reluctant native societies is not a helpful one. The leaders of native societies were agents in this process – albeit agents with markedly less power – assessing their new situation and improvising with the means available to them to obtain advantageous outcomes. The rulers of the tribes of northern Britain can hardly have been unaware of the early encroachment of Roman military power in southern Britain. They will already have begun to consider their own responses to this process, and to consider their options.

Apart from the appeal made to Claudius by the ousted Atrebatan king, Verica, there may have been a number of other factors involved in the emperor's decision to launch his invasion in AD 43. There was, of course, the natural tendency of empire to expand its boundaries – 'wider, still, and wider, shall thy bounds be set', as was sung of a much later empire. Acquisition of territory and peoples, exploitation of their wealth and resources, was always a prime consideration. But Britain was not initially regarded as the richest new territory that the Romans might have sought. Indeed, Cicero had written to his good friend Atticus in 54 BC that, 'It has become clear that there isn't an ounce of silver in the island, nor any prospect of booty except for slaves'. But shortly afterwards Strabo had a more positive estimate of the likely profitability of a British invasion, pointing out that Caesar had obtained 'slaves, hostages and other booty', and noting that several British kings were seeking the friendship of Caesar Augustus. Among the products of Britain Strabo lists are 'grain, cattle, gold, silver, and iron. These things, accordingly, are exported from the island, as also hides, slaves, and dogs that are by nature suited to the purposes of the chase.' Likewise, Tacitus' *Agricola*, towards the end of the first century, lists 'gold and silver and other metals, as the prize of conquest', along with 'pearls, though of a dusky and bluish hue'. It seems that in the decades following Caesar's adventure, during which there had been direct contact between Britain and Rome, the view of the island had changed. Certainly, by AD 43 the Romans had a more positive view of Britain's likely profitability as a new colony, worth the investment of a full invasion.

In addition to economic considerations, Rome must have considered the security of the empire. Like any other polity of the time, it had enemies on every boundary. There were two possible responses to security threats from those outside the empire: one was to create defensive boundaries and keep the enemy out; the other was to expand continually and to neutralise the enemy's threat by incorporating their land and people into the area of control. In Britain, at least at this time, the policy seems to have been to pursue the latter option as far as possible.

We should also consider Claudius' personal motives. His predecessor and nephew, Gaius Caligula, had been killed by the Praetorian Guard in Rome in AD 41, and within hours they had adopted Claudius as his successor. He was a surprise choice: physically disabled, he was widely regarded – though wrongly – as suffering from a mental disability, and he belonged to an imperial family whose reputation had been badly damaged by Caligula's years of misrule. For such reasons as these his rule was not secure, and there had been an abortive coup against him by the governor of Dalmatia in AD 42 – a move that had received some support in the Roman senate. Simply in order to survive, Claudius had to act decisively, to show himself worthy to rule the empire, and to show the army that had brought him to power that he would support their interests. An invasion of Britain would serve these purposes very well.

Four Roman legions sailed to Britain in AD 43, each containing a nominal force of 5,000 professional soldiers, mostly Roman citizens, highly trained, and well equipped with personal armour and weaponry and the back-up of specialist troops and equipment such as catapults. Along with these came about 20,000 auxiliaries, mostly at this stage drawn from *peregrini*, non-citizen subjects of the empire from the provinces occupied by Rome, many of them probably Celtic-speakers.

This massive, disciplined, well-equipped force, with its complex administration, its written communications and its efficient organisation of supply, fort construction and bridge building, had an overwhelming impact on the Britons who were, apart from a small elite, 'farmers under arms' rather than warriors. For the most part they lacked armour, they had nothing like the command-and-support structures of a large army, and they lacked the material resources to undertake long-term warfare away from their lands, livestock and harvests. We should also note that different groups of Britons often had very different political intentions and different relationships with the empire, and so were as likely to fight each other as to join in common cause against Rome. Many of the British elite, looking across the Channel to Gaul and seeing the lifestyle of some of their Gaulish peers who were already living in villas and enjoying public office and wealth under Roman rule, will have hoped to share in such benefits. For this reason, many Britons in the 40s and beyond were brought under Roman rule not by force, but by negotiation and treaty. A triumphal arch erected in Rome in AD 51 commemorates Claudius' British victories. A reconstructed text derived from the badly damaged inscription indicates that he accepted the surrender of eleven British kings who were 'subdued without any losses'. The reconstruction is hypothetical but scholarly; its general drift is confirmed by Suetonius' *Life of the Caesars* written in the 120s or 130s, which claims that Claudius 'without any battle or bloodshed, received the submission of part of the island, and returned to Rome within six months of leaving the city, and celebrated a triumph of great splendour'.

In spite of their material and organisational disadvantages, the Britons were still able at times to mount an effective resistance to the Roman invasion, and some – especially the Catuvellauni on the north side of the River Thames – paid a high price for their resistance. Claudius himself came to Britain in support of his troops, bringing reinforcements (including elephants) and taking formal command of the army. Hailed several times as *imperator* by his troops, Claudius' conquest of the southern part of Britain was more or less complete by AD 47, while initial encounters with peoples further north also began. It may seem far-fetched, but in the late first or early second century the Roman poet Juvenal declared that the Romans 'have recently advanced our arms beyond the shores of Ireland and the recently conquered Orkneys'. The fourth-century historian Eutropius also claims that Claudius added the Orkneys to the empire. We should not take these claims at face value; Ireland and the Orkneys were highly symbolic as the limits of the known habitable world. But the fact is that Roman pottery of a type that went out of production about AD 60 has been found at the broch of Gurness in Orkney, suggesting some kind of contact at a very early stage of the conquest.

There would be various revolts and acts of resistance against continuing Roman advance, but these need to be understood as examples of the constant improvisation by native leaders that we have already mentioned, rather than a simple and continuous rejection of Roman rule. For example, as Tacitus tells the story some decades later, the Iceni in what is now East Anglia appear to have sided with the Romans during the invasion of AD 43, but on the death of their ruler Prasutagus, following excessive Roman demands, his widow Boudica led a rebellion in AD 60 or 61 which caused huge Roman losses – 70,000 dead according to Tacitus. The resistance was finally crushed with the slaughter of 80,000 Britons. In spite of such disasters, Roman consolidation continued and the area occupied grew, with most of Britain south of the Humber, even including Cornwall and parts of Wales being occupied by the 60s.

To the north, the Brigantes, occupying a huge area, roughly between the Humber and the Solway Firth, entered into a treaty with Rome as a client kingdom. It was an unstable situation, however, and internal political tensions among the Brigantes led to conflict with Rome in the 50s, with hostilities continuing until AD 71 when Petillius Cerialis was made governor and, with the Ninth Legion (*Hispana*), crushed Brigantian resistance east of the Pennines, erecting a fort at York. This fort would remain for centuries the most important Roman base in the north of Britain. Meanwhile Julius Agricola commanded the Twentieth Legion (*Valeria Victrix*) as it moved north through Brigantian territory on the west side of the Pennines and built a fort at Carlisle. Dendrochronology shows that the timber used to build the Carlisle fort was felled in AD 72.

It is actually possible that Roman forces had already penetrated into Scotland by the early 70s. Cerialis' predecessor as governor, Vettius Bolanus (AD 69–71), was commemorated in a poem by Statius which rejoiced that his glory 'exalted Caledonia's plains', and described natives there pointing out the place where he had administered justice. This may owe something to literary invention, but it is suggestive of early Roman activity in Scotland, and, as we shall see in due course, there is also archaeological evidence of a Roman presence in Scotland in the late 60s or early 70s.

But the first clear account of Roman penetration into Scotland in anything other than a scouting or exploratory expedition comes with the return to Britain of Julius Agricola, now appointed as governor. We owe our picture of his governorship to the Roman writer Tacitus and his book *Agricola*, especially for its description of his hero's campaigns in the north to conquer Caledonia. For Tacitus, writing in about AD 98, 'Caledonia' is the name of 'a large and irregular tract of land which juts out from Britain's furthest shores, tapering off in a wedge-like form'. The 'furthest shores' envisaged here are probably the southern banks of the Firths of Clyde and Forth. 'Caledonia' in Tacitus' mental map is therefore all of Scotland to the north of that line.

As Tacitus' *Agricola* is the only detailed account of Roman activity in Scotland in the first century, and much of what we think we know about Scotland in the first century is drawn from it, we will consider it at some length. But we must read it with caution. Tacitus was Agricola's son-in-law, and his work is clearly intended to promote Agricola's reputation as a man of integrity and courage, an honest political and military figure in a dishonest age, and a conquering hero of new territory for Rome. Agricola had served the empire during the reign of Domitian (AD 81–96), and Tacitus wanted to show that his father-in-law's integrity was not compromised by having served an emperor now regarded as despotic and corrupt. Tacitus also sought to promote a particular political view, criticising the tyranny of emperors and their violence against the organs of state, which corroded the virtues of the Roman people. At the beginning of *Agricola* he declares that 'as a former age saw the utmost freedom, so we have seen the depths of servitude'. Reading Tacitus' work, therefore, we meet Julius Agricola as a symbol of all that was good about Roman values and virtues.

Tacitus describes Agricola's arrival in Britain in midsummer in AD 77, or perhaps 78, and his rapid and successful military action in north Wales. He appears as both a military commander and an ideal governor, manifesting justice and political good sense, moderating taxation, judging fairly and mercifully, administering his territory honestly and abolishing oppressive practices by Roman officials. Tacitus also remarks on Romanisation as a cultural process encouraged by Agricola: city building, erecting schools for the sons of British chiefs, erecting temples and public buildings as well as private houses. Tacitus says that Britons who had formerly hated and feared *Romanitas* began to long for Latin eloquence and took to wearing the toga. The conquest of British tribes is presented as a process designed not to annihilate or enslave them, but rather to convert each tribal elite into the ruling class of a Roman *civitas*, incorporating them into the wider *Pax Romana*. Their identity would in theory not be lost, but transformed, 'rebranded' under Rome.

In his third year of campaigning, Agricola pressed north, encountering new peoples and building forts in their territories, marching as far north as an estuary called the *Taus* – probably the Firth of Tay. The following season he 'secured what he had overrun', building a line of forts from the Clyde (*Clota*) to the Forth (*Bodotria*), 'two estuaries separated by a narrow space of land'. All the territory to the south of this line, Tacitus says, was now occupied by Rome, while the enemy to the north was 'driven back as if into another island'. If this northern territory is to be understood as the 'large and irregular tract' that Tacitus has already referred to as the territory of Caledonia, it confirms the idea that Caledonia stretched down as far as the Forth–Clyde line in Tacitus' mental map. The image deployed by Tacitus here is of an early frontier: enemies to the north and Roman-occupied land to the south, separated by a line of forts or guard posts (*praesidia*).

In the fifth year of his governorship, Agricola sailed across an un-named stretch of water and in a series of successful battles subdued various groups (*gentes*) who, until that point, had been unknown. This may have been an expedition into modern Argyll, crossing the Firth of Clyde, or perhaps to Galloway, sailing across the Solway. It was, however, on the west coast, since Tacitus records that the governor posted troops there looking towards Ireland, in the hope of conquering that island. Agricola also gave signs of friendship to a minor king (*regulus*) from Ireland who had been driven into exile in Britain by 'domestic sedition'. Agricola presumably hoped that when an opportunity arose this Irishman might return to power with Roman support as a client-king and so provide a Roman toe-hold in Ireland.

In his sixth year Agricola moved northwards and eastwards

again, beyond the Forth (*trans Bodotriam*), fearing a general movement of the tribes there. Sending the Roman fleet ahead to prey on coastal areas, he pushed north with infantry and cavalry and found that the people of Caledonia were indeed preparing for war. Dividing his own troops into three divisions, he advanced. At this point the Ninth Legion (*Hispana*) was nearly defeated by a night-time attack, and were saved only by the arrival of reinforcements from Agricola's other troops.

In Tacitus' account Agricola's army then decided to fight their way through the depths of Caledonia to discover the furthest limit of Britain, advancing as far as a mountain that he calls *Mons Graupius*. Meanwhile the enemy – Tacitus calls them *Britanni* rather than *Caledonii* – 'in assemblies and with sacrifices, formed a sworn confederacy of their tribes' (*conspirationem civitatum*). More than 30,000 of them had already come together according to Tacitus, and among the many leaders one outstanding man, Calgacus, made a stirring speech to the massed warriors of Britons, while Agricola made a corresponding speech of encouragement to his own troops.

The speech attributed to Calgacus contains a number of interesting themes. First he sees himself as addressing a host whose valour in battle will mark 'the beginning of freedom for the whole of Britain' (*initium libertatis totius Britanniae*). The people of Caledonia are in this view simply the Britons who remain unconquered. He goes on to describe the greed of the Romans, 'robbers of the world' who plunder the rich and oppress the poor:

> They call it 'empire' (*imperium*) to steal, to kill and to despoil by false claims; and where they make a desert they call it 'peace'.

He warns that men's families will be taken away into slavery, their women dishonoured, their wealth taken in tribute, their harvests seized, and their very hands and bodies will be forced to labour 'under blows and insults' building fortifications in forests and marshes. He calls on the assembled Britons to choose: 'on one side you have a general and an army; on the other you have tribute, the mines, and all the other sorrows of slaves'.

Tacitus then relates Agricola's speech to his men, and the course of the dreadful battle, culminating in his description of the slaughter of the Caledonians. 'Then, indeed, in the open plain was an awful and cruel spectacle. Our men pursued, wounded and captured them, only to kill them when they came across others.' The Britons fled the field in terror and 'everywhere were weapons and bodies and wounded limbs, the earth drenched in blood'. Three hundred and sixty Roman soldiers fell, while 10,000 Britons were slain. After the battle, as the summer campaigning season was over, Agricola decided to return south to his winter quarters. At the same time, he ordered his fleet to sail around the entire island, terrifying those whom it approached, while he himself marched slowly south with his infantry and cavalry. On the way he took hostages from a tribe called the *Borestii* – their location is not known and they are not shown on Ptolemy's map.

The battle of *Mons Graupius* is the climax of Tacitus' book, dramatic and powerful writing. But we must remember that Tacitus had his own ideological and personal commitments, and was not an impartial observer. Indeed, he was not an observer of any sort, but a creative writer using other men's reports of events that had happened many years earlier and many miles away. Scholars have often sought to identify the site of *Mons Graupius*, but there is no agreement on the matter. It must lie north of the Forth if Tacitus' account is to be trusted, and the presence of a line of Roman temporary camps of the Flavian period (AD 69–96) running north from Strathcathro through Aberdeenshire and up to the Moray Firth, almost as far as Inverness, may indicate the movement of Agricola's troops in this campaign. Some, however, have denied the existence of *Mons Graupius*, suggesting that it is a literary device of Tacitus, while the great definitive battle may also be an invention (or the exaggeration of a minor battle) designed to portray Agricola as a latter-day Julius Caesar, a brilliant commander, a great conqueror and a worthy hero of the empire. While there is little doubt that battles took place during Agricola's invasion of Scotland, we cannot place too much weight on Tacitus' narrative of one great climactic conflict.

The speech attributed to Calgacus is magnificent and has become a central text in the popular imagination of early Scottish history, but it is a literary composition by Tacitus. The purpose of the speech is to heighten the narrative of the battle and to show the bravery and warlike character of Agricola's enemies; there would be no glory in defeating an army of Caledonian cowards, though, in fact, elsewhere Tacitus' Agricola does accuse them of cowardice, of being 'spiritless and fearful'. Tacitus may also be understood to have had an ideological purpose in his sympathetic account of Calgacus' speech. It is a speech of fiery defiance against enslavement, the loss of freedom, the humiliation of forced labour and the impoverishment which tribute to the Romans would bring. The moral contrast between the Caledonian Britons and the Romans in Tacitus' mind is important: here, at the end of the world, these barbarians value their freedom and are prepared to fight and die for it, while under the reign of despotic emperors such as Domitian the integrity and love of freedom of the Roman people had seeped away.

Tacitus does show, by the speech given to Calgacus, a real sympathy with the vanquished, an understanding of why they might resist what Rome had to offer, allowing the Caledonian leader to express what must have been the experience of many native peoples in newly conquered Roman territories. Slavery, for example, is a key issue. After a Roman attack, survivors were taken away as slaves. Of course the soldiers themselves would not abandon their legion to take prisoners to a slave-market. There were merchants among the civilian hangers-on who travelled with the troops, ready to buy captives and take them to market. Caesar describes the aftermath of his siege of Alesia in Gaul in 58 BC, when 53,000 Gauls were sold into slavery; 'this number was given by those who bought them' (*ab iis qui emerant*), presumably the traders. The capture of men and women as slaves was a significant part of the economics of warfare as the Roman Empire expanded, and was also an important part of the frontier economy. The huge population of slaves (estimates for the late Roman Empire's slave population cluster around the 4–6 million mark) had to be maintained –

slaves were mortal, and dead slaves had to be replaced, while some owners freed their slaves after years of service. It has been calculated that the empire required more than 250,000 new slaves every year simply to keep the population of slaves at a steady level. Many of these would be *vernae*, people born into slavery. But the frontiers of the empire acted as a sort of pump, sucking new men and women into the servile state on which Rome depended. Some of these slaves were captured by Roman troops during engagement with enemies, but the presence of the Roman army on a frontier also created a local market for slaves captured by others. Tribes outside the *limes*, already familiar with slave-raiding on their own account, now sought to profit from the trade opportunity on the frontier by increasing their raids and selling their captives to Roman traders.

Calgacus is also made to rage against the prospect of taxation. One can understand that conquered peoples might resent in principle being taxed to pay for the cost of their occupation by foreigners. But the effects of taxation could also be crushing, and its administration inevitably led to over-enthusiastic tax collectors and to oppression. Tacitus records in his *Annals* that in AD 28 excessive taxation in Frisia led to the people losing their livestock and their lands. Finally, when they were forced to sell even their wives and children into slavery to pay the tax, the Frisians revolted, with significant losses to Rome. This may be an extreme example, but it is an extreme example of a more general pattern.

We have relied heavily in the past on Tacitus' account, partly because there is no other comparable historical source, but we have seen that there are reasons to doubt its accuracy. Archaeology provides other reasons to doubt it, as Liverpool University's archaeologists in the Gask Ridge Project have found. First, as we have seen, Tacitus portrays Agricola's frontier as running along the Forth–Clyde isthmus. But the strongest evidence for a *limes* in Agricola's time is the archaeology of military installations further north. It consists of two broad elements: one is a line of forts, fortlets and watchtowers along what is known as the Gask Ridge; the second is a much longer line of installations running parallel to and northwest of the Gask Ridge, more or less coast-to-coast, from Barochan in Renfrewshire in the southwest, then mostly along the Highland Line from Drumquhassle near Loch Lomond to Strathcathro in the northwest. Many sites on this second line are known as 'glenblocker' forts, named for their position at the bottom of glens running north into the Highlands, while one is the great legionary fortress at Inchtuthil. The two linear features are seen as interdependent elements of a complex of military control. The 'glenblocker' forts were too small to resist an organised attack from the north, but they must have had a role in policing, and perhaps as stations to support troops carrying out military operations in Highland territory.

The archaeological evidence coming from these military posts suggests that they were occupied for considerably longer than the three or four years between Agricola's invasion and the sudden withdrawal of troops in AD 86 or 87. Some were rebuilt and developed over their lifetimes: Cargill shows evidence of as many as six separate stages of reconstruction, indicating a longer period of occupation than that implied by Tacitus. He sought to present Agricola as the conqueror of new barbarian territory

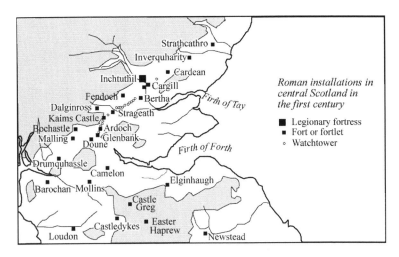

The Flavian frontier

hitherto unoccupied by Rome, but if these military installations were abandoned in AD 86 or 87 as coin evidence indicates, and if the evidence of rebuilding suggests a longer occupation than three or four years, then we must suppose that many of these installations were established before Agricola's arrival, before his crossing of the Forth in his sixth season (AD 81 or 82).

Tacitus' portrait of Agricola as the conqueror of new territory is also called into question by the presence of pottery from the reigns of Nero (d. AD 68) and Vespasian (AD 69–79) as far north as Strageath on the Gask Ridge, suggesting a pre-Agricolan Roman establishment here. There are also a number of coins in Scotland from the reigns of Nero and Vespasian, some of which were hardly worn when lost, suggesting that they were lost in the late 60s or the 70s. All this points strongly towards a Roman presence in Scotland before Agricola arrived.

Having cast doubt on some details of Tacitus' narrative, we might consider it in a more general way. He portrays the encounter between Roman forces and native peoples in Scotland as almost always hostile, but if the Roman presence in first-century Scotland is longer than the short period described by Tacitus, we might doubt this. A period of several years of Roman occupation would normally imply some degree of native collaboration. As we have seen in Gaul and southern Britain, the pattern of Roman advance was conducted by a combination of military and diplomatic means. Some evidence in Scotland also points towards various *civitates* having entered into alliance with Rome at an early stage: the Votadini may have been one of the first. A treaty might explain why there are no Roman forts or camps, and no Roman road, in their territory east of the Roman road whose route is followed by the modern A68. This road may in fact have run along the western boundary of Votadini territory and been a protection for them. Likewise, there is little evidence of Flavian occupation in Fife, perhaps because the tribe or *civitas* that occupied Fife, apparently known to Ptolemy as the *Venicones*, had a treaty with Rome which protected them from military occupation. Tacitus reports that the *Borestii*, somewhere south of *Mons Graupius*, gave hostages to Agricola, which suggests that they too had made a treaty of some sort.

Archaeology on the Gask Ridge also suggests that Romans and native people sometimes achieved a stable *modus vivendi* in the Flavian period. Pollen evidence shows that the area was almost treeless when the Romans arrived, indicating an agricultural and settled society of farmers. But the same evidence also shows that farming intensified during the occupation. If the Roman–native encounter had been universally hostile, farmers would have fled, or at least had their production disrupted. The intensification of farming activity indicates that farmers stayed put and increased their productivity. This is best explained by the development, as usually happened in the areas around Roman garrisons and settlements, of a new market in which local people supplied produce to Roman troops, requiring a degree of collaboration and trust between Roman and native communities.

There are also numerous Iron Age native settlement sites in the areas of Roman occupation. These are mostly isolated farmsteads rather than villages, and they are largely undefended, suggesting that a peaceful agricultural life was possible in these areas. Much more archaeological investigation of these settlements is needed, but evidence is emerging of Roman–native liaisons. At East Coldoch near the Roman fort at Doune a large roundhouse contained a quantity of Roman pottery and bottle-glass, reminding us that wine-drinking was one of Rome's great gifts to northern Europe. There is also evidence of wheaten bread being eaten at East Coldoch, but pollen evidence indicates that no wheat was being grown in the area, which suggests that grain or flour was being imported from elsewhere in some kind of trade system.

The Iron Age settlements built close to Roman military installations suggest that native people were attracted to these places. They might have been traders or members of local elites who found an advantage in living close to Romans, or craftsmen or the owners of prostitutes selling their services to Roman troops. In the same way, features known as 'souterrains', underground constructions that probably served as food storage facilities, are often found close to Roman sites. Were these the infrastructure of a farming community whose agricultural surplus was stored underground until being sold to Roman soldiers and merchants? There are other possible interpretations of the evidence, but these are at least serious possibilities, and correspond to patterns of collaboration between native and Roman that we find in Gaul and southern Britain.

AGRICOLA AND PTOLEMY

If Tacitus' story offers rather shaky evidence, perhaps we can get a clearer picture from Ptolemy's map mentioned above. He composed it in the mid-second century, but depended on earlier sources that may ultimately derive, at least in part, from surveys conducted during Agricola's military operations in Scotland. The marching troops and fleet will have recorded information that they regarded as potentially useful for subsequent Roman operations in Britain: the topography of the island, the names of its population groups, the locations of their power centres. All these appear on Ptolemy's map.

One striking feature of the map is the contrast between the distribution of two groups of names. One group consists of coastal and tribal names, and they are fairly evenly distributed around the country. The other group is the names of *poleis* 'cities', that is, settlements (which may be native power centres or Roman installations, or both), which are mostly limited to the southern half, lying south of a line between the Firth of Tay (*Tavae Aest*) and Loch Long (*Lemannonius Sinus*), though three are shown in the northeast. This imbalance between the two groups of names may reflect the modes of collection during the Agricolan campaign. The tribal and coastal names are those that could have been collected fairly easily by the fleet that Agricola sent out during the *Mons Graupius* campaign when it sailed all round Scotland without collecting detailed knowledge of the local people. The names of settlements, power centres and forts are a different matter, however. To identify and map them would require some familiarity with the landscape, the

settlements and the routes between them. The distribution of
the *poleis* on Ptolemy's map coincides with those areas where
Romans had 'boots on the ground', military installations and
regular contact with native Britons – mostly south of the Gask
Ridge line, but some in the northeast of the country whose data
may have been obtained during Agricola's expedition to *Mons
Graupius*.

Ptolemy's map also gives us, in a way that Tacitus' *Agricola*
does not, a picture of the political geography of Scotland in
the first century. Tacitus names only one tribe in Scotland: the
Borestii. He names *Caledonia* as a territory – the land north
of the Forth–Clyde isthmus – but does not name the people
as *Caledonii*. Ptolemy, on the other hand, names fourteen or
fifteen *poleis* in Scotland, from the *Cornavii* in the far north to
the *Brigantes* in the south whose territory, mostly in northern
England, may have extended into southern Scotland as suggested
by a sculpture of their patron goddess, Brigantia, at the Roman
fort of Birrens, though this may have been erected by Brigantian
troops from further south serving at Birrens. Some of Ptolemy's
names find echoes in place names and tribal names that occur
again centuries later. The name *Votadini* reappears as *Guotodin*
in the ninth-century *Historia Brittonum*, and as *Y Gododdin* in
an Old Welsh poem of that name. The *Caledonii*, the people of
Caledonia, appear in Perthshire, and their name survives there
in Dunkeld, 'fort of the Caledonians' (or 'of Caledonia'), and in
Schiehallion, 'fairy hill of the Caledonians'. These modern place
names represent survivals of the territory known to Tacitus as
Caledonia.

Although Ptolemy's coordinates seem to locate the *Caledonii*
in Perthshire, and modern place names seem to confirm this location, it seems likely that the name also had a wider application.
The sea on the west coast of Scotland, far from the core territory
of the *Caledonii*, is called *Oceanus Duecaledonius* by Ptolemy,
and we may recall that for Tacitus Caledonia was the name of all
the territory to the north of the Forth–Clyde isthmus. Subsequent
Roman writers would also treat Caledonia as the name of a
much larger territory than that of any particular tribal group.

Cassius Dio, in his florid descriptions of barbarian Britons, refers to the Caledonians (Καληδόνιοι) as one of two British tribes, the other being the Maeatae (Μαιάται), adding that 'the names of the others have, so to speak, been merged in them'. The testimony of Tacitus, Ptolemy and Dio suggests two ways of using the name *Caledonii*: one refers to a particular tribe, another to a federation of tribes, perhaps under Caledonian leadership. Agricola's invasion may actually have been the cause of the formation of this federation; as we have seen, Tacitus says that these *Britanni* 'formed a sworn confederacy of their tribes' to resist the Roman invasion. Ptolemy's map may therefore show some of the tribes who belonged to this federation: *Vacomagi*, *Venicones* and *Taezali* in the east, and the *Epidii*, *Creones* and *Carnonacae* in the west, though they were separated from the presumed eastern theatre of war by the mountains of Drumalban. Even the tribes further north might have been involved.

AFTER AGRICOLA

In his *Histories* Tacitus portrays the recall of Agricola from Britain by the Roman Emperor Domitian as a disaster, stating that 'Britain was conquered and immediately given up'. The claim fits well with his ideological agenda – the praise of Agricola and the damnation of Domitian – but it is overstated. Britain was never conquered in the simple way that Tacitus suggests, nor was it lost as a province after Agricola's recall. But there was a significant Roman withdrawal from northern Britain shortly afterwards. The Gask Ridge complex and its associated frontier positions were abandoned. The legionary fortress of Inchtuthil, whose construction may have started around AD 84, was never completed. In AD 86 or 87, it was not only abandoned, but was systematically dismantled. Its abandonment can be dated by the appearance at the site of several coins of AD 86, many of which have suffered little wear indicating that they were fairly new when they were lost, and by the absence of coins of AD 87.

The destruction of the Roman forts of lowland Scotland, and the gradual withdrawal of troops to the Tyne–Solway line, was not the result of local hostilities. The archaeology shows a careful decommissioning as the Roman military pulled southwards, and it was primarily the consequence of events more than a thousand miles away. On the eastern frontier on the River Danube, the Roman Empire had suffered serious military defeats in the mid-80s at the hands of the Dacian kingdom. This frontier lay far closer to the heartlands of the empire than did the Scottish lowlands, and its defence was therefore more urgent. The Second Legion (*Adiutrix*) stationed at Chester was quickly sent to defend the eastern front, while the Twentieth Legion, which had served in Scotland under Agricola, was withdrawn further south. While this meant loss of territory in the north, it meant that the Roman presence and authority further south could be consolidated, preventing disturbance among the recently conquered Brigantes and others.

Further crises on the Danube in AD 101–2 and AD 105–6 may have intensified the impetus for withdrawal. For the following decades the Tyne–Solway line became the effective frontier formed by a Roman road, the 'Stanegate', which had probably been built in Agricola's time. It was now strengthened at various points and in some places (Corbridge and Carlisle) older forts were demolished around AD 103, and new forts built on the sites within a short time.

From AD 87 there is something of a gap in the evidence for Roman Scotland until the beginning of the reign of Hadrian, Trajan's cousin and successor (117–38). It seems that during their reigns Rome's expansion came to a halt and the challenge of barbarian neighbours was now met not by invading and conquering them, but by excluding them, or at least by controlling their access to Roman provinces, by creating *limites*, defended frontiers which would demarcate the areas of direct Roman control and help to defend those areas against attack from outside. This happened in northern Britain along the Tyne–Solway line, but also in Germany where the River Rhine functioned as a natural *limes*, separating Roman territory from *Germania Libra*. In the far southeast of the empire at the same time the *limes Arabicus* was developed as a series of forts and watchtowers along a line some 930 miles long, together with a road of 267 miles built by Trajan and developed by Hadrian. Hadrian spent many years of his rule away from Rome, travelling the provinces – including Britannia – and strengthening these *limites*.

It may be that this early second-century halt to imperial expansion was unavoidable, that having extended her authority over such a vast area Rome's military and administrative abilities had reached a natural limit, and that this limit was reinforced by particular local difficulties (by the 'forests and marshes' of Caledonia and Germania, for example, or by the deserts of Arabia) which made further expansion too difficult to contemplate. But the creation of such *limites* could only give rise to a new kind of problem for Rome. By creating militarised frontiers instead of conquering her neighbours, Rome displayed to them the wealth and sophistication of the empire, but at the same time restricted their access – creating desire while simultaneously frustrating it. The 'barbarian' neighbours across the frontiers would now have plenty of time to learn about Roman arms and to develop their own responses, copying Roman weapons and developing their own tactics to counter those of Roman troops. These neighbours also began to coalesce into larger-scale polities, a process whose beginning we saw in the confederation of Caledonians that appeared in response to Agricola's invasion of the north. The barbarian 'other' who lived on the far side of the *limes* may once have been represented by a large number of disparate *civitates*, tribes or self-governing farming communities, but in response to the political and military pressure of a huge empire these groups would coalesce to form new polities with new forms of hierarchical organisation which would eventually prove more dangerous to Rome. In the short term, however, during the reign of Hadrian and his immediate successors, the policy of strengthening the *limites* did bring a measure of peace and stability.

As we have seen, the line across Britain from coast to coast was initially a road connecting a sequence of forts a short day's march apart, built to connect two northbound roads which ran far into Scotland: Dere Street in the east, and on the west coast a road running north via Carlisle (*Luguvalium*) and into southwest Scotland. Its development under Trajan did not substantially change this arrangement, but under the Emperor Hadrian a new and dramatic development took place. When Hadrian had taken power in 117, the *Historia Augusta*, a collection of biographies of second- and third-century emperors, noted that the Britons 'could not be kept under Roman control'. Useful as this is to know, we cannot tell from this source whether the disruption was occurring within the Roman province of Britain itself or in Scotland beyond the *limes*. The Libyan Roman writer, Cornelius Fronto, writing *c.* AD 162, reminded Antoninus Pius that 'under the rule of your grandfather, Hadrian, what a number of soldiers were slain by the Jews, what a number by the Britons!' This seems to confirm the record of resistance in the *Historia Augusta*, but again it leaves us wondering on which side of the *limes* these Britons should be located. Fronto, it should also be noted, was not writing history, but rather making an impassioned exhortation to Antoninus: speaking in the voice of Mars, the god of war, he recites various military disasters which he (Mars) has brought on great Roman commanders in order to remind Antoninus that Rome's greatness has always come at a terrible cost and that he should not lose heart in the face of defeat. It would not be wise, therefore, to place too much historical weight on a passing and rather rhetorical reference to a massacre of Roman soldiers by Britons.

In spite of the vagueness of the written record, however, the fact is that in AD 122 Hadrian ordered the construction of a great wall across the Tyne–Solway isthmus, and this strongly suggests that there had been incursions of northern Britons – perhaps the Selgovae who dwelt near the wall, or perhaps Caledonians or another group from further north. The *Historia Augusta*'s description of Hadrian's arrival in Britain supports this interpretation of events:

> He set out for Britain, where he corrected many abuses, and he was the first to build a wall, eighty miles long, which separated the barbarians from the Romans. (*Historia Augusta*, Hadrian: xi, 2)

The image here of barbarians on one side and Romans on the other is perhaps a little simplistic, as there were surely disruptive Britons to the south, as well as Roman clients and sympathisers to the north. But it is a revealing simplification, and one that accords well with the suggestion that the attacks on Rome had come from the north.

Unlike the Stanegate, which mostly ran along lower ground, Hadrian's Wall was built on higher ground to the north of the road, offering commanding views over the country further north. The wall was built of stone for most of its 73 miles. Impressive though it was, it is important to realise what this wall was not. It was not an effective defence against invasion from the north, since a host of armed men could easily have breached the wall or sailed around either end of it. Neither was it intended by the Roman establishment to define a limit to imperial control, as Roman forts continued to be manned north of the wall, and Roman control of Britons beyond the *limes* could also be maintained by diplomatic means: Rome paid subsidies to client states to gain their military support or to buy immunity from attack; she supported more tractable rulers against their rivals; and she threatened devastating military incursions against hostile tribes. The *limes* did allow Roman troops to be stationed at regular intervals along its line, and it provided a road for rapid troop movements to defend the frontier from outside aggression wherever it should occur. The wall and its fortified installations also provided the means for policing the population, controlling movement in and out of the province, preventing small-scale raids, disarming suspicious travellers, protecting legitimate travellers and taxing traders. It could be a springboard for military action into *barbaricum*, should that be required, and for more routine intelligence-gathering operations and for the collection and transport of supplies for the army. The *limes* of northern Britain should be understood therefore as a broad zone, rather than a single line: it was a defence 'in depth', a pattern of interlocking devices intended to create a secure province in the south. Hadrian's Wall was a key element in this pattern, but it was only part of it.

The Emperor Antoninus Pius, unlike his predecessor Hadrian, never left Rome during his rule (138–61), but he took an active interest in Britain where Lollius Urbicus acted as governor from AD 139 to 142 or 143. The *Historia Augusta* records of Antoninus that 'he waged several wars through his legates. He conquered the Britons through Lollius Urbicus, his legate, building a second wall of turf and driving off the barbarians.' This 'second wall of turf' is the one built on the Forth–Clyde isthmus, a line that, according to Tacitus, had already been adopted and fortified by Agricola in the 80s, although without a wall. Now, enhanced by a road along its southern side, a wall stretched 37 miles from Old Kilpatrick to Carriden, forming part of a system of policing and administrative control.

The new 'Antonine Wall' built around 142 or 143 reflects the outcome of this 'driving off the barbarians', but, again, there is some confusion about who exactly these barbarians were. The natural assumption would be that they were the Britons on the north side of the wall, or perhaps between the walls; but a brief reference by the contemporary Greek geographer Pausanias says that Antoninus 'deprived the Brigantes in Britain of most of their territory' because they had attacked a people friendly to Rome. As most of the Brigantes lived south of the Hadrianic *limes*, and as they were considered to be a *civitas* within the Roman province, with an impressive capital at Aldborough, this sounds more like a disturbance within the province than an invasion from the north. It may be a mistake, however, to place too much weight on the passing remark of a distant Greek writer about the details of such struggles in Britain. It is also quite possible that there was both a crisis with the Brigantes within the province and a quite separate intrusion of barbarians from the north.

It is not clear why Antoninus chose to build a new wall on the Forth–Clyde line, about a hundred miles north of Hadrian's Wall. A number of possibilities may be considered. First, it may have been that an invasion from the north had been initiated in Caledonia, and that the Hadrianic line was thought to lie too far from these enemies. The creation of the Antonine

Wall would bring troops further north and give Rome more effective military and political reach into Caledonian territory. Certainly, once the Antonine Wall was built, Roman garrisons were replanted to the north of it, with a road running from the wall northwards via Ardoch and Strageath as far as Bertha (near Perth), and there is evidence of the re-occupation of these forts and of those even further north at Dalginross and possibly Cargill. The Antonine Wall was clearly not intended to mark the limit of Roman power.

Second, we might consider that there were reasons for incorporating the tribes of southern Scotland into the empire – peoples such as the Votadini, Damnonii and Selgovae. Some of them were probably client states of Rome, or had been during the Flavian occupation. If these were the barbarians 'driven off' by Lollius Urbicus, rather than the Caledonians, the incorporation of their territory into the province could be seen as a practical Roman response to a troublesome or unreliable barbarian neighbour. It is worth recalling that native *civitates* were not motivated by some generalised anti-Roman Celtic consciousness, but were negotiating for their own advantage in a complex political and military environment, conducting a constant cost–benefit analysis. Episodes of native violence may sometimes have been an attempt to 'throw off the Roman yoke', but they might sometimes have been a way for a *civitas* to re-negotiate its relationship with Rome. Client kings in southern Scotland may have felt that Hadrian's Wall was disadvantaging them, that they were being excluded from some of the advantages of *Romanitas*, even if they were being paid for their collaboration. They may have felt that Rome should have offered them more protection from their Caledonian enemies to the north. The creation of the Antonine Wall, therefore, may not have met with general opposition from the people of southern Scotland.

This may be especially true of the Votadini in the Lothians and further south. The archaeology of the Roman fort at Inveresk (NT342720) reveals a *vicus* to the east of the fort, a civilian settlement with a bath house and an amphitheatre. Also nearby are field systems showing agricultural settlement clustering around the military installation, while surviving pottery at the fort demonstrates its occupation during the Antonine period. This close spatial relationship between Roman fort and civilian settlement indicates a stable relationship between the empire and the Votadini. This is especially revealed by the presence of an amphitheatre in the civilian area. The amphitheatre was the place in which Roman order was demonstrated. Before an audience seated according to social rank and class, public spectacles asserted imperial power over the colonised or conquered peoples, over slaves and over nature itself. Those who attended the games were taught to know their place within the Roman world. The creation of the Antonine Wall had symbolically declared these people to be Romans, and they (or some of them) may have been glad of it. Perhaps it simultaneously declared the people across the Forth – whose land they could see from their seats in the amphitheatre – to be barbarians.

A third reason for the creation of the Antonine Wall may arise less from conditions in Britain than from the politics of Rome. To make himself a credible ruler Antoninus had to show prowess as a military commander, even though he never went anywhere near any of his legions. He chose Britain as a theatre where he could manifest his power and obtain his imperial triumph. Following his campaign, Antoninus was declared imperator in AD 142, and in AD 155 a coin showed him on one side and Britannia on the other, the divine personification of the island province, seated and accompanied by a Roman shield and *vexillum*, or military flag. Britannia's posture has suggested to some that she is in mourning, defeated by Rome; others have proposed that she is sitting quietly at peace, content to be surrounded and protected by Roman military power. In either case the coin, like all Roman coins, was an instrument of Antonine propaganda, an image that made its statement every time it changed hands.

Instability in Britain continued, however. In AD 154, Julius Verus was appointed governor, and came to Britain from Germany with a large body of troops to help in the suppression of a revolt, perhaps the revolt of the Brigantes mentioned by

Pausanias, and the Britannia coin of AD 155 may commemorate the outcome of Verus' intervention. Such disturbances persuaded the Roman authorities that the neglected and somewhat dilapidated Hadrianic frontier was, after all, a more practical way to defend the province. An inscription at Heddon (NZ1366) of AD 158 records repair and restoration work on Hadrian's Wall by the Sixth Legion, suggesting that the authorities were already reconsidering their strategy, even before Antoninus died in AD 161, in favour of a restored Hadrianic line. As the restoration of the Tyne–Solway frontier progressed, including the addition of a new road alongside the wall, the Antonine frontier was gradually depleted. There is some evidence of continuing Roman presence on the Antonine Wall for some years, however: a coin with the inscription Lucilla Augusta, datable to 164×169, has been found at Old Kilpatrick, while an inscription on an altar at Castlecary has been dated to 175×190. Furthermore, Dio wrote in the early third century, but probably using material that he collected in the 180s, about the Maeatae living 'close to the wall which divides the island in two'. As we shall see in due course, this must refer to the Antonine Wall, suggesting that it was still seen as a significant feature in the 180s, perhaps enjoying a re-occupation at that period. The final withdrawal to the Hadrianic frontier may not have occurred until the reign of Septimius Severus (192–211), about the year 197.

When Marcus Aurelius became emperor in 161 we hear that 'war was threatening Britain and a certain Calpurnius Agricola was sent against the Britons'. This probably refers to trouble on the northern frontier, but we cannot be certain. It was during this emperor's reign, in AD 175, that a large unit of Sarmatian cavalry was sent to Britain to serve in the Roman army. The Sarmatians had been a major threat to Rome's eastern frontier, but Marcus Aurelius marched against them on the Danube, intending their complete extermination. Finally, however, Sarmatian rulers accepted terms of peace from Rome, including the obligation to supply 8,000 cavalrymen for the Roman army. Of these, 5,500 were sent to Britain, where they may have served on Hadrian's Wall, although inscriptions mentioning their cavalry units appear only in Ribchester (Lancashire) and Catterick (Yorkshire). The interest of this movement of thousands of eastern horsemen to Britain is partly in the fact that it is an early instance of what would become a common practice in the later empire: the recruitment of large numbers of barbarian warriors to serve in Roman provinces. Unrest in Britain continued in the 180s when according to Dio's *Roman History*:

> The greatest struggle was the one with the Britons. The tribes in that island, crossing the wall that separated them from the Roman legions, proceeded to do much mischief and cut down a general together with his troops. (lxxiii, 8)

The Emperor Commodus responded in AD 180 by sending Ulpius Marcellus to be governor of Britain, who 'ruthlessly put down the barbarians of Britain'. It is commonly understood that the wall crossed by the attacking Britons was Hadrian's Wall, but it appears from another passage of Dio, already cited, that he regarded the Antonine Wall as the significant division of the island at that time. He writes that:

> There are two great nations of Britons, the Caledonians and the Maeatae (Καληδόνιοι καί Μαιάται) and the names of the others have been merged in these two. The Maeatae live next to the cross-wall which cuts the island in half, and the Caledonians are beyond them. (lxxvii, 12)

The Caledonians, as we have seen, had their core lands in highland Perthshire, but the Maeatae can be located by modern place names which contain their name – Dumyat and Myot Hill – both lying a few miles north of the Antonine Wall, though the Maeatae may have occupied land south of the wall as well. Marcellus fought this incursion until about AD 184, but the final outcome was his withdrawal to the Hadrianic frontier. No doubt violence had been visited on the Britons to the north, but if Marcellus had hoped to dominate lowland Scotland between the Tyne and the Forth, he could not do it.

Following the assassination of the Emperor Commodus at the end of AD 192 a power struggle disturbed the Roman Empire during 'the year of the five emperors'. The contest between

Decimus Clodius Albinus and Septimius Severus, both of them Roman provincials from North Africa, was the most serious. Its resolution in favour of Severus, and the fact that Albinus had been governor of Britain and had been proclaimed emperor by the army in Britain meant that one of the first tasks of the triumphant Severus was to dismantle Albinus' power base in Britain, confiscating his estates and executing his former supporters, while at the same time dealing with any native insurgency which had arisen during the power struggle. This task was assigned to Virius Lupus, appointed governor by Severus in 197. Dio implies that there had been an insurrection of the Maeatae during the 190s:

> Inasmuch as the Caledonians did not abide by their promises and had made ready to aid the Maeatae ... Lupus was compelled to purchase peace from the Maeatae for a great sum; and he received a few captives. (lxxvi, 8)

Clearly Lupus was not in a strong military position at this point, since he had to buy peace rather than imposing it by force of arms. It is not clear what is meant by his receiving captives: perhaps they were Roman provincials who had been captured by the Maeatae in some earlier raid, now being returned; or perhaps they were hostages handed over to Lupus by the Maeatae as a guarantee of compliance. Interestingly, Dio's claim that the Caledonians had broken a promise by conspiring in this way indicates that they had earlier made some kind of treaty with Rome. The episode is another illustration of what we have called the political and military 'improvisation' of native societies in the face of Roman power.

The peace purchased by Lupus was not the final outcome of the dispute, however. Septimius Severus arrived in Britain early in AD 208, and Dio tells us, 'desiring to subjugate the whole of it, he invaded Caledonia'. The legionary fortress at Carpow on the south bank of the Tay was built at this time, and was probably the starting point of the invasion proper. The size and position of Carpow suggests that Severus really was, as Dio says, intent on conquering the whole of the island and occupying it, but his expedition was in many ways a failure. Dio writes of the forests, rivers, mountainous country and swamps hindering and harming Severus' troops, wearing them down as if the very countryside was a barbarian force – a topos often used by Roman writers. The archaeology of Severan marching camps in Scotland shows that the campaign, which began in AD 208, extended far into the northeast, roughly the same area as that traversed by Agricola in the first century. Meanwhile, the Caledonians, wishing to avoid a pitched battle, pursued a guerrilla strategy of harassment against the Romans. Dio says that Severus 'forced the Britons to come to terms on condition that they should abandon a large part of their territory', but there is no evidence that any such abandonment actually happened. The northerners seem to have accepted a treaty without suffering any major loss. But Dio goes on to say that this treaty did not hold. Within a short time, probably in AD 210, the Caledonians and Maeatae were again in open revolt, and Severus commanded his soldiers to conduct a campaign of extermination in the north, killing everyone they met. In Dio's account Severus quotes the words of Homer's *Iliad* as his standing orders to his troops:

Let not one of them escape sheer destruction
and the might of our hands.
Nay, even the child whom his mother bears in her womb –
Let not even him escape destruction.

It is unclear to what extent this genocidal slaughter actually took place; perhaps it began in the late summer of 210 and continued for some months. But Severus died in February 211 and his two sons and heirs, Caracallus and Geta, seem not to have shared their father's interest in conquering Caledonia. Proclaimed joint emperors by the army, they may have allowed their father's northern campaign to continue for a while after his death, but they had more urgent demands to attend to – in particular, how to deal with the difficulty that they had inherited a shared empire. Caracalla dealt with it by murdering his brother.

Severus had issued coins bearing his own image on one side and on the other side a winged Victory looming over tiny bound captives and bearing the inscription VICTORIAE BRITTANNICAE, but his victories were hardly what he had hoped for. His great fort at Carpow was probably abandoned before 215, as was the important fort at Cramond on the Forth – an Antonine foundation, rebuilt under Severus as a harbour and depot for the fleet to supply troops in the north. The end result of Severus' campaign in Britain was little more than a handful of treaties with his enemies and, as the *Augustan History* notes, a good deal of reinforcement and new construction on Hadrian's Wall. The Tyne–Solway line once again became the northern frontier. But it was a frontier that now seems to have become more effective: the savage assault on the Maeatae and Caledonians by Severus and Caracalla may have weakened their military capacity, or the subsequent treaties may have given them sufficient reasons for accepting the Roman presence. In any case, the area north of the Wall remained comparatively quiet for some time after the Severan campaign. Perhaps for this reason we have less evidence from Roman writers about the affairs of north Britain for this period.

We may wonder, however, about the internal dynamics of the northern tribes during the third century. We have seen how some had formed a provisional alliance in the first century against Agricola, and how the Maeatae and Caledonians joined together against the armies of Severus. Likewise, in the eastern empire the smaller tribes of the Rhine frontier were beginning to coalesce into larger entities. Roman writers began to identify new confederacies with such names as *Alemanni* and *Franci*. Their wealth was increasing, partly as a result of trade with Rome and subsidies from Rome to client kingdoms, and this brought new forms of social, political and military hierarchy, together with new military threats. An army of Goths attacked the Balkans in the 250s and slew Decius, the first emperor ever killed by barbarians; in the same decade the Alemanni invaded the empire and reached the outskirts of Rome before being defeated. The organisation and power of newly emerging groups in the east would increasingly threaten the Roman world.

Similar processes were occurring during the third century

north of Hadrian's Wall, where non-Romanised groups were
being awarded a new common identity by Roman observers.
In AD 297 they were all referred to as *Picti* by Eumenius – the
first use of an ethnonym that would survive for several more
centuries. They are characterised in that first occurrence, along
with the Irish (*Hiberni*) as having been enemies of the Britons
during the time of Julius Caesar. His use of the name in this way
is anachronistic, of course, since there were no *Picti* in Caesar's
time; Eumenius is projecting his view of northern *barbaricum*
into the distant past. But it is significant that this first mention
of the Picti portrays them as enemies of the Britons, for this is
how they must have appeared to Eumenius when *Picti* from
the north were troubling the Roman province of Britain. This
broad definition of *Picti*, incidentally, leaves open the possibility that the Romans included in this group any hostile tribes
living between Hadrian's Wall and the Forth–Clyde line. In the
eighth century, Bede would locate the *Picti* north of the Forth,
but we cannot assume that this was Eumenius' perception four
centuries earlier.

What the Romans meant by *Picti* has been much discussed,
but there is some consensus that it meant simply 'the painted
ones'. Herodian, in his *Roman History* in the early third century,
says of the Britons that 'they tattoo their bodies with coloured
designs and drawings of all kinds of animals; for this reason
they do not wear clothes, which would conceal the decorations
on their bodies'. While this may not be an accurate observation
of daily behaviour among the northernmost Britons, it illustrates the perception of these 'barbarians' by writers within the
empire. But Roman use of the term *Picti* does not mean that they
called themselves by this name, or even that there was any long-
term coalition of tribes or groups who identified themselves as
a single people, rather than occasional ad hoc alliances between
smaller polities. For Roman writers it is likely that *Picti* was a
rather slangy catch-all term for 'barbarians up there'. Indeed, it
was probably fairly pejorative too, an 'othering' and devaluing
of their culture. The word *Picti* might have associated them in
Roman eyes with others who were commonly tattooed: slaves,

rebels, criminals and those convicted of sacrilege. Tattooing was something the powerful did to those in their power. It did have some less dishonourable meanings: Roman conscripts were tattooed, but even that was done so that deserters could be identified, suggesting that it was hardly seen as a respectable form of self-adornment. The term *Picti* now enabled Latin-speakers to make a clear distinction between Roman Britons and inferior barbarian Britons who lived beyond Roman control. Just as the Pictish landscape was barbaric in Roman descriptions, all swamp and mountain and forest, so now was the Pictish body.

While the eastern frontier of the empire was under threat from outside, other changes would arise within the empire itself. Rome depended increasingly on barbarian recruits, many of them with loyalties that embraced not only some general notion of *Romanitas*, but far more local or particular interests. In the provinces there was a growing dependency on the recruitment of new frontier troops from among the sons of serving or retired legionaries, recruited to serve locally in the province in which their fathers had served and settled, creating similar local loyalties and new Roman–native hybrids of cultural and political life. Eventually, the men on Hadrian's Wall would be mostly recruited from among the families of veterans and serving soldiers based there, and so would be serving close to their own kin.

From time to time a Roman legion would proclaim its commander as emperor, going to war with other units who had proclaimed their own emperor elsewhere, as we saw in the struggle between Clodius Albinus with his Britons and Septimius Severus with his Illyrian troops. Likewise in AD 280 the governor of Britain declared himself emperor, requiring Probus (emperor from 276 to 282) to send a Moorish general, Victorinus, to destroy him. Further rebellion by Romans in Britain occurred in AD 286 or 287, when the general Carausius declared himself emperor. He was slain by his treasurer Allectus in 293, who in turn declared himself emperor and ruled in Britain until he was slain by the Emperor Constantius Chlorus in 296. This instability in the southern part of Britain may have had some effect on the northern neighbours, the *Picti* and the tribes of southern Scotland, but it is hard to discern. It may have given the impression of a weakened empire, one that could be raided with a degree of impunity. It may also have disrupted the flow of goods from the Roman province to the northern rulers, and this would encourage expressions of dissatisfaction – expressions which could take military form. But such incursions as there were from the north were not serious threats at this stage. It is worth noting that the panegyric of Constantius in AD 297 stressed the obedience of the northern barbarians to the emperor. Had he gained this obedience by a great military victory, the panegyrist would surely have mentioned it. The evidence suggests a degree of stability in the north, an impression confirmed by the statement (in a eulogy of Constantius' son, Constantine) that Constantius, when he went to Britain in 305, chose not to acquire 'the forests and marshes of the Caledonians and other Picts'.

While Constantius and his son Constantine were at *Eboracum* (York) in 306, the father died. His troops immediately proclaimed Constantine as Augustus (senior emperor), at the instigation of Crocus, an Alemannic king who had rebelled against Rome, but was now a commander serving under Constantius in Britain. For several years Constantine's energies were poured into the effort of taking sole control of the empire, putting an end to its fragmentation, and fighting off challenges from rival claimants. In AD 324 he achieved his aim, gaining control of both eastern and western parts of the empire and moving his capital from Rome to the newly re-founded *Constantinopolis* – 'Constantine's city'. But it was not his British proclamation, nor his military success, that made Constantine important in Britain. It was the fact of his conversion to Christianity, and the 'edict of toleration' which he made in Milan with Licinius in AD 313, putting an end to the persecution of Christians that had been in force since an edict of Diocletian in 303. The Diocletian persecution may have had little direct impact in Britain, though there were already churches here, but the conversion of Constantine heralded a new phase in the relationship of Christianity and Rome.

Constantius' grandson and ruler of the western empire, Constans, visited Britain in the 340s. He appears to have made use of troops sometimes referred to in modern literature as *areani* – in fact, this may be an error for *arcani*, 'secret ones', that is, spies or scouts operating on or beyond the frontier. This would suggest that whatever anxieties there may have been about the north, they were not being dealt with by open armed conflict. The appointment of *arcani* may simply have been a measure to ensure that northern polities were observing the conditions of whatever treaties were in force at the time, rather than responding to some crisis.

Up to the 350s the main threat to the *Pax Romana* in Britain was internal conflict arising from various usurpers claiming the purple, rather than incursions from *barbaricum*. But in AD 360, Ammianus Marcellinus reports that 'the wild tribes of the *Scotti* and *Picti* broke their undertaking to keep peace, laid waste the country near the frontiers, and caused alarm among the provincials'. The involvement of the *Scotti* may imply the existence of a fleet from Ireland (or perhaps from Scotland, Gaelic-speaking western parts of which may already have been seen as *Scotia*) sufficiently powerful to challenge Roman sea power; the *Picti* also may have raided by sea rather than simply marching south. Such ships certainly did not appear overnight; they must have been used by the traders sailing between Ireland and western Britain in the years prior to 360, during the decades of British prosperity when Ammianus implies that a treaty of some sort was in force. The massive-walled Roman fort at the harbour of Holyhead on Anglesey, built around AD 300, had presumably been built to help police the Irish Sea trading zone, defending merchants and repelling pirates, functions which it shared with the forts at Cardiff and Lancaster, and with the chain of forts running round the coast of Cumbria (Ravenglass, Moresby, Maryport).

Responding to these raids the Emperor Justinian, unable to leave Gaul because of the threat of the Alemanni, sent a commander called Lupicinus to resolve the situation. Ammianus' account states that the *Scotti* and Picts were attacking 'near the frontiers' – presumably in the north, though a sea-faring host might also have attacked further south on the coast or made incursions by river. But Lupicinus is said only to have landed at Richborough (*Rutufiae*) and made his way to London. There is no indication of his having mounted punitive expeditions against the *Picti*. His concern seems to have been limited to a pacification of the Roman territories rather than a more aggressive approach to the raiders' home territories.

A few years later, however, another attack on Roman Britain took place. Ammianus states that 'Britain was being reduced to the direst need by a barbarian conspiracy (*barbarica conspiratione*) and that Nectaridus, the commander of the coastal territory, had been slain, probably by sea-borne Germanic warriors; meanwhile Fullofaudes, the *dux Britanniarum* (the military commander of the north), had been captured by an enemy plot.' The language of 'barbarian conspiracy' for the events of AD 367 suggests a degree of international coordination between hostile forces in Britain and on the Continent, and so it may have seemed to Roman eyes, but there is no reason to suppose that these disparate attackers actually conspired together. In Britain, however, there may have been collusion between a northern coalition and the Roman *arcani* who had been bribed to give military information to Rome's enemies, instead of acting as intelligence-gatherers for the Roman army.

Ammianus names various ethnic groups involved in the attack on Roman Britain. First are the *Picti*, who he says were divided into two groups, the *Dicalydonae* and *Verturiones*. The former were probably a development of those we earlier met as *Caledonii* or *Caledones*, perhaps now a bipartite coalition, suggested by the prefix *Di-*. The *Verturiones* were from north of the Mounth – a group whose successors we shall come across again in Chapter 2. Another group are the *Scotti*, who had already joined with the *Picti* in the raids of 360. Ammianus names another group involved, the *Attacotti*, whom he describes as a 'warlike nation of men', but there is no certainty about their place of origin. They may have been an Irish federation distinguished in some way from the *Scotti*; but they may also have been from Britain, as the scholarly monk Jerome believed when he met them in Gaul in the 360s:

> I saw the *Atticoti*, a British tribe, eat human flesh ... it is their custom to cut off the buttocks of the shepherds and the breasts of their women, and to regard them as the greatest delicacies.

Jerome's strange and negative mythologising does not encourage confidence in his evidence, and in any case, we know that Jerome was capable of confusing Britain and Ireland. Elsewhere, for example, he accused the British Pelagius of having grown up stuffed with Irish porridge.

Ammianus says that at the same time *Franci* and *Saxones* were attacking Gaul by land and sea, placing further pressure on the Roman army and keeping the Emperor Valentinian busy there. His commander Theodosius brought four units from the Roman field army with him from the Continent to take control in Britain. He attacked and defeated various bands of invaders, and restored Roman towns, strengthening and rebuilding damaged forts on the frontier, and bringing deserting troops back under control. He suppressed the *arcani* who had colluded with the enemy, and he may also have mounted attacks on some of the lands from which the raids had come. Some years later various units of *Atecotti* are listed as serving under Roman commanders in a document known as *Notitia Dignitatum*. If Theodosius had made war on *Atecotti* territories, these units may have been composed of men recruited into the Roman army under the terms of a recent surrender or treaty.

The attacks on Roman territory in 360 and 367 should perhaps be understood against a background of shifting Roman policies and attitudes. It is likely that for the *Picti* and *Scotti* the advantages of peaceful co-existence with Roman Britain had sometimes outweighed the disadvantages. There were many ways in which some non-Roman elites could take advantage of Roman power, including increased wealth through trade, bribes offered by British governors, access to prestige goods, having their sons serve in the Roman army, and new forms of political life with new opportunities for the exercise of power. If during the internal disruptions of empire the access of *barbaricum* to these advantages had been eroded, these peoples might well have turned to hostile action not out of anti-Roman sentiment so much as out of a desire for a greater share of that *Romanitas* which they now regarded as theirs by right. And it does seem that there had been a reduction in the flow of Roman goods into Scotland beyond the Forth. Faced with such a reduction, the newly emerging warrior groups could only hope to renew their claim as forcefully as possible.

The disruption caused by these raids in Britain was serious, but it could be mended, and Roman resources – including the four regiments brought by Theodosius – were able to re-establish some kind of order within two or three years. But this was not true on the Continent, where many more hostile actions took place over the coming years and increasing demands, as a result, were placed on the Roman army. The pressure on Roman Britain from its neighbours, *Picti* and *Scotti*, continued. Ammianus Marcellinus records that in the 370s Valentinian sent troops to support the Britons who 'could not endure the hordes of enemies who were overrunning their country'. In AD 381 Magnus Maximus, a senior army official in Britain, usurped imperial power, and the following year repulsed another attack by *Picti* and *Scotti*. But in 383 he took troops from Britain to Gaul to pursue his quest for power, depriving the Britons of much of their defence. It is possible that Maximus was the *superbus tyrannus*, or 'proud tyrant', so hated by the British writer Gildas for having introduced the fierce Saxons to the island. He may have introduced Germanic *foederati* to replace the troops he had taken with him. And, given that the *Picti* represented the main threat to the Britons, such German troops would most likely have been posted on the Hadrianic *limes* in the north. Maximus is certainly the one responsible, in Gildas' view for stripping Britain of its security:

> After that Britain was despoiled of her whole army, her military resources, her governors, brutal as they were, and her sturdy youth, who had followed in the tyrant's footsteps, never to return home. (*The Ruin of Britain*, §14)

There was a long-standing presence of Germanic troops in Roman Britain, for the Romans recruited regularly from among *Alemanni* and *Franci*, Germanic peoples from east of the Rhine frontier. The introduction of Saxons by the 'proud tyrant' to free Roman field troops for fighting in Gaul would have been simply an expansion of this policy. Over a considerable period a North Sea zone had been developing, with regular economic, cultural and military exchange between Britain, Gaul and Germanic peoples – some of them consensual, some of them more hostile. Attacks by sea-borne Germanic groups, as well as disruption from within Roman Britain, are probably associated with a gradual withdrawal of troops from the Pennine forts at this time. The Hadrianic frontier continued to be manned, however, as evidenced by coins found there dating after AD 383. But the troops on the wall were not legionaries; they were *limitanei* (units dedicated to border duties) tied to the area. They may have included leaders of the local tribes who had been granted the title of imperial officers, the sons of retired soldiers who had settled locally, and incoming Germanic militia. Most of them will have had local interests, which included not only defending the wall and its settlements, but also the cultivation of land they held nearby and their own positions within local power structures.

During earlier periods large quantities of coin had been brought to Britain to pay the army, but from around AD 400 coins are missing from the archaeological record. It seems that Stilicho, the Roman general responsible, was in such military and financial difficulty on the Continent that he was no longer able to pay the British troops in the usual way, and that new forms of military service were appearing in which the *limitanei* or barbarian troops who kept order did so in return for grants of land instead of cash payment. In 406, the western empire was overwhelmed by large numbers of Alans, Sueves, Burgundians and Vandals; they were never removed. The empire was also shaken by internal conflicts, including a series of revolts in Britain in AD 406 and 407, where Marcus, Gratian and Constantine III set themselves up as emperors in rapid succession. The last of these took an army to Gaul to confront the invaders there, leaving Britain at the mercy of Germans in the south and east of the island, and of *Picti* and *Scotti* in the north and west. The Visigothic ruler Alaric first invaded Italy in AD 401, and by 408 was besieging Rome itself, eventually sacking the city in August 410. In this year it has conventionally been thought that British *civitates* begged for imperial help against encroaching enemies, but the Emperor Honorius replied that they must see to their own affairs and defend their territory – hardly surprising given the collapse of Rome before Alaric's forces. He had long been encouraging other provinces of the western empire to do likewise. It has been suggested that Honorius' letter was actually addressed to the leaders of Bruttium, now Calabria in southern Italy, but whether Honorius wrote to Britain or Bruttium hardly matters in the broad picture. This is the moment usually and understandably imagined as the collapse of 'Roman Britain'. And in a sense it was: Roman provincial government, the collection of Roman taxes and the military defence of the provinces by imperial troops were all in a state of collapse.

But though these aspects of the Roman imperial order were important, their collapse did not mean 'the end of Roman Britain'. For almost four centuries the whole island had undergone huge cultural transformation as a result of the Roman presence. We might give the name *Romanitas* to the new elements of culture – a shifting and varied pattern of behaviours, values, technologies and symbols. These changes were not simply forced on passive British provincials by occupying Roman forces and governors, and they cannot be assumed to have occurred solely within the area of Roman imperial control, south of the *limes* (whether Hadrianic or Antonine). This is made clear by the appearance of *Romanitas* in Ireland. Though never part of the Roman Empire, never having suffered a military invasion by legionaries, Ireland also adopted aspects of *Romanitas*. In the eastern part, facing Britain, a quantity of Roman goods survives, giving evidence of a lively sea trade between Ireland and Roman Britain. We should recall Ptolemy's second-century map of Ireland in this context, with its names for tribes, centres, promontories and rivers. Unlike his map of Scotland, which may rely on military surveys, Ptolemy's map of Ireland must be derived from mercantile informants since no military campaign was ever undertaken there. Such a view is supported by Tacitus who says of Ireland that 'most of its approaches and harbours are known [to us] through trade and from merchants'.

Roman goods obtained by trade – and also perhaps on occasion by raiding in western Britain – show one of the vectors by which *Romanitas* entered Ireland. Another element that spread beyond the frontiers of the empire, not only in Ireland but also, for example, in Germany, was writing. In the east, German-speakers developed a way of representing their language in letters, which they derived from Roman and Greek alphabets. The runic alphabet or '*elder futhark*' shows this derivation. Consider the similarity between the following runic letters and their Latin equivalents:

F = ᚠ
R = ᚱ
C = ᚲ
H = ᚺ
B = ᛒ
S = ᛋ
T = ᛏ

The Irish also developed a technology for writing their language, creating a writing system called *ogam*, probably around the fourth century. Unlike the *futhark* of the Germans, however, Irish *ogam* letters bear no visual relationship to Latin letters. Each letter of the *ogam* alphabet is formed by a number (from 1 to 5) of dots or lines carved on or across a single axis. The creators of *ogam* were guided by their knowledge of Latin letters and were familiar with Latin-language spelling conventions, as also with the Roman practice of raising stones marked with personal names, but they created a completely new symbol system to represent their own language. They did so primarily, it seems, to commemorate named individuals on stones erected for this purpose. What is remarkable is that the distribution of the Roman-inspired *ogam* carvings in Ireland is quite different from that of Roman trade goods. While trade goods are concentrated in the east, on the coast facing Britain, *ogam* stones are concentrated in a broad band across the south of Ireland, facing Gaul. While both distributions are evidence of *Romanitas* penetrating a society that was not subject to Roman imperial authority, the difference between them reminds us that *Romanitas* should not be seen as a monolithic all-or-nothing construct. It shows that native societies had different kinds of contact with the empire, and that their appropriation of *Romanitas* could be selective, a discriminating process conducted by active and assertive participants in cultural exchange.

The army also provided a means for Romanising people beyond the frontiers. The *Notitia Dignitatum* lists large numbers of Roman military units from *barbaricum*. As we have seen, some were *Atecotti*, British or Irish fighters who had earlier been enemies of Rome. Others from Scotland also served in the army. A stone at Colchester (*Camulodunum*) dateable to AD 221×235 honours the god Mars-Medocius and the victory of the emperor. It was erected by Lossio Veda, who describes himself as a Caledonian (*Caledo*) and states that he is the grandson (or descendant) of Vepogenus, a name that may mean 'born in Fife'. There is no mention of Lossio Veda's military affiliation, but the dedication to Mars and to the emperor's victory suggest that he was in the Roman army. Those who served in the Roman army might eventually return home – a pattern we see clearly in the archaeology of *Germania* – to high social positions, bringing with them Roman ideas and practices.

In addition to men from Scotland serving in the Roman army, there were people within Scotland living cheek by jowl with Roman soldiers. As we have seen, even in the first century native dwellings began to cluster around Roman forts. Later civilian developments appear at such places as Carriden, at the east end of the Antonine Wall, where a stone altar records the presence of *vicani*, people living in the *vicus* or civilian community attached to a Roman military site. At Cramond there was a large civilian settlement to the south and east of the fort, and another lay beside the Roman fort of Inveresk, as we have seen. At sites such as Cadder (NS616725), Inveresk and Bar Hill (NS707759), the remains of field systems attest to the presence of farmers using the land under the shadow of Roman fortifications. At Bar Hill archaeologists have found more than 300 shoes belonging to men, women and children, even babies – clear evidence of a civilian presence. Some of these settlements may not have lasted more than a few decades around the time when the Antonine Wall was occupied, but they were a medium of cultural transmission.

Coins provided another medium by which those who used them were bound together throughout the empire and beyond. They served to articulate Roman values and ideas, as they passed from hand to hand, bearing their messages of imperial authority, the cult of the emperor as a divine figure, the power of the military and its victories over barbarian nations. About AD 314 a document known as the 'Verona List' (*Laterculus Veronensis*) named various barbarian tribes, including *Scoti, Picti* and *Caledoni*, who had flourished 'under the emperors' (*sub imperatoribus*). None of these peoples lived within the empire, but the phrase accurately reflects strong elements of *Romanitas* among the societies beyond the frontier. Even if they were not directly under Roman rule, they were partners in various ways: they crossed frontiers, buying and selling in the empire's marketplace; their children were sometimes sent to Roman towns to be educated or as hostages.

Another aspect of *Romanitas* that transformed native societies was religious cult. Roman soldiers came to Scotland from all over the empire, along with officials, administrators and merchants. Among the ideas they brought with them were the names of gods and the cultic practices associated with them. Some Roman gods could be easily accommodated by native British ideas by the strategy of *interpretatio romana*, the process whereby non-Roman deities were identified with Roman gods with similar profiles. Lossio Veda's dedication to Mars-Medocius, mentioned above, is a good example where

Mars, the Roman god of war, is linked to Medocius, probably a British god with military interests. The two names are treated jointly as the name of one deity. The pattern is well attested throughout the empire, and in Scotland we see Roman visitors (of whatever ethnicity they were) adopting native cults. At Bar Hill the soldiers of the First Hamian Cohort erected an altar 'to the god Mars-Camulus' (DEO MARTI CAMVLO). This means that a company of Syrian archers were culting a British deity called Camulos (he is commemorated in *Camulodunum*, Colchester) as the equivalent of Mars. The Celtic god Maponos was identified with Apollo at Corbridge near Hadrian's Wall in an inscription to APOLLINI MAPONO.

As well as twinning Roman with native gods, the Romans may even have helped to create 'Celtic' deities. Inscriptions honouring *Dea Brigantia*, the presumed tribal goddess of the Brigantes, were erected by Romans, including an altar and statue of the goddess at Birrens. It is possible that Brigantia was an ancient tribal deity of the Brigantes, but she may also have been a Roman or Romano-British creation intended to personify the conquered *civitas* of the Brigantes and the landscape where they lived. It was certainly not unknown for Roman troops to deify and worship the supposed essence of their conquered territories – perhaps slightly nervously, in the hope that by appeasing these deities they would make their conquest safe and pacify the conquered people. This instinct must have inspired the dedication of an altar erected by the centurion Marcus Cocceius Firmus at the fort of Auchendavie (NS666745) on the Antonine Wall: GENIO TERRAE BRITANNICAE, 'to the protecting spirit of the British land'.

The interplay of Roman and native British gods was complicated by the fact that the imperial troops and officials who were sent to Scotland brought with them countless gods from their own home countries as well. At Birrens fort an altar was erected to a Germanic goddess, DEAE RICAGAMBEDAE, by a Tungrian military unit who also erected an altar to Minerva. Another altar at Birrens was erected by an apparently German *architectus* called Gamidiahus, inscribed as 'sacred to the goddess Harimella' (DEAE HARIMELLAE SACRUM) – a goddess whose name occurs nowhere else in the record, but was presumably one that Gamidiahus had worshipped in his homeland.

It is in this context that we should see the earliest appearance of Christianity in Britain. In the empire the constant movement of soldiers, officials, merchants and slaves carried cultures from one end of the known world to the other, including religious ideas. Christian faith was spread not on the whole by missionaries, but as the unintended consequence of this movement. Tertullian noted, c. AD 200, that 'haunts of Britons, inaccessible to Romans, are subject to Christ', though he is unlikely to have known much about Britain, and we should make some allowance for hyperbole here.

The Emperor Constantine's conversion to Christianity in the early fourth century and his subsequent promotion of the faith meant that its position in the empire was transformed. In AD 314 bishops of the western empire attended a church council at Arles, three of them coming from Britain. The faith that had once spread by a discreet osmosis was now promoted in more public ways: imperial coins bearing the Greek letters *chi* and *rho* (χ and ρ, the first two letters of the name of Christ in Greek) were a constant reminder of the presence of Christianity and a proclamation of the emperor's support for the Church. The Gospel continued to spread in more informal ways of course: Christian slaves introduced their faith into the homes of their owners, so that Prosper (*c.* AD 455) could report that those captured by enemies 'have handed their masters into the possession of Christ's Gospel'. Marriages brought pagans and Christians together in one household, allowing the exchange of ideas.

What is surprising, given the new public acceptability of Christianity, is the comparative lack of archaeological evidence for it in Britain. We know there were Christians, and we have some material traces – lead tanks embossed with *chi–rho* symbols in southeast England, Christian mosaics in Roman villas, a cross carved on a stone on Hadrian's Wall – but the material evidence is thin. A congregation might pray in a room in a villa, or in a small building in a fort, without leaving a very distinctive archaeological footprint. Some of the best material evidence for Roman Christianity in Britain is perhaps the sub-Roman remains (some of which we will look at in Chapter 2) that show a late fifth- and sixth-century church, which is clearly a survival from the period of the Roman occupation. Early British literature also suggests that the Christianity of the sub-Roman Britons was a survival from the Roman period.

Most of Scotland never endured any Roman conquest or long-term occupation at all. Attempts to establish a *limes* along the southern edge of the Highlands, or on the Forth–Clyde isthmus, were short-lived. And there were good reasons for this. First, much of Scotland is not very agriculturally productive. There would be little to be had from the Highlands and the Cheviot Hills. Rome did sometimes conquer highland territory, as in Wales and Spain, but these mountains promised mineral wealth while the Scottish mountains did not. Much of the lower land in the Central Belt of Scotland was marshy in the Roman period, and while there were more productive areas – Lothian, Fife, Angus, the Mearns – even these were much marshier before modern drainage than they are now. In Britain, as elsewhere in Europe, the Roman frontier corresponded roughly with the general limit of intensive agriculture, reflecting the fundamental cost–benefit analysis that had to be made in any colonial expansion: does the territory to be occupied promise to repay the cost of occupation?

There were other reasons why Rome might have sought to occupy Scotland. One was the possibility of neutralising a barbarian threat in the north, but the threat could be contained by creating a wall and its associated defences – the boundary between Scotland and the Roman provinces being a comparatively short one – and this was easier than attempting to occupy and dominate Caledonia. Romans did have a powerful sense of their own destiny to save the world by Romanising it, but this sense of mission seems to have been more fruitful in areas where there was already a degree of urbanisation, an agricultural surplus capable of supporting a number of non-farming specialists, and a hierarchical political system that could be absorbed into Roman administration. They found this in Gaul and southern Britain, but perhaps insufficiently in most of Scotland.

There were military incursions, of course, and repeated devastations of the landscape which must have reduced thousands to hunger and destitution – possibly killing more people than were killed in battles. The sources for our period have little to say about the suffering of these people. But the Roman presence shaped the societies of Scotland in many other ways over nearly four centuries. In some parts people seem to have chosen *Romanitas* or some aspect of it as part of their identity. This is not to deny that they celebrated more local ethnicities as well. As a third-century soldier had engraved on his gravestone near Aquincum (Budapest): FRANCUS EGO CIVES [sic] ROMANVS MILES IN ARMIS, 'I am a Frank, a Roman citizen, a soldier in arms'. One did not have to choose between one's native ethnicity and one's acquired Roman identity.

2

'Tumult among the Nations' (Psalm 2:1)
The Development of Sub-Roman Kingdoms

The last chapter concluded with events that have been described as 'the end of Roman Britain', but, as we have seen, what came to an end was regular imperial government of the British provinces – in essence, military control, taxation, a money economy. That did not imply the end of *Romanitas* conceived in broader terms. For many centuries people both within and beyond the limits of empire had sought to benefit from access to Rome, and this continued to be the case in Britain. Even those who had never lived under direct Roman rule continued to be attracted to aspects of *Romanitas*, while those who had lived in the Roman provinces continued to think of themselves as Romans long after the supposed 'end'. It is a fruitful exercise to look at different ways in which communities continued to assert their *Romanitas* after the political collapse around AD 410. I will refer to aspects of the culture of this period as 'sub-Roman', but this is not meant to imply a decadent form of Roman culture, a falling away from past glories. The 'sub' serves here as it does in the word 'subsequent' to suggest following on: in a changed political context, *Romanitas* was given new forms, its symbols and content partially renegotiated, resulting in a continuity that is not always sufficiently recognised.

In Gwynedd in northwest Wales a late fifth-century stone commemorates Cantiorix, a *magistratus*.

People and places in Chapter 2

CANTIORI HIC IACIT VENEDOTIS CIVE FVIT [C]ONSOBRINO // MAGLI
MAGISTRAT[I]
Here lies Cantiori[x]. He was a citizen of Gwynedd, the cousin of
Maglus the magistrate.

Clearly people here continued to conceive of their community
and its leaders using Roman models, as citizens and magistrates.

A degree of continuity of Roman administration was also
provided through the officials of the Church, the clergy. So in
the later fifth century the British-born St Patrick describes his
family origin in a *villula* ('small farm') near a *vicus* ('village')
where his father had been a *decurio*, a local Roman official
responsible for tax-collection, and also a clergyman (a deacon),
which suggests that he had lived in the Roman civilian zone in
southwest Britain (not in Kilpatrick on the Clyde where much
later legend claims he was born). His grandfather had been a
priest, and Patrick himself was a priest and eventually a bishop,
but he would also have been expected to inherit his father's
office of decurion had he not spent most of his adult life in
Ireland. This intertwining of civil and ecclesiastical authority
in a single family neatly illustrates the continuity of this aspect
of *Romanitas* and its often ecclesiastical flavour. As one might
expect of such a man, Patrick's writings (his *Confession* and
his *Letter to the Soldiers of Coroticus*) are in Latin. Apart from
a few short inscriptions, his works are the only writings that
survive from these islands for the whole of the fifth century. If
the offices of *magistratus* and *decurio* show the survival of some
aspects of Romano-British organisation, so does the evidence
of sub-Roman occupation of Roman villas in southern Britain.
Here it seems that local rulers living in these villas continued to
extract some kind of tax from those subject to them, probably in
ways which continued aspects of Roman taxation.

During and immediately after the Roman occupation Latin
seems to have remained almost the only form of literacy in
Britain. There are a tiny number of exceptions to this rule: out
of about 130 'curse tablets' found at Bath, all are in more or
less intelligible Latin, but two may have been written in British.

St Patrick's own Latin writings show that Latin education in Britain continued in the fifth century, and this means that there were schools, teachers, students, books, scribes and libraries. This literate culture could have survived only if the sub-Roman elite continued to invest in such costly things, and this would be likely only if they thought that such investment would help to sustain the social and cultural – and perhaps political and economic – forms that they valued.

In addition to the Latin of a literate and scholarly elite, who may often have been closely associated with the Church, there is also evidence in southern Britain that Latin had become a widespread vernacular language, in some areas perhaps the main spoken language. This was Latin with a British accent, and the kind of speech that is sometimes called 'Vulgar Latin', the non-classical form of the language that in different parts of the empire gave rise eventually to the Romance languages (French, Spanish, Italian and so on). Curse tablets at Romano-British shrines in the south, notably at Bath and Uley in Gloucestershire, show a fairly consistent Vulgar Latin, and these were probably made by or for local farmers and town-dwellers, Britons who used this language in their daily affairs.

A similar conclusion may be drawn from the fifth-century stone commemorating Cantiorix that we have just looked at. The workman who made it, or the person who commissioned it, clearly spoke Vulgar Latin. In proper classical Latin the monument's *cive* 'citizen' should have been written *civis*, while *consobrino*, 'cousin', should be *consobrinus*. But in fifth-century Britain *consobrino* should be seen not as a mistake, but as a typical spelling of Vulgar Latin as it was spoken and sometimes written (compare the word *sobrino*, 'nephew', in modern Spanish as an exact parallel to Cantiorix's description as a *consobrino*).

Another possible indication that Latin was the vulgar tongue of southern Britain may be the fact that the Germanic language spoken by invaders and settlers in Britain at this time had very few words borrowed from British speech (fewer than ten have been identified with any confidence), but many more borrowed from Latin. This might suggest that the spoken language first encountered by Germanic settlers in Britain was Latin rather than British. We cannot be certain about this, however, as it may be that settlers in these areas of Britain picked up their Latin loan-words in various parts of Romanised Germania, and we should also consider that some of the earliest Germanic settlement in Britain before AD 410 comprised units of the Roman army. This might also explain why Latin was eventually so much more influential on Anglo-Saxon than British was.

The strength of Vulgar Latin as a spoken language in Britain is also demonstrated by its impact in Ireland. As the Church developed in Britain in the fourth and fifth centuries, it began to reach out westwards to Ireland. The conversion of the Irish to Christianity involved the creation of several new words in Gaelic for Christian concepts, and many of these new words were borrowed from Latin, and in particular from British Latin – a Latin that had in turn been shaped by the sound-world of the Celtic language of Britain. This can only have happened if the British Christians who shared their beliefs with the Irish were regularly speaking this kind of British-influenced Vulgar Latin themselves.

ROMANITAS IN SOUTHERN SCOTLAND

We have so far discussed the evidence of continuing *Romanitas* in southern Britain, the civilian zone of the province. But *Romanitas* took different forms in different areas. In some ways the variation is a matter of degree: the southern zone, with its villas, civilian government and so on, might be expected to offer more Roman evidence than the northern zone, especially north of Hadrian's Wall. But even in the north there is evidence of Latin speech and Roman practices. Various sub-Roman inscribed stones in southern Scotland show a knowledge of Latin in the fifth and sixth centuries. Kirkmadrine in the Rhinns of Galloway has three early stones, each marked with a *chi–rho* symbol. One stone commemorates two *sacerdotes*, 'priests', or more probably 'bishops', Viventius and Mavorius – the first a Latin name, the second a Latinised Celtic name (from *Magurix*). It has the

Greek letters alpha and omega above the *chi–rho* symbol, referring to the words of Christ: 'I am the Alpha and the Omega . . .
the beginning and the end' (Rev. 22:13). Another stone commemorates someone called Florentius and another person whose
name has been almost entirely obliterated. A third stone bears
the words *Initium et Finis*, 'the beginning and the end', referring like the alpha and omega to Christ. These stones are the
remains of an important sixth-century sub-Roman church at
Kirkmadrine, where Latin and Celtic names co-existed.

A similar interweaving of Celtic and Latin names appears a
short distance to the east at Whithorn. The 'Latinus Stone' is a
fifth-century artefact commemorating two local people:

TE D[OM]INVM
LAVDAMV[S]
LATINV[S]
ANN[O]RVM
XXXV ET
FILIA SVA
ANN IV
IC SINVM
FECERVNT
NEPVS
BARROVA
DI

This may be translated as follows: 'We praise you, the Lord.
Latinus, aged 35 years, grandson [or descendant] of Barrovadus,
and his daughter aged 4 years, made a sign here'. What was
the 'sign', or *si[g]num*, that they made? The word was once
thought to refer to a damaged *chi–rho* symbol at the top of this
tall stone, but that has been shown to be illusory, so maybe the
stone itself is the sign. Though his grandfather was called by
the Celtic name Barrovadus, the stone was inscribed in Latin by
Latinus. The opening phrase, *'Te Dominum laudamus'*, makes
their Christian faith clear, but there is nothing ecclesiastical
about the stone, and its principal purpose is probably not religious at all. Its intent is probably the more secular concern to
assert kinship, which is probably connected to property, using

the language of Roman authority. This stone might also be evidence for spoken Vulgar Latin in Galloway in the fifth century. The spelling *sinvm* for *signum* reflects the pronunciation of British Latin-speakers.

Earlier commentators saw these stones at Kirkmadrine and Whithorn as evidence of some Latin-speaking mission from Gaul, the first toe-holds of a Continental outpost in southwest Scotland. But scholars now see them as a continuation of the native *Romanitas* of northern Britain, some in a more formal and book-learned ecclesiastical Latin, some in a less formal and secular Vulgar Latin.

Other early stones in Scotland support these conclusions. In Peebles a stone was inscribed, probably in the late seventh century:

NEITANO SACERDOS
Neitan the priest

The personal name Neitan is a Celtic one, a name shared by various kings of Picts recorded in Gaelic sources as *Nechtan* and by Bede as *Naiton*; a warrior called *Nwython* appears in the early British poem *Y Gododdin*. But in Peebles the name is that of a bishop or priest, and in spite of his presumed church education in whose 'correct' Latin he would have appeared as *Neitanus*, he is represented on the stone as *Neitano*, showing the decay of nominal endings characteristic of oral Vulgar Latin.

Other stones of a more secular character also show the use of Vulgar Latin in southern Scotland. At Yarrow a stone made in the sixth century is inscribed:

HIC MEMORIA PE[RP]ETUA
IN LOCO INSIGNISIMI PRINCI
PES NVDI
DVMNOGENI HIC IACENT
DVO FILII
LIBERALIS

Here [is] a perpetual memorial. Here lie, in [this] place, the most distinguished princes, Nudus and Dumnogenus, the two sons of Liberalis

The two princes have Latinised British names, but their father, Liberalis, had a purely Latin name. The forms taken by these personal names, where *Nvdi* and *Dvmnogeni* are the subjects of the verb *iacent* 'they lie', are not Classical Latin, which would have rendered them *Nudus* and *Dumnogenus*. Here again the loss of case-endings suggests that the speech of the ruling class at this period included Vulgar Latin, though no doubt they spoke British too.

The *hic iacent* formula is diagnostically Christian, but like the Latinus stone, the actual intent of this stone has very little to do with the proclamation of theological or ecclesiastical ideas. It is a declaration of lordship, of a territorial power connected to kinship and patrilineal descent. The same could be said for the Catstane (NT148743), a fifth- or sixth-century stone commemorating Vetta, daughter of Victr... (perhaps Victricius), which lies not far from Cramond, an important Roman fort and civilian settlement. And on Hadrian's Wall another interesting stone, probably of the late fifth century, was found:

BRIGOMAGLOS
HIC IACIT
Here lies Brigomaglos.

The name is British meaning 'high prince', and the *hic iacit* formula is Christian. It was found at the Roman fort of Vindolanda, near a place where an early church seems to have been built on the ruins of the officers' quarters in the fifth century. At this former Roman power centre, within a century of the collapse of imperial power, a member of a sub-Roman British elite was buried and commemorated in Latin by people now Christian who were presumably using this site as a power centre of their own. A similar pattern of sub-Roman British occupation of northern Roman power centres is apparent at Carlisle, and at Birdoswald a series of three Dark Age halls were built on top of Roman granaries in the fifth and possibly the sixth century. Analogous to the sub-Roman occupation of Roman villas in the south, the sub-Roman occupation of Roman forts in the north suggests the continuity of an elite who conceived of themselves as heirs to Roman power in the region. We will return to this pattern in due course, as some of the evidence of sub-Roman occupation of these sites points to the presence not only of Britons but of Anglo-Saxons.

ROMANITAS NORTH OF THE FORTH

The Scottish evidence we have examined so far has been in the area between Hadrian's Wall and the Antonine Wall, but forms of *Romanitas* are apparent further north as well. Long cist cemeteries are heavily concentrated in the Lothians, but extend northwards in significant numbers into Fife and Angus, and beyond that in smaller numbers to Easter Ross, Sutherland and Caithness, and even to Orkney. These cemeteries began to be used in Pictland during or shortly after the Roman occupation of Britain, and may have had connotations of *Romanitas* for their creators. Many were Christian burials, though some may be pre-Christian. The large long-cist cemetery at Hallow Hill by St Andrews in Fife is one of the most impressive, with burials radiocarbon-dated to a period from the sixth to the ninth century. Among the earliest burials is one of a child whose body, in a dug grave (not a long cist), was accompanied by various Roman goods, including a ring, a brooch and a seal-box, leading the excavator to suggest that it may have been a foundation burial for the cemetery. The Roman goods may be two or three centuries older than the burial, perhaps having been held by members of an important family or having been acquired by trade. The later use of Hallow Hill in a Christian context is clear, and the name of the place, *Eglesnamin*, which survives to appear in twelfth- and thirteenth-century records, also indicates a Pictish church here, containing as it does the Pictish word *egles from Latin ecclesia. Other long-cist burials are sometimes found to contain Roman objects, such as the late Roman glass cup found at Airlie School in Angus (NO315501).

The influence of Rome north of the Forth can also be seen in the use of silver as an articulation of power and status. Silver was not mined in this territory, so any silver that was being used must have been imported, and the evidence suggests that it had a Roman origin. Silver Roman coins are found at various sites, and massive silver jewellery indicates the re-use of Roman silver by skilled native craftsmen in the service of the elite.

We have another glimpse of *Romanitas* north the Forth in the writings of St Patrick. Patrick tells us that he was captured from Britain by Irish pirates and taken to Ireland as a slave. After his escape and his eventual return to Ireland as a missionary bishop, we find him writing a pair of letters to the soldiers of a certain Coroticus. The first of these letters is lost, but Patrick refers to it in his second letter in which he denounces Coroticus and his men for having mounted an attack on Ireland and captured and enslaved many of Patrick's people, men and women. Coroticus appears to have ruled a British kingdom, though Patrick does not state this; his seventh-century 'biographer', Muirchú, is the earliest source to state explicitly that Coroticus was British – he may have been king of Alclud, 'rock of the Clyde', now Dumbarton Rock. But whatever the ethnicity of Coroticus himself, our interest is actually in his allies, the Picts, to whom Patrick refers twice. First Patrick refers to Coroticus' men as 'allies of the *Scotti* and of Picts and apostates' (*socii Scottorum atque Pictorum apostatarumque*). Later in the letter he speaks of the captives as slaves 'of the most vile, wicked and apostate Picts' (*indignissimorum pessimorum apostatarumque Pictorum*). The use of the term 'apostate' here strongly suggests that the Picts were Christians. You can only apostatise from Christianity if you are already a Christian. Patrick's point is not simply that these soldiers are wicked in a general way, but that by attacking and enslaving innocent Christians in Ireland they have forfeited a Christian identity that they claimed for themselves.

Coupled with the rhetoric of apostasy from Christianity is that of loss of citizenship. Patrick says he is writing to the soldiers of Coroticus: 'I do not say to my fellow-citizens, nor to fellow-citizens of the holy Romans, but fellow-citizens of demons' (*non dico civibus meis neque civibus sanctorum Romanorum sed civibus daemoniorum*). This highly charged word *civis*, 'citizen', is clearly being used to reflect not some residual attachment to the Roman Empire, but rather to Christianity. You cease to be a *civis* in Patrick's argument when you abandon Christian practice. A 'citizen' is someone who is Roman (a 'holy Roman' as Patrick says) not because he pays taxes or enjoys the protection of the Roman army, but because he belongs to the Roman religion, Christianity. In fifth- and sixth-century Britain, being in the Church became a key part of what it meant to be a Roman, to be a *civis*.

FOUR NATIONS, FIVE LANGUAGES

The English monk Bede gave a brief description of the linguistic geography of early eighth-century Britain. He stated that there were five languages:

> The language of the English (*Anglorum*), of the Britons (*Brettonum*), of the Gaels (*Scottorum*), of the Picts (*Pictorum*) and that of the Latins (*Latinorum*) which has become common to all of them through meditation on the scriptures. (HE i, 1)

Bede's division of the people of Britain into language groups corresponds closely – and problematically – with his division of the island into political territories. He narrates various legends of how different peoples arrived in Britain and how they took their respective territories. The Britons (*Brettones*), who originally occupied the whole island of Britain, had come from Armorica 'so it is said' (*ut fertur*), that is, northwest France, including modern Brittany. This legend presumably arose from the observation that there was a British-speaking community in Armorica, and this suggested to the creators of the legend that the Britons had come to this island from there. In fact, the British-speaking territory in Armorica was established by Britons moving in the opposite direction, some fleeing from Saxon (and perhaps Irish) aggression in the fifth and sixth centuries, though there was probably a certain amount of even earlier British settlement there. Gildas in the sixth century applies a verse of Psalm 43 to those fleeing Britain in the fifth:

They sought territories across the sea, with great wailing, singing under the folds of their sails, instead of a sea shanty: 'You have given us over like sheep to be devoured, and have scattered us among the nations'. (*de Excidio* § 25)

Bede says that the Picts came from Scythia, 'as they say' (*ut perhibent*), first to Ireland and then to Britain where they established their rule over the northern part of the island. A third nation, the *Scotti*, came from Ireland (*Hibernia*) and formed the kingdom of Dál Riata. The fourth nation in Britain is described by Bede as a complex of Germanic tribes, each of which is described as settling in a particular part of Britain and eventually establishing control there.

They came from three very powerful tribes of Germany, that is the Saxons, the Angles and the Jutes. (HE i, 15)

Bede's narratives are typical of the medieval conception of the origins of peoples, or 'ethnogenesis'. It corresponds to a particular model in which a group of people under a famous leader leaves its place of origin, travels a great distance and finds a territory that suits it. The newly arrived group, now acting as an invading army, seizes control of the territory by force of arms or perhaps by negotiation. The descendants of the leader are the rulers of this new territory, which now becomes a kingdom, making them kings. They and their people speak the same language and may have other customs which give the impression of cultural cohesion, marking them out as different from their neighbours.

This kind of ethnogenetic story-telling, the 'migration and conquest model' with its innumerable variations, was almost universal in the Middle Ages. It enjoyed the authority of both ancient Rome (Virgil's *Aeneid* in which Aeneas journeys from Troy to Latium, conquers the territory and becomes the ancestor of the Romans) and of the Bible (where the Hebrews escape from Egypt, spend forty years wandering in the desert, and conquer and settle in their 'promised land'). This model followed by medieval authors bore only a partial resemblance – sometimes not even that – to the historical processes which had actually shaped their world. Historians treat such narratives as accurate accounts at their peril.

BRITONS

The Britons known to Bede were not the result of a migration from northwest France, but a patchwork of societies speaking various dialects of a P-Celtic language, British. Their polities and ethnic identities had emerged from centuries of interactions among themselves and with people from overseas. Centuries of contact with the Roman Empire had shaped their sense of themselves. There had also been a great deal of political disruption and change in that period. Of all the territorial kingdoms in Scotland described by Ptolemy in the second century, the name of only one survived into the sub-Roman period of the sixth: the people whom Ptolemy called the *Votadini* reappear in sixth-century poetry as the *Gododdin*, and in the ninth-century *Historia Brittonum* (drawing on sixth- or seventh-century records) as *Guotodin*. The *Maeatai* mentioned by Cassius Dio in the early third century (but not known to Ptolemy) also survived into the early medieval period, and were mentioned by Adomnán of Iona in his *Life of Columba* in the late seventh century as the *Miathi* (VC i, 9). The survival of these two names, however, does not mean that the two polities had survived intact and unchanging throughout the intervening centuries. In the sub-Roman period there was probably much political fragmentation, and we should imagine a rather more improvised sort of lordship, low-level and more local rulers, petty chieftains governing and exploiting small territories with a few warriors.

Out of this fragmented political and economic world, new lordships appear in the earliest native records. The British poetry known in Welsh as *Hengerdd*, the 'old poetry' from the north, purportedly written in the sixth century though considerably reworked in the later Middle Ages, includes poems attributed to Aneirin and Taliesin and mentions various war leaders and rulers – perhaps we might call them 'kings'. But the territories over which they ruled and the places where they fought are sometimes difficult to place with any certainty. We hear, for example, of the lordship of Rheged. The poetry of Taliesin hails the courage of Urien:

> Battle's cloak, he'd no mind to flee,
> Rheged's lord, I marvel, when challenged.

He is 'Urien of Rheged', and 'Rheged's defender'. His son, Owain, is also praised as 'Rheged's lord' in a lament on his death:

> Soul of Owain ab Urien,
> may his Lord attend to its needs.
> Rheged's lord, a green burden hides him,
> It was no light thing to praise him.

Many scholars have located the kingdom of Rheged around Carlisle and the River Eden, and therefore believe that the Solway Firth is the body of water known in one medieval poem as *Merin Reget*, 'the sea of Rheged'. Others have suggested that Rheged was in the far west of Galloway, offering the place name Dunragit as 'the fort of Rheged' at the head of Luce Bay (which is therefore understood as *Merin Reget*). Another suggestion accepts both these locations for Rheged, and therefore envisages an extensive kingdom all around the shores of the Solway Firth and up to the Rhinns of Galloway – a larger territory than we might expect for a single kingdom at this point in British history. A fourth theory places Rheged further to the southeast on the basis that Urien of Rheged is also referred to as the ruler of *Catraeth*, usually identified with Catterick in Yorkshire:

> I saw a lord, most gracious his ways.
> I saw the ruler of Catraeth beyond the plains.

Urien may have 'ruled' *Catraeth* in some sense, but that does not mean that *Catraeth* was in Rheged. As leader of a war band, Urien is recorded by the Taliesin poems as raiding far and wide, making war on neighbours and on more distant peoples, such as those of *Manaw*, the area around Clackmannan:

His steed beneath him,
making for Manaw
and greater gain,
profit in plenty . . .

Likewise he is recorded in battle at *Cludfein*, probably 'Clyde Rock' (Dumbarton), and is praised as 'the defender of *Aeron*', which is probably Ayr and its surrounding territory, and 'bold against the Gododdin' in Lothian. None of these references indicates the location of Rheged; rather, they record the raiding and war-making of a sixth-century ruler, seeking cattle, slaves, tribute, hostages and overlordship. As an aside it is also worth remarking that nothing in Taliesin's verse on Urien suggests that his warfare was conducted with a particular view to ousting English invaders. Certainly, some of his enemies are 'Angles', or 'Lloegyr-men', but these do not stand out above Manaw, Powys, Ayr, the Ford of Alclud and Cludfein – all British places – where he also fought, presumably against British war bands.

The *Cludfein* just mentioned above as 'Clyde Rock' may simply name the location of a battle. There was a British fortress on the rock, which appears elsewhere as *Alclud*, 'rock of the Clyde', and is the place named in Latin in the seventh-century *Life of Columba* as *Petra Cloithe*, 'rock of the Clyde', where King Rhydderch ruled in the sixth century. Here the name of the fortress stands for the kingdom, but we have very little idea of the extent of the kingdom, nor of when it emerged; we certainly cannot simply identify it with the *Damnonii* of Ptolemy or with the kingdom of Strathclyde, which did not appear until the ninth century.

Other territories mentioned in the poems are even harder to place. We should not approach this material with any great confidence that it will enable us to draw a political map of southern Scotland in the sixth century, far less of the century before that, or after it.

GERMANIC PEOPLES

The peoples referred to by Bede as Angles, Saxons and Jutes, together comprising his *gens Anglorum*, or 'nation of the English', were all speakers of a Germanic language. Such people appeared in the third century as pirates raiding the east coast of Britain. The Roman army had also recruited many thousands of Germanic soldiers, and numbers of these men had for a long time been stationed in Britain. Cemeteries near Romano-British towns and forts contain quantities of pottery of a recognisably Germanic style from as early as the fourth century. The two army commanders in Roman Britain whose deaths in AD 367 were recorded by Ammianus were called Fullofaudes and Nectaridus, both Germanic names, and in AD 372 Fraomarius was king of the Bucenobantes, a tribe of the *Alamanni*, when Ammianus records: '[Valentinian] removed him to Britain, where he gave him the authority of a tribune and placed a *numerus* of the Alamanni under his command, forming for him a division strong in its numbers.' Where these German troops served is not known, but they may have been posted to the defence of the northern frontier, the Hadrianic line. Such defences are likely to have involved a number of troops originating in Germania or other parts of *barbaricum*, in addition perhaps to British troops. In fact, the distinction between native British and troops from the Continent must have become blurred as foreign troops were assimilated into frontier society, settling locally after retirement, marrying local women and having sons who were obliged by law to enter their fathers' units and continue to serve locally.

This late Roman elite in the frontier zone, with cultural and political ties to the north of the frontier (think of the soldiers of Coroticus who imagined themselves to be *cives*) did not disappear in 410 with the collapse of imperial control. They were probably the group from which the war bands emerged, which would eventually form some of the lordships and kingdoms mentioned in the poetry of Taliesin and Aneirin. If these war bands included men from Germanic units then we might imagine that even by the early fifth century there were Germanic elements in the culture of the British elite in the north.

Further south new burial rites appeared in the first half of the fifth century. In East Anglia, around AD 430, cremation burials began to be used in which the deceased had been burned and their ashes buried in ceramic urns, a rite that connected its practitioners to people in German-speaking areas on the Continent. Another new funeral rite began to be used in eastern Britain at about the same time: extended inhumation with various goods buried alongside a finely dressed corpse. This kind of burial may also suggest connections to German-speaking areas on the Continent, though there are other parallels too. It is not obvious, however, what brought about this cultural shift in Britain. One explanation is the arrival of numbers of Germanic warriors in these areas and the expulsion of native British communities. An invasion is envisaged by writers such as Gildas and Bede, while in the sixth century the 'Synod of the Grove of Victory' indicated the penance for people who assisted Germanic war bands in their raiding:

> Those who afford guidance to barbarians [i.e., Saxons], fourteen years [of penance] if no slaughter of Christians or bloodshed occurs, or dreadful captivity. If it does occur, however, let them do penance for the rest of their lives, laying down their arms.

Violence and the enslavement of British people by Germanic war bands is clearly an aspect of the cultural change. Population movement must be part of the explanation, therefore, whether of large numbers of people or of a warrior elite in smaller numbers, or of something in between.

But invasive barbarians are not the only factor in the spread of Germanic culture in Britain. We have already noted the role of German recruits in the Roman army. There were thousands of them, and for most of them there is very little archaeological evidence up to the end of the fourth century other than the names of their units and their gods found inscribed on stones. Otherwise, their archaeological footprint is very much like that of the other Roman units in Britain. Whatever their place of origin, they were Roman soldiers and enjoyed the status that this conferred on them. They had little reason in the fourth and early fifth century to proclaim their barbarian origin in an empire that often regarded barbarians as virtually sub-human. But in the fifth century, as imperial authority collapsed in Britain, there must have been a renegotiation of status and power among local elites. Such a renegotiation would entail fierce competition between rival groups and kindreds, and the competition would be played out partly in the ceremonies of death in which 'barbarian' practices took on new symbolic value.

Is it a coincidence that the distribution of Germanic cremation burials and furnished inhumations – mostly south of the Humber – generally overlaps with the distribution of Roman villas, towns, roads and coin finds? This might be because invading Germans were immediately attracted to the areas that had also attracted Roman settlement, and for the same reasons – richer farmland, ease of land and sea transport. But it might also be because some of the people who began to bury their dead in these ways were not invaders, but local people who had chosen to adopt Germanic cultural markers, a Germanic ethnicity of some sort. The success of a Germanic military elite would persuade many people in the fifth century and beyond that theirs were the symbols of power, and that they should adopt those symbols if they wanted to compete. Burial practices were symbols to be deployed in the quest for status.

Ethnic change in a given area can therefore be seen as the result of some combination of military invasion and occupation, migration and the adoption of the cultural practices of one group by another. The process of change varied in different parts of Britain: in some areas there must have been widespread expropriation of lands, large-scale settlement and the destruction of native British communities by violence, enslavement and expulsion. But in some areas the process was evidently a more complex interaction, where change went along with continuities between British and Anglo-Saxon identities.

The evidence for a pattern of co-existence and ethnic diversity in the area north of the Humber is many-stranded. Two

Anglo-Saxon kingdoms of the north come into view in the sixth century. The northerly one, Bernicia, expanded from its heartland in the lower Tweed basin and took in Bamburgh and Lindisfarne when they were captured by Ida in the mid-sixth century. We must assume that it was initially surrounded by British communities with their own lords or kings. Further south, across the River Tees, lay Deira, where more extensive Anglo-Saxon settlement appears to have taken place, and somewhat earlier, but even here we will see that British communities persisted. Both names, Bernicia and Deira, are British in origin, which in itself may suggest that, unlike kingdoms with thoroughly English names (West Saxons, East Angles, Mercia), there was some continuity of territory and even of lordship between British and Anglo-Saxon kingdoms of the north. The archaeology of the Bernician power centre at Bamburgh reveals continuous occupation by British and then Anglo-Saxon groups (insofar as these can be characterised by artefacts, burials and building types). Similar continuities are apparent at other high-status Bernician sites at Dunbar and Yeavering (British power centres whose sites and names were adopted by Anglo-Saxons). Likewise, just as we saw British occupation of Roman forts on Hadrian's Wall in the sub-Roman period, there is also evidence of early Anglo-Saxon occupation here, with Anglo-Saxon burials and artefacts at various sites on the wall. And we must remember here that the terms 'British' and 'Anglo-Saxon' in this context refer to an 'ethnic style' (e.g., burial types) and not to any racial characteristic. The evidence of ethnic change in some cases may therefore be due, at least in part, to the persistence of a single group whose members adopted new ethnic markers, rather than the displacement of one group of people by another. Ethnicity is a word for the culture by which people choose to represent themselves, and with which they improvise to assert identities and to negotiate such matters as status and power.

One of the most interesting illustrations of a multi-ethnic complex of Anglo-Saxon and British communities is in the territory of the Gododdin, to the north of Bernicia, with a power centre in the later sixth century at Edinburgh. Referring to this territory, the poem *Y Gododdin* ('The Gododdin') has long been understood as an account of a sixth-century raid by British warriors from *Din Eidyn* (Edinburgh) on an Anglo-Saxon settlement at *Catraeth* (Catterick in Yorkshire). The poem as it now stands – in two versions in a thirteenth-century manuscript – is the result of a process of transmission and re-modelling that lasted for centuries, including a possible seventh-century copying in the kingdom of Alclud. But it appears to contain a core of material that was composed in the late sixth or early seventh century, a collection of praise poems for warriors who had fallen in battle. In the traditional view of the poem as the account of an ethnic conflict between Britons and Anglo-Saxons, the name *Mynyddog Mwynfawr*, which appears several times in the text, is the name of the ruler of Din Eidyn, and it is under his lordship that the Celtic warriors rode south on an ill-fated adventure that ended in the death of them all.

But some re-interpretations of this poetry have been offered by modern scholars, among them John T. Koch, for whom Mynyddog Mwynfawr is not a personal name at all, but a place name meaning 'Mountainous Luxurious'. Certainly, none of the occurrences of the name in the poetry is clearly a reference to a person, and all could refer to Din Eidyn itself, or to the territory of Gododdin as a whole. The ruler of the war band of Gododdin in this view is not Mynyddog, but a man who appears as 'Eidyn's lord' (*ut Eidyn*) whose name is given as Uruei. The crucial stanza tells us:

> Natural – on a charger to defend Gododdin;
>   In the vanguard, swift his grey steed;
> Natural – that he should be fleet as a stag;
>   Natural – before Deira's picked men he'd attack;
> Natural – what he said, Golystan's son, would be heard,
>   Though his father was no high lord;
> Natural – on Mynyddawg's behalf, shattered shields;
>   Natural – a crimson spear before Eidyn's lord, Uruei.

This stanza portrays Uruei as 'the lord of Din Eidyn' who had feasted the warriors with wine and mead, and whose hospitality they repaid with their weapons and with their lives. And Uruei, though his own name is British, is the son of a man called Golystan, a name whose British orthography disguises its Anglo-Saxon origin: it is Wolstan, a variant of Wulfstan. The poem tells us that Uruei's father was not a 'high lord' (*guledic*), that is, not a British lord. The implication is that Uruei, the lord of Din Eidyn and commander of the Gododdin expedition to Catterick, was the son of an Anglo-Saxon. His father, Wulfstan or Golystan, may have married a British woman from a lordly family, perhaps because his own war band had posed a sufficient threat to Uruei's mother's kindred to demand her marriage to him as the price of peace. In this scenario there is a matrilineal dimension to Uruei's ascent to power since his father, not being a high lord or *guledic*, could hardly have passed on to him this social status.

If we follow this new reading of the poem we must abandon the old image of a titanic ethnic struggle between Celt and Saxon, between 'native' and 'invader'. Instead, we must imagine a scenario in which a multi-ethnic society in southeast Scotland and northeast England was composed of a number of lordships whose rulers were engaged in a continuous struggle for power. In each lordship men came to power by a combination of military force and some sort of hereditary right. At the moment envisaged by the poem, the leader of the Gododdin war band is a man with an Anglo-Saxon father, but he was able to draw on the support of warriors both from his own territory around Edinburgh and also from elsewhere in the north – at least according to the poem, which lists warriors in his band who came from elsewhere. These men may be Uruei's allies, fighting alongside him on a more or less equal footing, or they may be from peoples under his overlordship who were obliged to offer military support.

We may be able to glean further understanding of the multi-ethnic north if we consider this poem in relation to another one. A poem attributed to Taliesin, traditionally regarded as a contemporary of Aneirin, celebrates a battle at Gwen Ystrad. In this poem:

Catraeth's men set out at daybreak
Round a battle-winning lord, cattle-raider.
Urien he, renowned chieftain,
Constrains rulers and cuts them down.

The poem goes on to recount a great victory by Urien and
Catraeth's men over 'hordes of invaders', who came 'like waves
roaring harsh over land . . . savage men in war-bands'. Urien we
have already met as the ruler of the British kingdom of Rheged.
Here we find him leading '*Catraeth*'s men', the men of Catterick
in Yorkshire. Another poem in the *Book of Taliesin* calls Urien
'the ruler of *Catraeth*'. This presents us potentially with a striking contradiction of the ethnically charged idea that the expedition of the Gododdin to *Catraeth* was a Celtic attack on an
Anglo-Saxon kingdom, since for Taliesin the men of *Catraeth*
are led by a British war leader, Urien. One explanation for this
apparent contradiction might be that there were two battles, one
mentioned by Taliesin's poem on Gwen Ystrad and one mentioned by Aneirin's *Y Gododdin*. In between these two battles
the ethnic profile of Catterick changed from a British one (under
Urien) to an Anglo-Saxon one.
A plausible alternative scenario exists however: the two
poems may in fact commemorate one battle, not two, in which
a northern army comprising Gododdin warriors and their allies
fought a southern army led by Urien of Rheged, comprising
both British warriors of Rheged and an ethnically mixed war
band from *Catraeth* itself. We know from later accounts of
warfare between Northumbria and Mercia that both of these
Anglo-Saxon kingdoms fought with the support of troops from
British kingdoms over which they claimed overlordship. One of
the principal claims of overlordship was the ability to summon
warriors from subject kingdoms. In this scenario *Catraeth* was
not a monolithically Anglo-Saxon kingdom, but an ethnically
diverse power centre in the kingdom of Deira. It may be that
an Anglo-Saxon elite had already taken control (as it certainly
had by the early seventh century), but British warriors were
also part of the defence forces of Deira. The troops invading

from the north, as we have seen, were feasted by Uruei son of Wulfstan. In addition we must suppose that the Gododdin had ridden from their own territory of Lothian and then through the territory of Bernicia, to get to Catterick in Deira. But there is nothing in the poem to suggest that there was any defensive action by the men of Bernicia against this 'invasion' by the men of Gododdin. It may be that the Gododdin riding through Bernicia were not seen as invaders, but as allies. Indeed, it is possible that the battle commemorated in Y *Gododdin* was actually a battle between Bernicia and Deira, whose respective overlords had summoned troops from their subjects or allies, Bernicia calling on the Gododdin under Uruei, and Deira calling on Rheged under Urien. And if the Gododdin were in some degree of subjection to Bernicia by this point, might this not explain the apparent fact that 'Eidyn's lord' was the son of an Anglo-Saxon?

The interleaving of Anglo-Saxon and British power in this way does not sit well with the simple picture painted by Gildas and Bede for whom there was a natural opposition between Anglo-Saxon and British communities. But these writers were following the 'script' that we have already discussed, and other evidence supports our more complicated picture. For example, some early Anglo-Saxon laws envisage the co-existence of British and Anglo-Saxon communities cheek by jowl. Anglo-Saxon law set a value on a person according to their status. It was called *wergeld* and was the basis of legal compensation paid by an offender to the kin of his victim. The *Laws of Ine*, which purport to have been composed in Wessex in the seventh century, list the *wergeld* of various kinds of Welsh (i.e., British) people, implying that these people were incorporated into a legal community alongside Anglo-Saxons, able to take part in legal proceedings and to avail themselves of the law's protection. The British were at a disadvantage in the laws, however: the *wergeld* of an Anglo-Saxon *ceorl* (a free man with a hide of land) was 200 shillings, while that of a British person with a hide of land was only 120 shillings. This imbalance of legal rights would put British people at a marked disadvantage, and it must have encouraged the gradual 'Englishing' of such mixed polities as we are envisaging here. First, such a legal and financial disadvantage might push British farmers into poverty and debt, eventually losing them their lands and edging them into servitude of some sort; second, there would be great incentives for a Briton to make strenuous efforts to look like an Anglo-Saxon, to assimilate culturally and perhaps to marry into an Anglo-Saxon family, to escape from legal disadvantage.

The *Laws of Ine* state that a British person with five hides of land enjoyed a *wergeld* of 600 shillings – about half the *wergeld* of an Anglo-Saxon *thegn* with the same amount of land. But a Briton with five hides of land, even if he had a smaller *wergeld* than a *thegn*, may be assumed to have exercised a kind of local lordship similar to that of a *thegn*. The laws clearly envisage, therefore, communities of Britons within a wider Anglo-Saxon polity, with their own British lords. The law also mentions British horsemen 'who ride in the service of the [Anglo-Saxon] king'. This also points to British integration in Wessex. Such laws have also survived (albeit from a later period) from further north in England. The continuing British presence in northern Anglo-Saxon kingdoms is also illustrated in Stephen's *Life of Wilfrid*, written c. AD 710: the bishop raised an infant from the dead at *On Tiddanufri* (perhaps Tidover in Yorkshire) and told his mother that she must hand him over at the age of seven to serve God in the bishop's house. When the child was seven, however, the mother hid him 'among others of the British race'. This was evidently still within the Anglo-Saxon bishop's territory, and the bishop's prefect found the boy hiding there and took him to Ripon (§ 18). One wonders if he was found at Walton (i.e., 'Welsh town') a short distance to the north of Tidover, clearly a small lordship of some continuing British character when it received its name.

THE GAELS OF THE WEST

Bede's account of another 'nation' in the island of Britain concerns the *Scotti*. He recounts their origin legend, how they came from Ireland (*Hibernia*) under the leadership of Reuda, and obtained lands from among the Picts, 'either by alliance or by the sword', which Bede says they still held (HE i, 1).

The name *Scotti* (sometimes *Scoti*) is first used in fourth-century Roman writings to refer to the people of *Scotia*, Ireland. But in Bede's time the Gaelic language of the Irish was also dominant in parts of western Britain, particularly in the area of modern Argyll, and so for him this Gaelic-speaking region, which he identifies (HE i, 12) as lying north of the Firth of Clyde (i.e., in the west of Scotland), was also part of *Scotia*. Its people spoke the same language as the Irish and this, following the logic of Bede's view of ethnicity and politics, had to be explained by a migration from Ireland and the seizure of lands from the Picts. He also gives an explanation of the name by which these Gaels were known in his time, the Dál Riata, in terms of their descent from Reuda, their founding ancestor.

The picture of a Gaelic migration from Ireland to Scotland dominated the historical imaginations of medieval writers and, until recently, of modern historians too. In the last few years, however, archaeological evidence has been used to challenge the migration narrative. If there had been a significant migration of Gaels from Ireland to Scotland *c.* AD 500, as traditional accounts would have it, one would expect the migrants to have brought with them a fair amount of their material culture as well as their language. But archaeologist Ewan Campbell has noted that there is little evidence of a transfer of Irish material culture into Argyll at this period.

If there was no major migration, however, there was certainly long-standing and regular contact between Ireland and the west of Scotland. The North Channel of the Irish Sea had been for centuries a highway for the movement of people and goods, and so for cultural exchange. It is in this context that we should understand the presence of Gaelic-speaking people in western Scotland. The dramatic and effective barrier to communication between peoples and cultures was not the Irish Sea, but the *massif central* of the Scottish Highlands. Adomnán speaks of *Dorsum Brittanniae*, or 'the spine of Britain' – clearly a calque on Gaelic Druim Alban – which separated the Picts in the east from the *Scoti* of the west (VC ii, 46). Rather than ask how Gaelic got from Ireland to Scotland (the question that Bede's narrative was designed to answer) we might do better to imagine Ireland and western Scotland as a single linguistic zone in which Gaelic evolved.

What, then, of the supposed 'ancestor' of this Gaelic kingdom? Bede tells us that the Gaelic invaders were descended from an Irish leader called Reuda, from whom Dál Riata took its name, stating that it meant 'Reuda's part'. Descent from Reuda, or in Gaelic sources Réti, was claimed by at least part of the Gaelic west. Adomnán's *Life of St Columba* records the same people in the late seventh century using a slightly different name, *Korkureti* (Old Gaelic *Corcu Réti*, 'the kindred of Réti', VC i, 47). But in the earliest sources Réti is not presented as the ancestor of all the Gaels of the west. He was the 'Domangart Reti' recorded as dying or retiring AU 507, and in the *Annals of Innisfallen* he appears as *Domongairt Cind Tire*, 'Domangart of Kintyre'. His son Comgall died as king in AU 538, and another son, Gabrán, is recorded on his death in AU 558. These two sons of Domangart are supposedly the ancestors of the Corcu Réti in *Míniugud senchasa fher nAlban* ('the explanation of the tradition of the men of Scotland'), probably a seventh-century genealogical tradition, which defined two distinct polities in southern Argyll, *Cenél nGabráin* ('the kindred of Gabrán') in Kintyre and *Cenél Comgaill* ('the kindred of Comgall') in nearby Cowal.

But Adomnán's *Life of St Columba* also speaks of a wider group of Gaels, the *Scoti Britanniae*, 'the Gaels of Britain' (VC ii, 46), whose rulers evidently did not all see themselves as descendants of Réti. This is confirmed in an eighth-century genealogical tradition tracing the ancestry of the Gaels in northern Argyll not to Domangart Réti, but to his supposed grandfather, Erc. This text, *Cethri prímchenéla Dáil Riata*, 'the four principal kindreds of Dál Riata', sees some descendants of Erc (*Cenél Loairn* and *Cenél nÓengusso*) as part of Dál Riata (whence the title of the tract), but their rulers have acquired this identity without actually being descended from the eponym of Dál Riata, Domangart Réti. *Míniugud senchasa fher nAlban* likewise traces some *cenéla* (*Cenél nÓengusa* and *Cenél Loairn* in their various branches) to Erc without descending via Réti. Perhaps this is why 'Erc's region' appears in a seventh-century poem in honour of Columba, *Tiugrand Beccáin* ('the last verses of Beccán') – to stress that Colum Cille's power embraced a wider Gaelic community than the territories ruled only by the supposed descendants of Réti:

> Colum Cille, candle brightening legal theory,
> the race the hero ran pierced the midnight of Erc's region.

The Gaels of western Scotland comprised a series of kingdoms, each with its own ruling family or families and each seeking to dominate the others – Cenél nGabráin, Cenél Comgaill, Cenél Loairn, Cenél nOengusa, as well as other Gaelic kindreds with insufficient power to force their way into the genealogical records. Power relations changed as one kindred emerged as dominant, or fell under the overlordship of another. In this context genealogical fictions were constantly being created to give ancestral legitimacy to new political realities. These realities included the creation of a transmarine polity in which a Scottish Dál Riata and an Irish Dál Riata (roughly County Antrim) were joined to some degree in alliance. Genealogies should therefore be seen not as hard-to-handle evidence of ancient migratory kindreds, but as evidence of the relationships between various kingdoms and their ruling families at the time the texts were written and rewritten. It will do us no good to search these texts for 'what actually happened' to some supposed migratory kindred in the late fifth century.

The term 'Dál Riata', although (like Corcu Réti) it may origi-nally have referred only to the descendants of Domangart Réti in southern Argyll, is now used by historians to refer to all the Gaelic kindreds of the west who identified themselves in later periods as members of Dál Riata, and in the following pages I will also use it in that wider sense.

THE PICTS

The fourth nation of Britain in Bede's mental map of Britain is that of the Picts. For him they are identified by their language and by their location:

> They were separated from the Britons by two wide and long arms of the sea, one of which enters the land from the east, the other from the west, although they do not meet. (HE i, 11)

The two 'arms' are the Firth of Forth and the Firth of Clyde, so the Picts are for Bede the people dwelling north of that line – the old line, more or less, of the Antonine Wall. He places the *Scotti* north of the Clyde, so we should regard his *Picti* as those on the north side of the Forth and in the east. And he accounts for the Picts with his now familiar narrative of ethnogenesis: distant origin, migration, conquest and settlement. As we saw in Chapter 1, the word *Picti* was coined by third-century Roman writers as a term for Britons outwith the empire – the same people that Tacitus had described two centuries earlier simply as 'Britons' (*Britanni*). There is no evidence that these people thought of themselves as *Picti* during the Roman period, or even as a single people or culture, though they may have begun to do so in some ways as various groups coalesced during the Roman occupation of southern Britain. But we should hesitate to apply the term *Picti* to them at that stage in the sense that they would have recognised themselves in it.

One possible indication of an early sense of shared ethnic identity among people who would later identify themselves as Picts is the emergence of what have become known to modern commentators as 'Pictish symbols'. The application of the term 'Pictish' to the earliest of these rather begs the question: did the people who made them think of themselves as Picts? Certainly, the symbols continued to be used into a period when we can be certain that they did, but we cannot simply assume that the emergence of 'Pictish symbols' defines the moment when the Picts emerged. Nevertheless, these symbols, some clearly representational (salmon, 'beast', mirror-and-comb) and some apparently abstract forms (triple disc, double-disc-and-Z-rod) are found distributed around an area of Scotland that, for a variety of reasons, we now identify as having become Pictland. The symbols – at least, those that have survived – usually occur on standing stones, though some appear on portable objects, such as small stones, a pair of silver plaques or an ox bone. The last of these, found at the Broch of Burrian in Orkney (HY7651), is particularly important because bone can be radio-carbon dated (unlike stones or metal). The bone at Burrian, carved with a crescent-and-Z-rod, is dated between AD 570 and AD 655, lending support to the view that Pictish symbols first appear in the late sixth or early seventh century.

There are three occurrences of Pictish symbols outside the area Bede knew as Pictland: one at Dunadd in Argyll, one at Trusty's Hill in Dumfries and Galloway, and one at Edinburgh. The first two, unlike normal Pictish carvings, are carved onto living rock rather than onto deliberately erected monuments. The Trusty's Hill carving of a double-disc-and-Z-rod is stylistically rather dif-ferent from other occurrences of this symbol, as if it were a copy by someone who was not completely familiar with the genre. The Edinburgh carving is on a stone whose original location is unknown. It may also be significant that these three outliers are all at probable royal power centres, which again differentiates them from most of the symbol stones in Pictland.

Apart from these three outliers, all the Pictish symbols have been found in Pictland. Their meaning is unknown, but sugges-tions have included a form of writing, a symbolic representa-tion of kinship, a marker of territorial control (many are near boundaries) or a representation of Pictish personal names. Some aspects of this artistic practice may have had their origin in Roman or Continental images, which had been fed through the mill of a Pictish aesthetic or style to acquire their present form. It has been suggested that they emerged in Pictland as a reaction against Christianisation, that an established elite used the symbols to assert a native ideology against some per-ceived threat from the new faith. This seems unlikely, given that the symbols continued to be used for centuries, well into the Christian period, very often carved on the same stone as the Christian symbol of the Cross. It is unlikely that symbols with an original 'anti-Christian' meaning would then appear so regularly on explicitly Christian monuments. We should also bear in mind that when Christianity was first adopted in Pictland (whenever that was), it is just as likely that it was the native elite who adopted it first and therefore that these symbols may reflect their interest in this new international culture rather than a conservative resistance to it.

Whatever their meaning, the symbols were clearly of some public importance. The investment required to erect and carve these stones with their permanently visible symbols suggests that they proclaimed messages about power – perhaps in terms of personal names, territory or kinship, or some combination of these – in ways analogous to the stones inscribed with Latin letters south of the Forth–Clyde line. Assuming that Pictish symbols meant much the same thing throughout the territory of their distribution, it seems reasonable to treat them as evidence for the emergence of a shared identity – though whether we call this ethnic, political, legal or cultural is a moot point. Clearly, however, in areas where people would eventually call themselves Picts, a potent symbol system was emerging in the late sixth century that united people in a common understanding of important public proclamations and differentiated them from their British, Anglo-Saxon and Gaelic neighbours.

Although the tribes north of the Forth line had been in contact with Roman culture for centuries, there are indications that early Pictish identity was partly formed by a sense of not being Roman. The Picts erected inscribed stones on routeways, at gathering places and at boundaries, very much as their Romano-British neighbours did in the south, but they may have used this Roman-looking practice to make a statement about their not being Roman: the Britons to the south inscribed their stones with Latin letters, the Picts inscribed theirs with symbols. Could this have been a statement about 'how non-Roman we are'?

This may relate to the linguistic difference between Picts and Britons – and here we recall that Bede saw them as two different languages. Discussions of Pictish language in the nineteenth and twentieth centuries tended to focus on its obscurity and its otherness, in line with a lot of other notions of the Picts being 'mysterious' (a much abused adjective). It was suggested that Picts spoke a non-Celtic or even non-Indo-European language, an idea derived in part from the opacity of many inscriptions on stone in Pictland. The fact that no extended Pictish texts survived to illustrate the language did not help. But personal names and place names are micro-texts, and their intelligibility as P-Celtic, with good British cognates, is generally clear. The first element of the Pictish place name Aberdour also appears in Aberystwyth in Wales, and means 'estuary, outflow'; the second element *duvr* is related to Welsh *dwfr*, 'water'. In addition, some of the inscriptions that puzzled earlier scholars have in recent years been read more clearly, bringing the errant Pictish language back into the P-Celtic fold. In terms of its historical evolution, Pictish emerged simply as a northern dialect of British.

But in the former Roman province to the south, British had been spoken for centuries by people who had also spoken Latin, the language of official and high-status discourse in the empire. This sustained bilingualism in the south led to a Latinisation of southern British dialects which might not have taken place in the British dialect further north (i.e., in Pictland). The differences between a Latin-influenced southern British and a more conservative northern British may (a) explain why Bede saw Pictish and British as two distinct languages, and (b) have helped shape the Picts' own self-image as a non-Roman people.

This 'non-Roman' ethnicity appears to have been asserted by the Picts themselves. Bede records a letter of Nechtan, king of the Picts (d. 732), addressed to Ceolfrith, abbot of the Northumbrian monastery of Monkwearmouth–Jarrow. In it the Pictish king states that he and his people want to follow 'the customs of the holy Roman and apostolic church', even though they are 'far removed from the speech and nation of the Romans' (HE v, 21). We have to allow for a degree of rhetorical strategy here, however. The Pictish writer of the letter to Ceolfrith was probably aware of the old Latin tradition that defined Picts as barbarians. He was therefore making a subtle play: in order to portray his people as non-Romans he writes a letter in Latin and demonstrates his familiarity with Latin authors and their view of the *Picti*, thus showing the importance of *Romanitas* to his way of seeing the world and the Picts' place in it. He does this precisely to make formal overtures to the Northumbrians to enter into closer union with them, playing on their sense of being 'true Romans'.

This may seem strange, but it does point towards how Romanised the Picts needed to be in order to create their origin legend as recorded by Bede. He states that they were descended from Scythians, *ut perhibent*, 'as they (i.e., the Picts) assert'. If the Picts themselves are claiming descent from the Scythians, what can we infer? James Fraser has highlighted a wonderful irony: the Pictish claim of Scythian descent appears to be drawn from a reading of Virgil's *Aeneid* in which a people appear called the *picti Agathyrsi*, 'the painted Agathyrsi'. Servius, author of an authoritative commentary on the *Aeneid*, stated that the *picti Agathyrsi* were a Scythian people (*populus Scythiae*). When the Picts stated that they were descended from Scythians, they were proclaiming their supposedly barbarian origins and their difference from Roman-Britons, but at the same time proudly demonstrating their familiarity with Virgil, proving that in fact they were not barbarians at all, but sophisticated readers of Latin.

KINGDOMS IN FLUX

The idea that in the early medieval insular world there were strong and long-lasting kingdoms united by language, shared ancestry, territorial integrity and the authority of stable ruling elites is a seductive view of the world for historians, both medieval and modern. We have seen, however, that rulers exercised lordship over client or subject kingdoms who were ethnically different from them, that people created and re-created their own ethnicity, that people acquired new languages and cultural practices, and that kingdoms were in a constant state of flux in which intermarriage, tribute-taking, hostage-giving and a good deal of violence dissolved old entities and brought about new ones. We can trace these processes, with varying degrees of detail, in many moments of the early history of Scotland.

The early Anglo-Saxon kingdom of Bernicia emerged in a complex interleaving of British and Germanic ethnicities in the sub-Roman southeast of Scotland and northeast England. Although there seems to have been a degree of continuity between British and Anglo-Saxon groups and their leaders, there was also an emerging Anglo-Saxon political identity which saw itself as different from, and hostile to, surrounding British polities. There was also considerable hostility between rival claimants to power within the new Anglo-Saxon culture. Bede tells us that a man called Ida ruled from AD 547 to AD 559, and that the Northumbrian royal family traced its origin from him (HE v, 24). The second of these two claims does not mean, however, that he was king of all Northumbria. He is recorded, rather, as king of Bernicia, and the territory directly controlled by him was probably not extensive. The ninth-century *Historia Brittonum* (§ 61) states that Ida 'joined *Din Guaire* (Bamburgh) to Bernicia', suggesting that his territory was concentrated in that area.

The expansion of Bernician power continued at the expense of both British and Deiran rulers through the later sixth century and into the seventh century. In the 580s, Ida's successor as ruler of Bernicia was besieged on the island of Lindisfarne by four British kings, Urien, Rhydderch Hen, Gwallawg and Morcant. The ninth-century Welsh-Latin *Historia Brittonum*, probably relying on a considerably older northern history, reports:

> At that time sometimes the enemy and sometimes the British (*cives*) were victorious, and he (Urien) blockaded them for three days and three nights in the island of Lindisfarne (*Metcaud*) and during this campaign he was killed at the instigation of Morcant because of his envy . . . (§ 63)

Here we may note that in this ninth-century account, presumably echoing its earlier source, the term *cives*, 'citizens', refers to the Britons, giving the British struggle against Bernicia something of the savour of a Roman struggle against barbarians. The Anglo-Saxon king of Bernicia, Æthelfrith, whose reign began about AD 592, achieved a dramatic expansion of his territory and power at the expense of both Deira and the northern British kingdoms. With regard to the British, Bede states:

> He more than all the rulers of the English devastated the British people . . . For no-one among the military leaders nor among kings had made more of their lands either tributary to the English people or places for them to dwell, having exterminated or subjugated their inhabitants. (HE i, 34)

In that final phrase, *exterminatis uel subiugatis*, it is not clear exactly what Bede intended by the first term. It could mean either 'exterminated' in the sense of 'slaughtered', or perhaps – its original sense – 'forced out beyond the frontiers'. Elsewhere, Bede uses the word *exterminare* to mean 'slaughter', and that may be the case here. In either sense, however, the impression of overwhelming violence is strong. Æthelfrith's war-making must have been made against British lordships in the immediate vicinity and also Gododdin territory to the north, and to some degree in British territory to the west – perhaps lands under the kings of Alclud on the Clyde – or on the north shore of the Solway. But here we should note that British-Latin inscriptions, including the one at Peebles reading NEITANO SACERDOS, indicate continuing British lordship and church organisation in the hills and the upper valleys of the Tweed and Teviot, for example, which may have been the western part of Bernicia. In the same upland areas a higher proportion of British place names survives than in the more fertile lowland area to the east, suggesting that in these hills native Britons were made tributary rather than *exterminati*, their local lordships and church organisation surviving intact, but now under the Anglo-Saxon overlordship of Bernicia. Æthelfrith also turned his attention far to the southwest, probably in 615 or 616, attacking the British at Chester (HE ii, 2).

While Æthelfrith was making Bernicia the most powerful kingdom in northern Britain, far to the northwest another

dynasty was making its own aggressive moves against its neighbours. The territory of Dál Riata, north of the Clyde, had fallen
under the authority of the descendants of Domangart Réti
whose power base was in southern Argyll (Kintyre and Cowal).
Domangart's son, Comgall, had died in AU 538, succeeded by
his brother Gabrán, who died in AU 560, and then by his son
Conall. It seems that Conall mac Comgaill ruled not only over
Corcu Réti, but also over Gaels in northern Argyll (modern
Lorn), as is suggested by the fact that he was able to give the
island of Iona to Columba in AD 563. Five years later he took
part in a raid on *Iardoman*, the Inner Hebrides, in the company
of the Irish king Colmán Bec. This attack may have been an
attempt by Conall to regain control of the islands – including
Iona – following some act of resistance by the men of Lorn or
other northern Gaelic kindreds.

On Conall's death in AU 574, the rule of Dál Riata passed to
his cousin, Áedán mac Gabráin. It appears that Áedán's succession was challenged by members of the Cenél Comgaill when in
AU 576 there was a battle at Teloch somewhere in Kintyre 'in

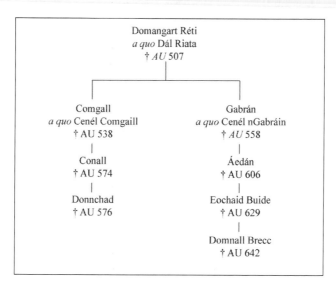

Descendants of Domangart

which fell Donnchad (*Dúnchad*) son of Conall mac Comgaill, and many other followers of the sons of Gabrán fell'. Having dealt with this challenge, Áedán consolidated his grip on Dál Riata and sought to project his power yet further. In AU 580, he raided Orkney, a Pictish territory whose king was subject to the overlordship of Bridei, a Pictish king whose power centre is recorded on the River Ness. Two years later Áedan won a battle in the territory of Manaw to the south (the area around Clackmannan). In AU 596, he was defeated, some of his sons being killed, in Circinn in the far east of Pictland. Adomnán's *Life of Columba* refers to another battle fought by Áedán against the Miathi – the people in the area near Stirling whose name survives in Dumyat, 'the dún or fort of the Miathi'.

In spite of his defeat in Circinn, Áedán mac Gabráin remained a powerful force in the Gaelic world, and probably beyond. The fact that one of his sons had a British name, Artúr, and another had an Anglo-Saxon name, Conaing, suggests that he had forged marital alliances beyond Gaelic Dál Riata which will have strengthened his hand. Certainly, he was still powerful enough in AD 603 to attack Æthelfrith in Northumbria 'with an immense and mighty army', according to Bede, who says that Áedán took this step in reaction to Æthelfrith's own expansionism (HE i, 34). Áedán's army met Æthelfrith at *Degsastan* ('Degsa's stone'), whose location is unknown. Interestingly, one manuscript of the *Anglo-Saxon Chronicle* says that Áedán was acting in concert with one Hering son of Hussa who 'led the army thither'. Now Hering's father had been king of Bernicia before Æthelfrith and, if the *Chronicle* is right, it seems that Hering, having been supplanted by Æthelfrith about AD 592, was using the support of Dál Riata in an attempt to remove Æthelfrith and return himself to power. Given his role in Áedán's attack, Hering may have been in exile in Dál Riata; Áedán would have hoped to increase his influence in Northumbria by installing his protégé or ally as king there. In spite of his 'immense and mighty army', however, Áedán was utterly defeated and his army slaughtered, though he himself survived.

The following year, strengthened by his destruction of

Áedán's army, Æthelfrith seized the kingdom of Deira, driving into exile a man called Edwin, son of the former Deiran king Ælle. The fact that Æthelfrith now ruled both Bernicia and Deira allowed Bede to speak of him as ruling 'the kingdom of the *Nordanhymbrorum*', the people dwelling north of the River Humber, Northumbria (HE i, 34). Æthelfrith also took Edwin's sister, Acha, as his wife at about this time. Although inheritance was essentially patrilineal in Anglo-Saxon society, there were many factors other than inherited paternal rights that actually determined who would gain royal power. Military success, wealth, the size of your retinue, and claims made on your wider kindred, including your mother's kin, would all help to determine who would rule a kingdom. By taking Acha as his wife, Æthelfrith ensured that his sons would be able to appeal to their maternal kinship in support of their claim to rule in Deira. Bede makes precisely this point when he states later that Æthelfrith's son Oswald was a fitting ruler of a united kingdom of Deira and Bernicia because he was 'the nephew of Edwin through his sister Acha' (HE iii, 6). This should be borne in mind when, in Chapter 5, we discuss the supposed matriliny of the Picts.

Æthelfrith's dominance came to a sudden end in AD 616 when Rædwald, king of the East Angles, defeated him in battle at the River Idle. Edwin, who had been sheltered by Rædwald during his exile, returned as king of both Deira and Bernicia, and Æthelfrith was slain, and his three sons, Eanfrith, Oswald and Oswiu, fled into exile in the north among the Gaels and the Picts (*apud Scottos siue Pictos*) according to Bede (HE iii, 1). Here these Anglo-Saxon princes not only found safety from their enemies, but also found themselves in the halls of Christian rulers where eventually they, and presumably their retinues of kinsmen, lords and warriors, were baptised by the clergy of the northern churches.

Meanwhile Edwin, ruling both Bernicia and Deira, married Æthelburh, the daughter of the king of Kent, bringing Edwin into an alliance with the southern kingdom, and also into the embrace of the Kentish Church which had been established some thirty years earlier during the papal mission led by Augustine, so

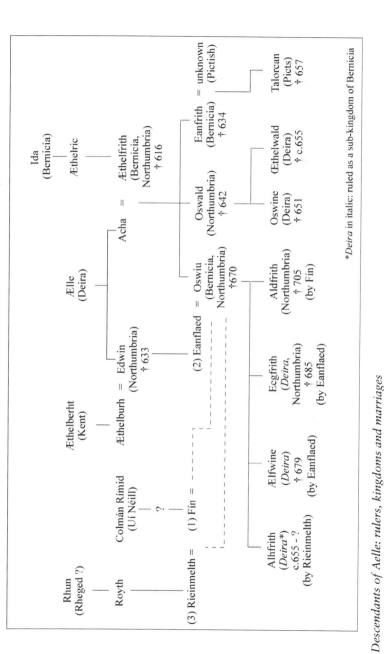

Descendants of Aelle: rulers, kingdoms and marriages

that Edwin was baptised in York at Easter in AD 627. Bede tells us that he dominated all the inhabitants of Britain, both English and Britons, except for the men of Kent. He even subjected to his rule the men of Gwynedd in northwest Wales, capturing Anglesey and the Isle of Man and gaining a degree of control of the Irish Sea. According to Bede, Anglesey contained 960 'hides' of land and Man contained 300, and the use of these terms suggests that Edwin was taking tribute from these islands, as the 'hide' or *familia* was the fiscal unit used for that purpose. The chances of Northumbrian warriors doing all this subjugating of Britain on their own are remote. Edwin would have relied on the military support of subject kingdoms and lordships, including Britons, who provided warriors to serve in his army.

Edwin's expansion was finally halted in AD 633 when he was defeated and slain by a combined force from Penda's Mercia and Cadwallon's Gwynedd, at a battle at *Hæthfelth* (Hatfield Chase, SE7304). The sons of Æthelfrith could now return from their exile in Scotland to their father's kingdom of Bernicia (though Deira was still separately ruled by a kinsman of Edwin). First to return was Eanfrith, who ruled Bernicia for only one year before being killed by Cadwallon – an act of divine vengeance, according to Bede, for having returned to paganism after coming to power. Eanfrith seems to have spent his exile in Pictland, for he had a son there: 'Talorcan son of Eanfrith, king of the Picts', died in AU 657. If his son was king of the Picts, it is likely Eanfrith had married a royal Pictish woman during his northern exile between 616 and 633 – an early link in a chain that would bind Pictland and Northumbria together in years to come.

Having devastated Northumbria for a year, Cadwallon was finally stopped and slain by a Northumbrian army, this time led by Eanfrith's brother Oswald who had been in exile with the *Scotti* – probably in Dál Riata, and possibly for some of that time on Iona. Having taken power in Bernicia, Oswald summoned monks and clergy from Iona to help him establish Christianity in his kingdom. He granted the island of Lindisfarne near Bamburgh to Iona monks as their base, probably in AD 635, creating a thoroughly Gaelic Church in his kingdom with monks or clergy arriving in numbers 'from the region of the Gaels' (*de Scottorum regione*) (HE iii, 3) – which for Bede could mean both Ireland and Scottish Dál Riata. At the same time Bernicia expanded militarily at the expense of British kingdoms. It was in Oswald's reign, in AU 638, that the siege of Edinburgh (*obsesio Etin*) is recorded, and this probably represents the final subjection of the Gododdin and the capture of its power centre by Bernicia. From now on, the rule of the kings of Northumbria would extend to the southern shore of the Firth of Forth. Across that body of water they looked north to the southern shore of Pictish territory.

Oswald was slain in AD 642 at a place known to Bede as *Maserfelth*, probably Oswestry in Shropshire, near the modern Welsh border (SJ2930). He was clearly seeking to continue his predecessor's expansionist thrust to the southwest when he fell, fighting Penda of Mercia, who was probably supported by British forces as he had been when he killed Edwin. From then until AD 670 all Northumbria was ruled by Oswald's brother Oswiu, with his sons ruling as under-kings of Deira, except for a period when two of Oswald's sons, Oswine and probably Œthelwald, ruled Deira apparently independently of him, leaving Oswiu with only Bernicia from AD 644 to about AD 655. Oswiu had a son by a British woman, Rienmelth, the granddaughter of Rhun. It is possible that her grandfather was Rhun the son of Urien, king of Rheged, though we cannot be certain about this. If he was, then her marriage to Oswiu might be seen as part of the absorption of Rheged into Oswiu's over-kingship. Certainly, the expansion of Northumbrian rule into the northwest of England – probably Rheged territory – is indicated by the description in the *Life of Wilfrid* of various lands in Lancashire around Ribble (*Rippel*, may be Ribbleton or Ribchester) and Yeadon (SE2041) and Catlow (SD8836) being given to Wilfrid's church of York in the 670s (§ 17). Though Oswiu was already dead by this point, it is likely that Northumbrian occupation of this territory was already taking place during his reign.

Oswiu's reign exceeded that of his predecessors in terms of his ability to extend his power over the northern peoples.

Having killed Penda of Mercia in 655, according to Bede 'he overwhelmed and made tributary for the most part even the tribes of the Picts and the Gaels who occupy the north of Britain' (HE ii, 5), and 'he subjected the nation of the Picts, for the most part, to the rule of the English' (HE iii, 24). As the ecclesiastical counterpart to his royal power, after AD 665 his bishop, Wilfrid, administered 'the see of the church of York, and of all the Northumbrians and of the Picts as far as the rule of Oswiu could extend' (HE iv, 3). As we have seen, Oswiu's brother Eanfrith had fathered a son, Talorcan, who was king of the Picts when he died in AU 657. His four-year rule in Pictland coincided with his uncle Oswiu's reign in Northumbria, so we may imagine that this prince with a Pictish mother and a Bernician father had taken power in Pictland – perhaps in southern Pictland only – with the support of his Bernician uncle, and that the price of this support had been a degree of subjection as described by Bede.

It has been plausibly suggested that during the reign of Oswiu a daughter of Edwin (we do not know her name) was married to the British king Beli. Two of his sons would become powerful kings in the north. The first of these was Owain of Alclud, whose army defeated Dál Riata at a battle in Strathcarron (*Sraith Caruin*) in AU 642, killing their king, Domnall Brecc, a battle which may have freed Alclud from a period of Dál Riata overlordship. A poem incorporated into a manuscript of *Y Gododdin*, perhaps because a copy was being kept in the kingdom of Alclud in the seventh century, commemorates the death of Domnall – here called Dyfnwal Frych – and describes his descent from Kintyre (*Pentir*):

> I saw a war-band, they came from Pentir,
> And splendidly they bore themselves around the beacon.
> I saw a second, they came down from their homestead:
> They had risen at the word of Nwython's grandson.
> I saw stalwart men, they came at dawn,
> And crows picked at the head of Dyfnwal Frych.

Beli's other son, Bridei, became king of Fortriu – we shall examine his career shortly. He is described in the *Historia*

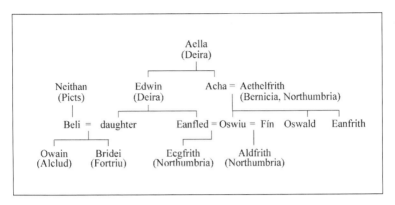

Descendants of Aella

Brittonum as having been a close kinsman, or *fratruelis*, of Ecgfrith of Northumbria, and it is this relationship that gives rise to the suggestion that a daughter of Edwin had married Bridei's father, Beli. Such a marriage would have given Northumbria influence in the lands of the Picts and of the Clyde Britons, and it is likely that the succession of Beli's son to the Pictish kingship was at least in part the result of leverage exercised by Oswiu and his son Ecgfrith.

It is Bridei son of Beli (Bruide mac Bile in Gaelic sources) who gives us a glimpse of how this leverage was exercised. It seems that Bridei's predecessor in Pictland, Drust, revolted against the Northumbrian overlordship of Oswiu's son, Ecgfrith. 'The expulsion of Drust from the kingship' is recorded in AU 672, probably obtained by the combined power of Ecgfrith and Pictish supporters of Bridei, who was then installed as king in Drust's place. This would explain the observation by Stephen in his *Life of Bishop Wilfrid* that in the 670s the 'bestial peoples of the Picts despised their subjection to the Saxons with a fierce disdain and threatened to throw off from themselves the yoke of servitude'. Ecgfrith gathered a small army together and defeated a vast enemy host, 'filling two rivers with corpses so that, amazing to say, the killers pursued the crowd of those fleeing, walking over the rivers dry foot' (§ 19).

Northumbrian hegemony in Pictland can be seen in the

installation of Bridei, Ecgfrith's kinsman; we can also hear
echoes of it in a document written in Rome during the papacy
of Agatho (AD 678–81) and mentioned in the *Life of Bishop
Wilfrid* in which Wilfrid appears to claim primacy over 'all the
northern part of Britain and of Ireland and the Isles which are
inhabited by the races of Angles, Britons, Gaels and Picts' (§ 53).
The exercise of Wilfrid's primacy can been seen in the installation of a Northumbrian bishop called Trumwine as 'bishop of
the Picts' in AD 681, though it is worth noting that he was unable
to live in his own territory, but had his see at Abercorn on the
southern shore of the Forth, looking across the water towards
his Pictish flock. This might suggest that the Northumbrian
hold of Pictland – even of southern Pictland – was still felt to be
slightly shaky.

The reign of Bridei son of Beli may have been inaugurated
with the assistance of a Northumbrian over-king, but he was no
lap-dog. In AU 676, many Picts were drowned '*i lLaind Abae*'.
This seems to be an error for '*i Lind Abae*', 'in Loch Awe', and
suggests that an aggressive Pictish regime was using Loch Awe
as a routeway for an attack on northern Dál Riata. In AU 682,
'the Orkneys were destroyed by Bridei'. The annals also record
the sieges of various power centres during his reign, some of
which may have been conducted by him, including the sieges of
Dunnottar in AU 681 and two years later Dunadd in Dál Riata.
A siege of Dundurn in highland Perthshire is recorded in AU
683, but it is not clear whether Bridei was the besieger or the
besieged in this instance – or neither. Finally, in AD 685 Bridei
would rebel against Ecgfrith and cast off the Northumbrian
claim of overlordship. We will return to this shortly.

Meanwhile Ecgfrith was continuing the westward drive of
his father. The eleventh-century *Historia de Sancto Cuthberto*
probably draws on earlier records in its account of Ecgfrith
granting the land around Cartmel (SD3878) to St Cuthbert, a
grant we should see as an ecclesiastical aspect of his colonisation of the area. It is interesting that the account states that 'the
king and all the Britons with him' gave the land to St Cuthbert,
indicating that some British lordship continued under the new

Northumbrian regime. Carlisle was also under Northumbrian control by AD 685, having a *reeve* (a royal official) called Waga and a royal monastery where Cuthbert visited Ecgfrith's queen in that year. The Anglian church at Hoddom in Dumfriesshire also shows the westward expansion of Northumbrian power in the seventh century (though this may have been absorbed during the time of Ecgfrith's father), as does, further west still, the Mote of Mark at the mouth of the Urr Water. It had been a British power centre in the sixth and earlier seventh centuries, and archaeology has revealed multiple ramparts and an impressive assemblage of imported luxury goods (glass beads and wine jars), and evidence of metal-working (clay moulds for casting penannular brooches). In many ways it looks similar to other high-status sites on the west coast of Britain – hill forts with evidence of feasting, luxury goods, and far-flung trade for foreign objects which would enhance the prestige and power of the lords who controlled their distribution. The Mote of Mark was destroyed by fire in the late seventh century, probably indicating a new phase of Northumbrian expansion.

Ecgfrith's aggression in the west reached its culmination in an attack on the east midlands of Ireland in AU 684: 'The Saxons lay waste the plain of Brega (*campus Bregh*), and many churches, in the month of June.' The event is dealt with in more detail, and with sharp moral condemnation, by Bede:

> In the year the Lord's incarnation 684, Ecgfrith king of the Northumbrians sent his ealdorman (*dux*) Berht to Ireland with an army, and he wretchedly devastated a harmless race which had always been most friendly to the English nation, and his hostile hand spared neither churches nor monasteries. (HE iv, 24)

The plain of Brega was ruled at that time by Fínsnechtae son of Dúnchad, alias *Fledach*, who was also king of Tara or 'high king' of Ireland at the time. We cannot be certain why Ecgfrith carried out this attack, but the fact that he took many captives at the time and took them back to Northumbria suggests that he was seizing hostages to ensure the 'good behaviour' of an Irish ruler. It may be that he feared Fínsnechtae or one of the Uí Néill kings of the northern part of Ireland was offering support to Dál Riata or Pictland in their efforts to shake off Northumbrian rule, and so he sought to protect his northern interests by this attack on the Irish. Another possibility is that Ecgfrith feared that Irish and Dál Riatan rulers were about to support a coup against him by his half-brother, Aldfrith, whose mother, Fín, was the daughter or granddaughter of the Irish king Colmán Rímid. Other possible motives must be considered, however, including a straightforward urge to expand Northumbrian dominion into Ireland (strongly suggested by his bishop Wilfrid's claim in Rome to have jurisdiction over 'all the northern part of Britain and Ireland' as discussed above).

THE EBBING OF NORTHUMBRIA

Whatever Ecgfrith's reasons, Bede saw this devastation of a harmless nation, and of their churches and monasteries, as a Northumbrian war crime that would be swiftly punished by God's vengeance, 'God's vengeance' came to Ecgfrith when, in spite of the warnings of his churchmen, particularly of St Cuthbert, he 'rashly led an army to lay waste the province of the Picts' (HE iv, 26). We must assume that his kinsman and under-king in Pictland, Bridei, was challenging Ecgfrith's overlordship. Ecgfrith sought to reassert it by a military campaign, and in May 685 he led his army far into Pictland. The place where Ecgfrith's and Bridei's armies met is called Dún Nechtain in the *Annals of Ulster*. Bede does not name the place where the battle occurred, but says that Ecgfrith's army was lured by the enemy 'into the narrow passes of inaccessible mountains'. In the twelfth century, Symeon of Durham recorded an English tradition about this battle which names the battle site as '*Nechtanesmere, quod est stagnum Nechtani*' ('Nechtansmere, that is Nechtan's lake'). For a long time the battle has been thought to have occurred at Dunnichen in Angus, principally because the name Dunnichen resembles the name *Dún Nechtain* recorded in the *Annals*. But Alex Woolf has recently made a strong case for locating it far to the north of this, near Dunachton on Speyside, beside Loch

Insh, which would therefore be Symeon's *Nechtanesmere*. This site corresponds much better to Bede's description of the place among 'inaccessible mountains'.

At Dún Nechtain, Ecgfrith's host was crushed and he himself slain and his body taken to Iona for burial. The defeat marked a turning point for Northumbrian power north of the Forth–Clyde line. As Bede remarks:

> From that time the hope and strength of the kingdom of the English began to ebb and fall away. For the Picts regained possession of their land which the English had held, and the Gaels who were in Britain and also some of the Britons gained their freedom, which they have now had for around 46 years. (HE iv, 26)

Bede tells us that many English were slain and Bishop Trumwine, who had claimed authority over the Pictish Church from his see at Abercorn, retired to Whitby in Northumbria.

By the end of the seventh century, then, Northumbrian overlordship in Dál Riata and Pictland had collapsed, as it had in some British areas. Other British territories continued to be under pressure, however. In Galloway the expansion of Northumbrian domination eventually brought about, according to Bede, the takeover of the British church at Whithorn by Northumbrian bishops, probably around AD 700. Bede mentions Pehthelm as the new bishop in Whithorn. In fact, he states that 'the number of believers has so increased in the church of Whithorn in recent times that it has been made into an episcopal see, and he names Pehthelm as its first bishop' (HE v, 23). This presents us with something of a puzzle, for Bede has already told us elsewhere (HE iii, 4) that the first bishop of Whithorn was a Briton called Nynia (usually now rendered as Ninian), that he had preached to the southern Picts and converted them to Christianity, and that his see was under English rule at the time of Bede's writing around AD 731. This contradiction in Bede's two accounts should make us suspect the accuracy of his Ninian story. And we might suspect it on several grounds.

First, doubt has been expressed about the historical existence of St Ninian. Thomas Clancy noted in 2001 that the cult of St

Ninian was almost completely absent from the early medieval landscape of Galloway, that it does not appear in place names in the area around Whithorn, and that, by contrast, the name of the British saint Uinniau appears rather frequently in the place names of the region. Clancy suggests that the cult of Ninian or Nynia was actually the result of a Northumbrian scribal misreading of Uinniau. The medieval misreading of *u* as *n* was fairly common (it explains, for example, the late formation of the name 'Iona' out of an original *Ioua Insula*).

It is also likely that some of the 'biographical' details offered by Bede for Ninian are pure invention. Bede claims that Ninian went to Rome to be correctly instructed, and that he had converted the southern Picts to Christ. These implausible claims are possibly made partly by southern Picts themselves, eager to align their Christianity with the supposedly 'Roman' Christianity of Northumbria (as we shall see in Chapter 3). Northumbrian hierarchs of a colonial mind-set, imagining that they had controlled Pictland until AD 685 and hopeful that they might do so again, also had an interest in promoting this narrative. If Ninian had converted the southern Picts, then the southern Pictish churches would all be in some sense 'daughters' of Ninian's church at Whithorn. And as Northumbrian bishops now ruled Whithorn, the Ninian story would justify Northumbrian control of the southern Pictish Church.

A further challenge to Bede's narrative is offered by archaeology. The earliest ecclesiastical remains in this southwestern corner of Galloway are not at Whithorn at all, but at Kirkmadrine in the Rhinns, twenty-two miles to the west. There, as we have seen, three sub-Roman stones survive commemorating bishops or senior clerics from what must have been an important church centre. At Whithorn, by contrast, the earliest stone commemorates not a *sacerdos*, but a secular ruler and his daughter, and the early archaeology points not to a church but to a secular power centre. There is no archaeological evidence of a shrine or a church at Whithorn in the pre-Anglian period. The evidence is of feasting and wine-drinking, with imported luxury goods from the Continent (amphorae and glass vessels) such as are more commonly found found at secular power centres like Dunadd and Mote of Mark. The presence of numbers of early burials at Whithorn is not necessarily evidence of an early church, since burial at church sites was not the norm until the eighth century.

Finally, we might consider a puzzle relating to the distribution of two important markers of Northumbrian control: place names and stone-carving. The toponymic cults of St Cuthbert and St Oswald, two Northumbrian saints, appear regularly in areas of southern Scotland subject to Northumbrian control. Likewise, finely carved free-standing crosses were erected in the eighth century at important Northumbrian church sites in the same area, and presumably express the newly Anglicised church culture there. But there is a clear gap in the distribution of these markers: they do not appear west of the River Cree, leaving the Rhinns of Galloway (including Kirkmadrine) and the Machars (including Whithorn) entirely free of such signs of Northumbrian authority. The map suggests that there was an area where the local church may have resisted Northumbrian encroachment at the time when these crosses were being erected. Recalling that Trumwine was unable to reside in Pictland even though he claimed authority there, we might also wonder if Whithorn and the Rhinns were as thoroughly Northumbrian as Bede suggests in the early eighth century, and even whether Pehthelm was normally resident in Whithorn.

The persistence of Anglo-Saxon bishops of Whithorn throughout the eighth century and beyond suggests that any such pocket of resistance was temporary, however; Pehthelm was followed by other men with good Anglo-Saxon names: Frithweald, Peohtwine, Æthelbeorht, Beadwulf and Heathored (c. 833, the last known Northumbrian bishop of Whithorn). The Northumbrian takeover of southwest Scotland continued, extending northwards from Galloway into Ayrshire, as recorded in AD 750 when Eadberht of Northumbria 'added the plain of Kyle (campum Kyil) and other lands to his kingdom' according to Bede's continuator. It is likely that the seizure of Kyle was at the expense of the kingdom of Alclud which lay on both sides of the Firth of Clyde.

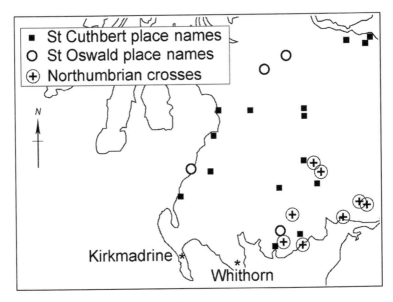

Cuthbert, Oswald and Northumbrian crosses

THE PICTISH CONQUEST OF DÁL RIATA

The collapse of Northumbrian rule north of the Forth–Clyde line after the battle of Dún Nechtain made space for the rapid rise of a powerful Pictish state. Bridei son of Beli ruled until AU 693 as 'king of Fortriu', the northern part of Pictish territory whose name echoes the *Verturiones*, the Latin name given by Ammianus in the fourth century. This is the area where we suppose that Bridei had defeated Ecgfrith's army. Bede describes a Pictland divided into two parts: the 'northern Picts' and the 'southern Picts', separated as he says 'by high and craggy ranges of mountains' (HE iii, 4), the mountains now called 'the Mounth'. The bipartite nature of Pictish political geography is confirmed by annal entries, such as that of AU 782 in which 'Dubthalorc, king of the Picts on this side of the Mounth ... died'. Further subdivision of Pictland into smaller kingdoms is also evident. Bede refers to the northern Picts as containing several *prouinciae*, a word which he sometimes uses for kingdoms, while Adomnán's *Life of Columba* mentions a sub-king (*regulus*) in the Orkneys who is subject to Bridei, king of the Picts in the sixth century (VC ii, 42). There are minor kingdoms in southern Pictland, too, such as that of Atholl, whose king was drowned by Unust, king of the Picts, in AU 739. Just as happened in Dál Riata, rulers of various Pictish under-kingdoms fought each other for the over-kingship, and out of this turbulent process powerful rulers emerged capable of unifying all of Pictland, or much of it, at least some of the time.

A single over-kingship of all of Pictland may be glimpsed in the guarantor list of the 'Law of the Innocents' promulgated in AD 697 (we will discuss the law in Chapter 4). Adomnán, abbot of Iona, obtained the support of ninety-one kings and bishops in parts of Ireland and Britain where the law was in force, and among them we can identify only one royal guarantor from Pictland: *Bruide mac Derilei rí Cruithintúathi* ('Bridei son of Der-Ile, king of the Picts'). This may simply indicate that one of the various Pictish territories supported Adomnán's law and the others did not, but that seems unlikely, given the extensive support that Iona had throughout Pictland at the time. The alternative explanation is more plausible: that Pictland was sufficiently centralised under a single king for his guarantee of the law to suffice for the whole of Pictland. This impression is confirmed by Bede's information that two decades later the Pictish king Naiton (*Nechtan mac Der-Ile* in Gaelic) accepted the Easter-dating system used by the Northumbrians:

> Without delay he enforced what he had said by royal authority. Immediately, by public order, the nineteen-year Easter-cycles were sent to be copied, learned and observed by all the provinces of the Picts, and the erroneous eighty-four year cycles to be obliterated everywhere. (HE v, 21)

Again the picture is of a centralised command structure, with a king issuing proclamations to the rulers or under-kings of all his *prouinciae*.

Such powerful Pictish rulers were able to put military pressure on the Gaelic west, as we have already seen in the case of Bridei son of Beli. There are many other signs thereafter of Pictish aggression against Dál Riata. One is the claim put about by Pictish kings, and repeated by Bede, that it was a king of the Picts who had given the Irish the right to settle in what became Dál Riata, and that another Pictish king had given the island of Iona to St Columba. To assert such 'facts' was to claim Pictish rights of lordship, both secular and ecclesiastical, over Dál Riata. At the same time, the kindred of Cenél Loairn in northern Dál Riata was displacing the power of southern *cenéla*, and they were probably doing so with the support of the king of Picts as an expression of his claim to overlordship.

In AU 734, the Dál Riatan noble Talorc son of Congus was held captive by his brother and handed over to the Picts, who drowned him, probably during an attack on southern Argyll by the Pictish king Unust together with Cenél Loairn. In the same year, Talorcan son of Drostan the king of Atholl was apprehended and chained near Dunollie in Argyll, probably also by men loyal to Unust who had him drowned in AU 739. Two years later, according to the same source, 'Unust son of Uurgust, king of the Picts, laid waste the under-kingdoms (*regiones*) of Dál Riata and seized Dunadd, and burned Creic, and bound in chains two sons of Selbach (ruler of Cenél Loairn).' A battle is recorded in the same year between Dál Riata and Fortriu at '*Cnoc Coirpre in Calathros uc Eter Linnddu*', possibly in the territory of Cenél Loairn. Finally, AU 741 records 'the smiting (*percutio*) of Dál Riata by Unust son of Uurgust'. This word *percutio* is an unusual one in annalistic writings, and suggests a cataclysmic blow to the Gaelic kingdoms of the west. It is significant that after this there are no further records of kings of Dál Riata until twenty-seven years later when AU 768 records 'a battle in Fortriu between Áed and Ciniod'. These two men were probably Áed mac Echdach, king of Dál Riata (died AU 768), and Ciniod, 'king of the Picts' (died AU 775).

The rulers of Dál Riata were now part of and subject to an expanded Pictish *imperium*, 'Fortriu', understood not merely as the northern part of Pictland, but as a power that embraced the Gaelic west as well as the rest of Pictland. In AU 789, a battle took place between Constantin king of the Picts and one Conall son of Tadc, who appears to have been a king of Dál Riata. But the *Annal* describes it as a battle *inter Pictos*, 'between the Picts' themselves. The kings of Dál Riata had become 'Pictish', in the sense that they were sub-kings in a Pictish dominion which stretched from coast to coast. We will return to this Pictish expansion in Chapter 6.

THE GAELICISATION OF PICTLAND

The subjection of the Gaelic west to Pictish *dominium* is a dramatic shift, but it is only one half of a two-way process. As Pictish and military power had moved west, Gaelic cultural and religious influences – and Gaelic-speaking people – were moving east into Pictland and transforming that society. The evidence for the Gaelicisation of Pictland is plentiful. One of the earliest signs is the numerous stones carved with *ogam* script, which began to appear in eastern Scotland in the sixth or seventh century. *Ogam* was a script developed by Gaelic-speakers in Ireland to represent their own language, and its subsequent transmission to Pictland can therefore be understood as evidence of Gaelic settlement in the east. There are many *ogam* stones in Scotland, and it is a little puzzling that most of them are in the eastern parts of the country, what was once Pictland. Why, if this was a script created by Gaels in Ireland, are there only four *ogam*s in the whole territory of Gaelic Dál Riata and one on Lewis in the Western Isles, but twenty-one or more in the Pictish east? Might there have been Gaelic influences in Pictland which owed nothing to the mediation of Dál Riata and which provided the means of transmitting *ogam* from Ireland – even from southern Ireland where *ogam* is more common – directly to eastern Scotland? Whatever the reason for this pattern, the distribution of *ogam* stones in Pictland points to early Gaelic influence and settlement there.

Another indicator of early Gaelic influence in Pictland is Adomnán's *Life of Columba* with its stories of Columba travelling 'across the Spine of Britain' into Pictland and being honoured by a Pictish king. Though these accounts may be read as seventh-century propaganda to support Iona's claims of jurisdiction in Pictland, they are surely not merely propaganda. There is confirmation of very early Columban influence in Pictland in the poem *Amra Choluim Chille*, written *c*. AD 600, which claims of the saint:

> His blessing turned them, the mouths of the fierce ones
> who lived on the Tay, to the will of the King.

And even if we were to read Adomnán's stories as evidence of Gaelic expansion at the time of writing rather than in Columba's own lifetime, they still reveal something interesting about the process, showing the importance of the Church as a channel for the transmission of Gaelic culture. Columba and Iona monks may not have been the very first preachers of the Gospel in Pictland, but they nevertheless exerted a powerful and enduring influence there. Adomnán observes that Columban monasteries in his own day are still greatly honoured among both Gaels and Picts (VC ii, 46). In addition to Adomnán's stories, we can see other signs of Gaelic-speaking churchmen moving into Pictland: a broad scatter of place names commemorating Iona saints such as Colum Cille, Adomnán, Céti (the first bishop of Iona) and Dúnchad, while the Columban church of Dunkeld became the principal royal church of Pictland in the mid-ninth century, and Columban relics were translated there from Iona in AD 849, further attesting to the enduring influence of Iona, its saint and its language in the Pictish east. And we should not suppose that the Columban *familia* were the only Gaelic-speaking clergy to influence Pictland, for Pictish churches culting non-Columban Gaelic saints might indicate other vectors of Gaelic influence. We might think of St Blane culted at Dunblane, and his kinsman St Cattan at nearby Aberuthven and Muthill, whose cults appear to have been imported from the island of Bute in Cenél Comgaill territory. The foundation legend of the important royal monastery of Abernethy, linking it to St Brigit of Kildare in Ireland, may also point to a non-Columban strand of Gaelic influence.

We might also see the monastic reform movement known as

the *Céli Dé* ('clients of God') as another aspect of Gaelic cultural expansion. The Céli Dé first appeared in Ireland at the end of the eighth century, but the surviving texts of the movement show a strong orientation towards Iona, often citing the customs of Iona monks, such as Columba or the ninth-century abbot Diarmait, as authorities for Céli Dé practice. Céli Dé monasteries became some of the most important churches in Pictland, many of them enjoying royal patronage: Dunkeld, St Andrews, Abernethy, Dunblane, Muthill, Monymusk, Brechin and Loch Leven all had Céli Dé communities. The movement was primarily concerned with the proper conduct of community life under a monastic rule, but also took a view on pastoral care, the role of bishops and priests, and the proper relationship between the Church and secular authorities. The Gaelic flavour of the Céli Dé movement, and of so much other church activity in Pictland, must have infused the pastoral and monastic culture there, certainly. But Gaelic-speaking clergy must also have formed the backbone of an administrative class serving Pictish rulers, which will have helped to promote the growth of Gaelic in in the east.

A more striking, but more secular, Gaelic penetration of Pictland took place in the seventh century when Dargart, a member of the royal Cenél Comgaill kindred of southern Argyll, married a woman called Der-Ile, who was from a royal Pictish family, probably in the 660s or in the 670s at the latest. For Dargart to have been a worthwhile marriage prospect for her kindred we must assume that Cenél Comgaill had considerable political and military leverage in Pictland. Dargart's kindred presumably used this same leverage to ensure that two sons of this marriage subsequently became kings of the Picts: Bruide (Bridei in Pictish) ruled from *c.* AD 697 until his death in 706, and his successor Nechtan (Pictish Naiton), who ruled until 724, retired into clerical life, and finally re-emerged from retirement during a violent struggle for the kingship to rule again from around 728 until his death in 732.

It seems that the Cenél Comgaill power base which supported Dargart and his sons lay not only in Dál Riata, but also in southern Pictland, notably in Strathearn and a little to the east of that. This is suggested by the foundation legend of the monastery of Culross on the Forth, which appears in the *Life of St Serf* and says that the land was given to Serf by *Brude filius Dargart* (Bruide son of Dargart). The *Life* as it stands may have been written *c.* AD 1200, but the foundation legend seems to contain material much older than that. A monastery does not easily forget who founded it: one of its *raisons d'être* is to pray for the souls of its founder and his family. If the legend does contain a core of truth, it seems that in the late seventh century Bruide held territory which included Culross. The fact that he is referred to in this text as Bruide son of Dargart, rather than son of his mother, Derile, suggests that his claim over these lands came from his patrilineal kin rather than from his Pictish mother. And this in turn suggests that lords from Cenél Comgaill had acquired land in this area.

Confirmation of Cenél Comgaill settlement in this area is found in a Gaelic tract on the mothers of saints in which Serf is described as the founding saint of Culross 'in Strathearn among the Comgall folk' (*hi Srath Erenn hi Comgellaibh*). The important church of Dunblane, which became the episcopal see of Strathearn, may be a religious expression of that Cenél Comgaill settlement in the area. Dunblane, originally *Dulblaan*, means '(St) Blane's haugh or water-meadow'. Now Blane's original church had been at Kingarth on the island of Bute, probably the principal church of Cenél Comgaill in the west, where Blane was held to have been the bishop. The earliest records of Kingarth refer to later bishops there in AU 660 and AU 689, but thereafter AU records only abbots, not bishops, among the churchmen of Kingarth in 737, 776 and 790. The change from bishops to abbots at Kingarth is unusual. What happened to the episcopal status of St Blane's church at Kingarth, the chief church of Cenél Comgaill? It is possible that when Cenél Comgaill dynasts moved eastwards into Strathearn and carried the cult of St Blane to *Dulblaan* with them they also took Blane's episcopal successors to establish a new see in their new territory.

The introduction of this Gaelic royal kindred into Pictland can be seen as one stage in the systematic absorption of powerful Gaelic lords – together with their military retinues – into the Pictish body politic in the seventh and eighth centuries. Pictish kings could harness the otherwise dangerous military energy of Gaelic kingdoms in the west by intermarriage and by granting lands within Pictland to Gaelic lords, who would then offer them political and military support. This pattern may explain the existence of provinces of Pictland with names that seem to derive from the names of Gaelic kindreds: not only *Comgellaibh* from Cenél Comgaill, as we have seen, but Gowrie from Cenél nGabráin and Angus from Cenél nÓengusso. Another territory showing early signs of Gaelic settlement is Atholl. Its name represents **Ath-Fhotla*, 'new Ireland', which must reflect a polity with a strongly Gaelic dimension certainly by AU 739 when Atholl appears with its own king. These territories all lie in southern Pictland, and this may suggest that kings of Fortriu in the north sought to maintain their control in the south by planting loyal Gaelic-speaking lords there. By marriage and military alliances some of these imported lords came to be regarded as kings of Pictish sub-kingdoms and will have entered into the group of men eligible to become *rex Pictorum*, as we have seen that the two sons of Dargart did.

As Pictland became more ethnically mixed, so it seems that the P-Celtic Pictish language was also being Gaelicised. Bede mentions a place on the Forth which the Picts called *Peanfahel* (HE i, 12); it is modern Kinneil. The name *Peanfahel* means 'wall's end' – referring to the Antonine Wall which ended nearby – but the Pictish form of the name should have been **Penguaul* (like the British form given by Nennius in the ninth century), but the form given by Bede contains Pictish **penn*, 'head, end', joined to Gaelic *fál*, 'wall'. This supposedly Pictish name is therefore a hybrid. It suggests that the language spoken in the early eighth century, even if it was still regarded as Pictish, was being Gaelicised. The name would eventually become Kinneil, representing Gaelic *cenn fháil*.

During the last decades of the eighth century, Pictish power had embraced the far west, while Gaelic culture had spread to the east. Dál Riata remained a Gaelic-speaking territory ruled by an eastern Pictish over-king. But Pictland, however powerful its rulers, was becoming more Gaelic – a change no less dramatic for being one of gradual infiltration rather than the direct result of *percutio* or 'smiting'.

3

'Happy the people whose God is the Lord' (Psalm 32:12)

The Church in Early Medieval Scotland

As we saw in Chapter 1, Christian belief and practice seeped into Scotland by the kind of osmosis of ideas, practices and institutions that the Roman empire carried with it, and that came also through trade and international travel. There had been no great mission of conversion, but in the summer of AD 441 Pope Leo might well have had Scotland and Ireland in mind when he observed that Rome was now enjoying a wider influence in the world through the preaching of the Gospel than she had ever had obtained as head of her empire: 'you have come to preside more widely by godly religion than you ever did by worldly domination'.

In Scotland the growth of Christianity would bring multiple transformations to society. It brought not only the preaching of Christ, but also literature, new theories of kingship and cosmology, new forms of social organisation and artistic traditions. To properly understand this change we really should have some idea of what society looked like in both its pre-Christian and Christian phases, and this raises an immediate problem for us. Christianity is, as they say, a 'religion of the book', or rather it is a religion of countless books – texts and commentaries on texts, the writing and re-writing of stories, poetry, the inscription of property rights, the records of great deeds by the living and the dead. There are materials to guide us around the Christian culture.

The pre-Christian culture of Scotland, in sharp contrast, left almost no written record of its own. We may infer something from what others wrote. The first group of these 'others' were strangers – men like Tacitus, Ammianus, Julius Caesar. Some, like Tacitus, wrote about people in Scotland, but said little about their culture. Some, like Caesar, did write about culture and cultic practices, but mostly observed those on the Continent and in southern Britain, not in Scotland. And in any case these strangers had their own agenda, seeking to portray their subjects sometimes as 'noble savages', sometimes as prime candidates for Roman occupation whose cult was similar to that of Rome, and at other times as barbaric and bloodthirsty savages whose crushing by Roman arms was a moral imperative.

The second group of 'others' who wrote about the pre-Christian people of Scotland were medieval Christians. Adomnán writes in his *Life of Columba*, for example, of Pictish magicians whose sacred well afflicted people with dire diseases (VC ii, 11), but this kind of writing is part of a literary genre in which Christian writers created a 'pagan' past to act as a kind of theatre in which the drama of their saint's holiness could be enacted against a backdrop of 'pagan' error. So in the *Life of Columba* the saint transforms the Pictish magic well just mentioned into a source of healing where 'many ailments were cured among local people'. This 'pagan past' is to a great extent the invention of Christian writers who recycled popular stock motifs from earlier saints' 'Lives' or stories from the Bible to paint a picture of 'paganism'.

Not all Christian writings about non-Christians are literary fabrications of this sort, however. A fifth-century council of Arles was worried that non-Christians (*infideles*) 'light little torches and worship trees, springs and rocks'. In the sixth-century, the church fathers in council at Auxerre forbade 'disguising oneself as a calf or a deer' on 1 January. Such attempts by clergy to wean Christians from particular practices that they saw as incompatible with their faith may offer good insights into the pre-Christian cults of their own time and in their own country-side. Unfortunately, no such texts survive from Scotland, though it may be legitimate to infer some aspects of pre-Christian cult from Irish, British or Anglo-Saxon sources which do. In the fifth century, Patrick recounts that on his escape from slavery in Ireland he was taken on a ship by some sailors. They invited him into a bond of friendship with them which he accepted, though he adds 'I refused to suck their nipples, for fear of God', clearly distancing himself from a ritual he thought incompatible with Christianity. The same men offered Patrick some wild honey that they had found, having first practised a ritual in which they declared it a sacrifice or offering (*immolaticium*), presumably to some god: 'Thanks be to God,' Patrick exclaims, 'I tasted none of it.' Such stories give glimpses of pre-Christian practices in the fifth-century conversion period, though we do not know where these sailors came from, or why they might have invited Patrick to suck their nipples. Later in his *Confession*, Patrick contrasts those who worship the sun ('they shall come to a dreadful punishment') with those 'who believe in and adore the true sun, Christ', which suggests that he may have come across sun-worship among his contemporaries. This last illustration, however, may owe its inspiration to the Bible rather than to his observation of fifth-century Insular cult (Ezekiel 8:15–16). The so-called 'First Synod of Patrick' (probably not a synod, and certainly nothing to do with Patrick) envisaged a continuing non-Christian population in sixth-century Ireland, and forbade 'swearing oaths in the pagan manner before an *aruspex*' (a divinatory figure possibly associated with animal sacrifice). It is remarkable that when the Christian authors just cited distance themselves from 'paganism', they do so with reference to its practices rather than its ideas – though ideas must have underlain the practices, just as they did with Christian practices.

We may also seek information about pre-Christian cult from archaeology, but while this discipline may present us with pre-Christian artefacts, the meaning of those objects is not something to which we have direct access. From the dedication of an altar on the Antonine Wall to the god 'Mars-Camulus' we may infer that the British god Camulus had an interest in war and warriors, simply because he is paired with Mars, the Roman god of war. But this remains an inference, not something directly attested. In the absence of more substantial texts written by the practitioners of pre-Christian cult, we must be tentative in making any observation about the meaning of its artefacts.

The words 'pagan' and 'paganism' appear in quotes in the preceding paragraphs because the idea of 'pagan religion' is a problematic concept. First, the description of a non-Christian cult or person as 'pagan' was a Christian view that was almost always negative. Second, to divide the world at this conversion stage into 'pagans' and 'Christians', as if there were two different religions, two belief systems, easily distinguishable and more or less opposed to each other, is quite misleading. Certainly, Christians thought of themselves as Christians, but there is no reason to think that 'pagans' thought of themselves as pagans. Christians had a sense of themselves as a body of believers with shared ideas, authoritative books and shared liturgical and social practices; they took the Latin word *paganus* ('rustic', with implications of simplicity and lack of education) and used it to refer disparagingly to things which differed from Christian beliefs and practices. But pre-Christian practices that we would now regard as 'religious' may not even have been understood in such terms by their practitioners. In addition, a good deal of pre-Christian culture continued to thrive among Christians, while some did not. The description of any pre-Christian custom as 'pagan' therefore tells us merely that Christians did not adopt it. Pre-Christian communities practised marriage, for example, and the only reason that we do not regard marriage as a 'pagan' custom is because Christians practised it too.

In spite of such reservations about the concept of 'paganism' and the limitations of our sources of information, we may consider the archaeological evidence for pre-Christian beliefs and practices in the insular world. Many swords have been found deposited in rivers and lochs throughout the British Isles, often bent or broken before deposition. These are thought to have been offerings made to gods associated with the water, or with an underworld into which rivers and lochs may have been seen as entry points. There is reason to believe that some rivers were named after goddesses. Adomnán talks of the River Lochy as 'the river which can be called *nigra dea* ("black goddess")' (VC ii, 37).

Some offerings may have been made at shrines created especially for the purpose. A wooden figure found in a bog at Ballachulish and dateable to around 600 BC may represent a goddess. Wickerwork remains found around her figure suggest that she was enshrined in some way, and perhaps offerings were made to her by travellers crossing the dangerous narrows here, where Loch Leven opens into the sea (NN0559). In Roman cult also, shrines were the locus of offerings made with the implicit bargain *do ut des*, 'I give so that you may give' – a kind of deal made with the deity to gain some favour. Such favours included such things as a good harvest, protection from danger, the safe birth of a child, healing from disease or revenge on neighbours who have wronged you. More public offerings may have been celebrated with animal sacrifices. A hillfort at Broxmouth in East Lothian (NT7077), occupied and developed over many centuries, contained a collection of ox skulls under the foundation of a stone-built house, perhaps a sacrificial or votive deposit intended to protect or ensure the prosperity of the settlement.

It seems that sacrificial cults in Britain sometimes used human victims. Several Roman writers record animal and human sacrifices in Gaul, and this is confirmed by archaeology at Gaulish shrines, such as those at Gournay-sur-Aronde and Ribemont-sur-Ancre. Tacitus states that when Suetonius captured Anglesey in northwest Wales he destroyed the sacred groves there 'devoted to inhuman superstitions', which included the sacrifice of prisoners and divination by examination of their entrails. Evidence of human sacrifice in Britain may also be found in bodies occasionally preserved in bogs, such as that of 'Lindow man', discovered in 1984; he is thought to have been sacrificed and his body deposited in a bog in the first century AD. The burial of a large number of humans and animals in deep pits dug into the ground at the Iron Age fort at Danebury in Hampshire are also suggestive of sacrificial deposition, perhaps as part of a rite to protect the fort. The evidence is not so clear in Scotland, but the Gaulish and southern British examples suggest the possibility of such practices further north.

We should also remember that exposure to Roman practices

began to influence the cults of other societies. As we have seen, one aspect of the Romanisation of Britain was the merging of Roman and native deities in altars and shrines, and the culting of native gods in Roman monuments. An example of this is found in a Roman temple by the Severn Estuary at Lydney Park, where a lead curse-tablet honours a British god in Latin: 'To the god Nodens. Silvianus has lost a ring. He has given half [its value] to Nodens. Do not permit health among those of the name Senicianus until it is returned to the temple of Nodens'. Such interweaving of Roman and native cult reminds us that there was no timeless, unchanging 'paganism'.

CONVERSION: BRITONS OF THE NORTH

As we have seen, the Christian identity of British rulers in sub-Roman southern Scotland is shown by carved stones in such places as Kirkmadrine, Peebles, Yarrow and Whithorn, and also by early British poetry. Among the verses of Y *Gododdin* we find echoes of their faith:

Ceredig, beloved leader,
    Ferocious champion in battle . . .
May welcome be his among the host
    With the Trinity, in total unity.

Mead payment in mead-horn,
    It was made good by corpses.
Cibno will not say, after battle's furor,
    Though he took communion, that he had his due.

Clearly, the poet imagines these warriors to have been Christians. This has caused some scholars to suggest that the 'Christian' verses must have been later additions. They observe that the violence celebrated by the poem seems incompatible with a Christian ethos, and the poem must therefore originally have been 'pagan'. Such an optimistic view of Christianity's peace-making potential is attractive, but it is not supported by what we know of early medieval elites, even those who were Christians. The Church may have sought to restrict violence in some ways, as we shall see in due course, but warlords continued to behave in the ways celebrated by such poetry whether they were Christian or not. We see it again in the poetry attributed to Taliesin, who praises Urien ('savage your spear-thrust when battle is sounded') and his son Owain ('he punished them fiercely, like a wolf savaging sheep'), but it concludes with a prayer:

> Soul of Owain ab Urien,
> May his Lord attend to its needs.

As the religion of powerful British rulers it is likely that the sub-Roman Christianity of southern Scotland also made an early impact in Pictland. We may recall that Patrick's letter to the warriors of Coroticus implied that the Picts saw themselves as sharing in the Roman Christian religion of their British ally, Coroticus, whom Patrick was now excommunicating for his violence against the innocent. It may have been partly through alliances like this one with a British Christian ruler that southern Pictland adopted elements of Christian belief and culture.

We also see a number of place names in Pictland containing the Pictish word *egles*, 'church' (from Latin *ecclesia*, related to modern Welsh *eglwys*), and this also points towards a British evangelisation of Pictland since Gaels tended not to use a word derived from *ecclesia* for their early churches while Britons did. Perhaps, therefore, we should see British church names south of the Forth such as Terregles, Ecclefechan, Eglismalessok, Ecclesmachan and Eaglescairnie as sharing an early origin with Pictish *egles* names north of the Forth, such as Ecclesmaline, Eglismartin, Eglismonichty, Eglesnamin and Ecclesgreig. It is remarkable that all known *egles* place names in Pictland lie south of the Mounth apart from one (*Eglismenythok*, now Abersnithock at NJ6817). This suggests that Romano-British Christianity influenced church foundation in southern Pictland more than it did further north. Even if we reject the claim that the southern Picts were evangelised by 'St Ninian of Whithorn', we may accept in a more general sense that they were influenced by sub-Roman British Christianity.

CONVERSIONS: THE GAELIC WEST

The other important vector of Christianisation in Scotland was from the west, from Ireland. Christianity had made its appearance in Ireland probably in the late fourth century, certainly by the early fifth. The *Chronicle of Prosper of Aquitaine* records in AD 431 that 'Palladius was ordained by Pope Celestine for the *Scoti* who believed in Christ, and was sent as the first bishop'. Palladius was not sent to evangelise a pagan territory, therefore, but to provide episcopal leadership for an existing Christian community. The Irish themselves had probably requested this bishop from Celestine who had written, 'No-one is to be imposed as a bishop on the unwilling. The consent of the clergy, the people and the ordained must be obtained.' Linguistic evidence shows that Christianity had come to Ireland in great part from the Church of Britain: the form of ecclesiastical loanwords into Old Gaelic shows that they were drawn from British Latin rather than from that of the Continent. The process by which British Christianity appeared in Ireland is now obscure, but St Patrick states that many thousands of Britons had been taken to Ireland as slaves, and we may assume that many of these carried Christianity with them. Trade between Ireland and Roman Britain may also have had a role, combined with the prestige attached to Roman culture and possibly the influence of Irishmen returning home after serving in the Roman army.

We can see another dimension of the Christian culture brought to Ireland in the writings of St Patrick. In his *Letter to the Soldiers of Coroticus* he appeals to the practice of the 'Christian Roman Gauls' as if they were an authority to be followed: they spent large amounts of money freeing captives from the Franks and other nations. For Patrick, the Gaulish Church represents a touchstone of orthodoxy, or at least orthopraxis. And in his *Confession* Patrick writes from Ireland of his longing to see his British homeland and family again, and 'not only that, but to go to Gaul to visit the brothers, that I might seek the face of my Lord's saints. God knows that I longed to . . .' (Conf. § 43). Such a longing in his later life ('this is my confession before I die') is hardly likely to be idle curiosity. It is remarkable that the people he calls his 'brothers' are Gauls, not British clergy or monks. It may be, therefore, that Patrick had spent time in Gaul and felt that the Gaulish Church was his *alma mater* where he had found his vocation to work as a bishop in Ireland. Patrick's mission would therefore represent a Gaulish dimension in the nascent Irish Church.

The appearance of Christianity in the Gaelic west of Scotland should be seen as part of the growth of this Irish Church. The sources are silent on the actual conversion process here: no missionary, no early bishop and no converts to Christianity are named in Dál Riata. There is no reason to believe that Columba brought Christianity to Scotland when he arrived in AD 563. He was given the island of Iona for his monastery by Conall mac Comgaill, probably the over-king of Dál Riata, and we can therefore assume that Conall was already Christian. In addition, in Adomnán's *Life of Columba* the saint sailed from Ireland to Britain not as a missionary bent on converting pagans, but as a monk and ascetic, 'wishing to be a pilgrim for Christ'. He baptises no Dál Riata folk except for a small boy brought to him by his presumably already Christian parents (VC ii, 10). He came from northern Ireland to western Scotland at a time when these two areas shared a common language, a common political and legal culture, and – there is no reason to doubt – a common religion. There was, therefore, already a church in Scottish Dál Riata when Columba arrived, and presumably at least one bishop and some clergy.

CONVERSIONS: COLUMBA AND THE PICTS

If Columba was not a missionary to Gaelic Dál Riata, what of the Picts? Adomnán, writing over a century later, does show Columba travelling in northern Pictland, working miracles and baptising some Pictish individuals: Emcath by Loch Ness, the captain of a Pictish war band on Skye. But though Adomnán writes of Columba in various encounters with Bridei, the king of the Picts, at his fort at the north end of Loch Ness, he does not tell us that Columba baptised him. There are scenes of confrontation between Columba and Bridei of the sort that in most saints' 'Lives' usually result in the king being either converted and baptised or being cursed. Columba does succeed in filling Bridei and his people with unbearable fear (VC i, 37; ii, 33) and even receiving honour from the king (VC ii, 35), but nowhere does Adomnán speak of Bridei's conversion or baptism. This would be a staggering omission if Adomnán had any information that Columba had baptised Bridei. We must assume that, at least as far as Adomnán was concerned, Bridei either remained a stubborn pagan during Columba's lifetime or was already baptised when Columba met him.

Both are possible, but in favour of the latter explanation is the fact that recent excavations at the important monastery at Portmahomack on Tarbat Ness have shown that it probably existed during Columba's lifetime. Radiocarbon dating of two of the earliest burials under and close to the church building gives date ranges of AD 430–610 and 535–605. The excavators concluded that they were part of the earliest monastic phase, indicating that there may have been monks at Portmahomack when St Columba was visiting the Pictish king and his followers at a fortress some twenty-five miles to the southwest.

Contradicting Adomnán, Bede probably relies on Pictish informants when he says that Columba 'came to Britain to preach the word of God to the provinces of the northern Picts', and that in the ninth year of the reign of Bridei, a most powerful king, he 'turned that people to the faith of Christ by his word and example'. In consequence, Bede continues, the Pictish king gave the island of Iona to Columba so that he could found his monastery there (HE iii, v). There are reasons to doubt all this, even apart from Adomnán's testimony. Bede finished his work in AD 731 shortly after Nechtan, king of the Picts, had chosen to align his kingdom and his church with the Christianity of Northumbria. But Pictish rulers still had to work out what role the monastery of Iona and its many daughter-churches would have in their kingdom. By claiming that Columba rather than Ninian had converted the northern Picts, they had a narrative which made their church independent of any claims that Ninian and his Northumbrian successors in Whithorn might have had on them. The second element of Bede's story (which he probably received from Pictish sources) is that Bridei had given Iona to Columba, but that is unreliable too. The *Annals of Ulster*, which probably give Iona's own view of the matter, say that it was Conall mac Comgaill of Dál Riata who granted Iona to Columba (AU 574). The much later Pictish claim that it had been granted by Bridei can be understood as a claim that Bridei's successors, the kings of the Picts, had inherited rights over Iona. Bede's story would therefore legitimate Pictish ambitions in the west, not only over the most powerful monastery in Dál Riata, but by implication over the kingdoms of Dál Riata. The realisation of this ambition took place only a few years after Bede wrote his account, when the Pictish king Unust reduced Dál Riata to an outpost of the Pictish *imperium*.

A lament and prayer on the death of St Columba in AD 597 may suggest a rather different involvement of the saint in Pictland. The *Amra Choluim Chille*, attributed to a poet called Dallán Forgaill, contains lines that seem both to support the dating of the poem to the time of Columba's death and to offer an insight into his possible missionary activity.

> Great Áed pledged it for all people:
>   a solid song when the hero went to heaven.
> Not worthless, not slight, not contentious,
>   not a hero unvigorous towards Conall's covenant.
> His blessing turned them, the mouths of the fierce ones
>   who lived on the Tay, to the will of the King.

These lines indicate that the song was commissioned by Áed mac Ainmirech, a cousin of the saint and the ruler of the Cenél Conaill. Áed ruled not only Cenél Conaill, but for the last twelve years of his life (AD 586–98) he was king of Tara or 'High King of Ireland'. Given that he died in battle in 598, if he really did commission this work he must have done so within a year or so of the saint's death in 597. The phrase 'Conall's covenant' in the following couplet probably refers to an agreement made between the saint and Conall mac Comgaill, the king who had given him the island of Iona for his monastery and was regarded in some sense by the monks as their secular founder. The *Amra* suggests that contemporary observers saw Columba as having spread Christian influence in the area of the River Tay in southern Pictland. Another reference in the same poem confirms this:

> . . . for he does not return to us, he who would explain the true
>   Word,
> for we do not have the teacher who would teach the tribes of the
>   Tay.

Two things should be observed about these lines. First, neither reference implies that they were pagans before Columba taught them. A monk or priest might teach or preach to an already Christian community, turning them 'to the will of the King'. These verses may not tell us anything about the conversion of the Tay-dwellers to Christianity, therefore, but merely reflect the extension of Columban influence into already Christian 'tribes', or *túatha*. Second, it is not clear whether the 'tribes of the Tay' dwelt by the upper part of this river, or in the broad lands of the lower part, or indeed in Fife and Angus on either side of the Firth of Tay. If the upper reaches were intended, these fierce-mouthed people may have lived in the area around Loch Tay and Dunkeld where Iona seems to have had a strong influence a century after this poem was written, as dedications to Adomnán (the ninth abbot of Iona) and Céti (the first bishop of Iona) in the area suggest. Indeed, the name of part of the upper Tay area, Atholl, from *Ath Fhotla*, 'new Ireland', may suggest that Columba's influence extended into the upper Tay area because it was already becoming Gaelicised in his lifetime. If so this might explain why this part of Pictland lacks any place names coined in Pictish **egles*, 'church': its early ecclesiastical character was more Gaelic than that of the area further east where **egles* names are found.

The fierce-mouthed Tay-dwellers envisaged by the *Amra* may, on the other hand, have lived in the fertile plains of the lower Tay area. In any case, the verses are early evidence of the saint's influence in southern Pictland, rather contradicting the impression given by Adomnán and Bede of a Columban mission to the northern Picts. It seems it is not yet possible to give a clear account of Columba's activities in eastern Scotland, or to discern the traces of Columba's activity in his own lifetime amidst the storytelling of subsequent generations.

CONVERSIONS: ANGLO-SAXON

According to Bede, when Æthelfrith of Bernicia was slain in AD 616, his three sons fled north to Pictland and Dál Riata to escape the power of Edwin, who would then rule both Deira and Bernicia until 633. The seventeen-year exile of these young men exposed them to the culture and religion of their Christian hosts. Meanwhile, Edwin, the Deiran king of Northumbria, married Æthelburh, daughter of King Æthelberht of Kent and Bertha, a royal Frankish woman. Æthelburh was given to Edwin in marriage in AD 625 on condition that she was allowed to bring her Christian household with her to Northumbria, including some clergy. One of these, Bishop Paulinus, had been one of a group sent to Kent by Pope Gregory in AD 601 as part of the mission to the Anglo-Saxons. Bede describes the marriage of Edwin and Æthelburh as a kind of foreshadowing of the more important marriage that was its consequence: the heavenly union between the Northumbrian people and Christ, which would take place two years later when Paulinus baptised Edwin at York. Bede goes on to describe a thirty-six-day marathon of preaching and baptisms conducted by Paulinus, as crowds of Northumbrians followed the example of their king and, having been instructed, were immersed in the River Glen by Yeavering (NT9330).

On the death of Edwin in AD 633, Northumbria was divided again into two kingdoms. Eanfrith returned from his northern exile to rule Bernicia, while the southern kingdom, Deira, was taken over by Edwin's cousin Osric. Though both of these men had been baptised, they both 'returned to the filth of their former idolatry', as Bede puts it, and both were soon slain by the British king Cadwallon. Now Oswald, also a Christian after his exile among the Gaels in the north, took the kingship of both Bernicia and Deira. He killed Cadwallon in battle at *Denisesburn*, close to Hexham on Hadrian's Wall. Both Bede and Adomnán present this battle as a triumph brought about by God, albeit with slightly different emphases. Bede (HE iii, 2) says that before the battle Oswald set up a cross nearby, at a place that would be called *Hefenfelth*, 'heaven field', and knelt there with his entire army to pray for victory. Adomnán also attributes Oswald's victory to God, but he makes St Columba the means by which God's assistance was given. In his account – which he got from his predecessor Abbot Failbe, who in turn had heard it from the very lips of Oswald – Columba appeared to the king in a dream to reassure him: 'The Lord has granted it to me that your enemies will be turned to flight and your enemy Cadwallon will be delivered into your hands' (VC i, 1). This stress on the saint as victory-giver highlights the Columban flavour of the Christianity of the new Bernician elite. Adomnán adds that up to that time 'all that Saxon land was obscured by the darkness of paganism and ignorance, except for King Oswald himself and twelve men who were baptised with him while in exile among the *Scoti*'. He ignores all the Northumbrians who had already been baptised by Paulinus in AD 627 following the conversion of Edwin.

The story of the 'conversion of Northumbria' as envisaged by Bede and Adomnán focuses on the baptism of kings and their high-status followers. But though this was an important part of the process, it is only one part of the story. Other parts, however, are harder to trace in the historical record. Conversions among the lower strata of society, people whose lives are scarcely remarked on by early medieval writers except as a backdrop to the deeds of kings or saints, are less well attested. These lower social strata included Anglo-Saxon and British people living alongside each other for several generations, some of them in areas where the local lord was British and Christian. In other cases, a pagan Anglo-Saxon lord might rule an estate where many of his people were Christian Britons. What impression did it make on the commander of the Gododdin, the son of Anglo-Saxon Golystan/Wolfstan, when his British warriors went to church to take communion before riding off to battle? In a culturally mixed environment, we should imagine people adopting the cultic practices of their neighbours (a process that could go in either direction) in ways that are mostly invisible to the historian's eye. This means that we should not simply accept as fact Bede's statement that the 'unspeakable crimes' of the British included a refusal to evangelise their Anglo-Saxon enemies and neighbours. In some areas it is evidently not true: when Anglo-Saxons penetrated the West Midlands (roughly what would become Mercia) it seems that they found an organised British Church with British bishops, and some were converted by it. Bede does not report this – it would undermine his anti-British rhetoric. He does report, on the other hand, the consecration of Chad as bishop of York *c*. AD 664 at the hands of Bishop Wine of the West Saxons and two British bishops – though he cannot resist reminding his readers that these British bishops were not 'canonically ordained' (HE iii, 28).

There is also evidence that some English people became Christian through the influence of Iona before the exile of Æthelfrith's sons in Dál Riata in 616. Adomnán records that there were at least two English monks on Iona during Columba's own lifetime, men called Genereus and Pilu (VC iii, 1; 22). This indicates sufficient Christian conversions among Anglo-Saxons in the sixth century for at least two of them to enter a monastery. Adomnán gives no clue as to the process by which these men became Christians and monks. But if, as is most likely, they were Northumbrians, we may be able to discover a context for their conversion. We have seen (p. 89) that Hussa ruled Bernicia until his death in AD 592, when Æthelfrith began to rule. Hussa had a son called Hering, who appears in one version of the *Anglo-Saxon Chronicle* as the leader of an army of Dál Riata that attacked Æthelfrith at Degsastan in AD 603. One possible explanation of this record is that on the death of King Hussa his son Hering went into exile in Dál Riata, where he was protected by Áedán during those eleven years until Áedán supported Hering in a failed attempt to retake the kingdom of Bernicia. If Genereus and Pilu had been members of Hering's entourage during his exile of from 592 to 603 in Christian Dál Riata, might they have been so engaged by the religion they encountered there that they became monks of Iona?

GOD AND THE GODS

We have spoken so far of 'conversion' to Christianity as if we knew what it meant to those involved. The use of the word 'conversion' to describe a particular event – what happened to Edwin when he was baptised in AD 627, for example – seems to imply a straightforward process of sloughing off one state of mind and taking on another; abandoning one set of practices and adopting another. But this disguises the complexity of religious change in the early medieval world – or in any other world for that matter. To understand the process we must be alert not only to the changes in belief and practice that Christianity brought, but also to the continuities. We should also be sensitive to the local and the temporary: what happens in one place and time cannot be made to stand in some general way for what happens everywhere and at all times. What follows will therefore highlight certain aspects or moments of the conversion experience in Scotland, rather than attempting a general narrative.

'Becoming a Christian' entailed accepting a broadly defined doctrine, though the extent to which those becoming Christian were aware of its details must have varied. The fundamental elements were:

(1) the unity of God as creator of all things;
(2) Jesus Christ as God's revelation in history, and his death and resurrection as a source of hope for eternal life;
(3) the calling to moral goodness under the guidance of God's Holy Spirit; and
(4) the Church as God's people and the community where this faith was expressed and taught.

Those who assented to this doctrinal outline normally did so in a public way in the rite of baptism in which they symbolically 'died to the world' as they were immersed in water (or had water poured over them), and emerged to begin a new life in the Church, 'the Body of Christ'.

But once people accepted baptism, what difference did it make to their understanding of the world and their place in it? What did they have to do in order to persevere in the faith they had entered at baptism? The 'difference' it made to both thinking and practice was a matter of constant improvisation, as Christians, far from being passive recipients of a whole new culture, constructed their new identity out of the materials of their inherited past and the ideas and practices offered by their new-found faith.

Belief in one God, creator of heaven and earth, as proclaimed by Christianity was clearly fundamental. But Christians continued to find uses for the old deities. A fourth-century mosaic of Christ's head and shoulders at a Roman villa in Dorset portrays him as a ruler, as Lord; but the pomegranates on either side of his head refer to the goddess Persephone who was rescued from death and Hades by her loving mother, the harvest goddess Demeter. For the artist this story of pagan gods was still relevant to the story of Christ. It proclaimed that in Christ the deepest human hope, long manifest in stories of the gods, was fulfilled: that love can descend into the darkest places of human loss to restore men and women to life. So pagan gods could be made safe – and even useful – for Christian believers.

Such gods continued to operate in other traditions, too. In early Christian Ireland the existence of intelligent and responsive beings under the earth was treated simply as a neutral 'fact' of cosmology. Although we might now see these beings as 'gods', and therefore find it surprising that they survived the Christianisation of Gaelic society, in fact these beings were simply part of the world, like mountains, animals and people. Unlike the God of Christianity, these were not something to 'believe in', any more than one 'believed' in mountains. They were not 'supernatural', but part of nature – powerful, capable of interfering in your life for good or ill, and so needing to be dealt with in appropriate ways. Traditions of public assembly in

Ireland and Scotland included gatherings at *Lugnasad*, a feast named originally in honour of a deity called Lug. Celebrated with feasting, horse-racing, legal procedures and political negotiations, possibly including the inauguration of kings, its continuity for centuries under Christian leadership demonstrates the selective improvisation of early medieval Christians in regard to their own pre-Christian culture.

Another way of treating the old gods was to turn them into demons, opponents of the will of God and the work of the saints. Adomnán tells how the Pictish *magus* Broichan opposed St Columba by conjuring up a wind to prevent him sailing as he intended, but he sees the need to give an account of how *magi* can do such things:

> It is not strange that these things can sometimes be done by the art of demons, with God's permission, so that even winds and waters can be whipped up into violence. For so hosts of demons once attacked the holy bishop Germanus in the midst of the sea when, for the sake of man's salvation, he was sailing from the bay of Gaul to Britain. (VC ii, 34)

Among the Christianised Anglo-Saxons, similarly, there was a need to negotiate a *modus vivendi* between ancient deities and Christian belief. Bede may help us to understand the distinction that an Anglo-Saxon Christian was supposed to understand between falling into idolatry and damnation, on the one hand, and simply assimilating characters from a pre-Christian worldview into the new Christian faith, on the other. So in his account of Rædwald, king of the East Angles, Bede tells us that the king had been baptised while in Kent, but when he went home he was led astray by his wife and perverse teachers:

> He was seen to be serving both Christ and the gods which he had served before, so that in the one holy temple he had both an altar to celebrate the sacrifice of Christ and a little altar to offer victims to demons. (HE ii, 15)

This was something intolerable for Bede, who says that Rædwald's last state was worse than his first, his confusion worse than his previous honest paganism. But in another context Bede offered a more hospitable view of pre-Christian Germanic gods. Discussing various Anglo-Saxon kingdoms and their takeover of southern Britain, he offers genealogies for the ruling families. He says of two brothers, Hengist and Horsa:

> They were the sons of Wihtgisl, whose father was Witta, whose father was Wecta, whose father was Woden, from whose stock the royal families of many kingdoms trace their origin. (HE i, 15)

Bede must have known about Woden's significance as a god in pre-Christian cult, and we may be surprised that he is able to mention him in this way. But Woden was an important part of the Germanic ideology of royal power, and Bede – like other eighth-century Anglo-Saxon genealogists – used him to legitimate kingship and to create an impression of unity between various royal families. Woden might have been a threat to Christian monotheism, but Bede neutralised this threat by making him part of a human genealogy. The survival of such deities in everyday English speech (I write this paragraph on a Wednesday, a day which still commemorates the same god) testifies to a nuanced approach to the pre-Christian pantheon.

SAVING THE PAST

The gods were not the only aspects of pre-Christian culture that were dealt with in this way. The Hebrew Bible (the Old Testament) provided Christians with images of salvation which were of course pre-Christian, prefiguring the salvation that they saw fulfilled in Christ. Insular Christians could use this model to look at elements of their own pre-Christian past in a similar way as foreshadowing the Gospel, seeking to align the 'pagan past' with the Christian present. In this way, a pre-Christian legal tradition was seen as a precursor of Christian faith. We can see one moment in the negotiation between that native legal tradition and increasingly Christian conceptions of law in the eighth-century prologue to the Gaelic law-text *Senchus Már*, 'the great tradition'. In this text Dubthach maccu Lugair, 'the royal poet of the island of Ireland' (*rígfilid innsi hÉirenn*), represents the pre-Christian tradition. St Patrick 'blessed his mouth, and the grace of the Holy Spirit came on his speech'. The end result of the story is that native Gaelic laws are selectively absorbed into the new Christian worldview and practice:

> The judgements of true nature, then, which the Holy Spirit had spoken through the mouths of righteous judges and poets of the men of Ireland from when this island was settled until [the coming of the] faith, Dubthach showed them all to Patrick. Whatever did not clash with the word of God in the law of the letter [the Old Testament] and with the New Testament and with the consciences of believers was confirmed in the ordering of judgement by Patrick and by the churchmen and lords of Ireland. For the whole law of nature had been proper, apart from the faith and its duties and the joining together of church and people.

The argument here is that long before Christianity came to the Gaelic world, God had informed the hearts of judges and poets with natural justice. The view is expressed succinctly in a seventh-century text known as the *Canones Hibernenses* ('the Irish Canons'):

> If we find good judgements among the heathen which their own good nature has taught them, and if it does not displease God, we shall keep them.

In this view, the truths brought by Church and Gospel did not displace what was good in the native Gaelic laws, but tested and perfected it.

It is significant that in the *Senchus Már* story the representative of the old order, Dubthach, is a poet rather than a druid, for this enables him to represent the acceptable part of the pre-Christian tradition. Other figures in stories of the saints symbolise unacceptable aspects of the pre-Christian past. In Muirchú's *Life of St Patrick*, written in the seventh century, Loíguire, the king of Tara, is feasting with kings and princes and *magi*. The *magi* or 'magicians' presumably represent druids; they are hostile elements of the old order and refuse to rise at Patrick's arrival, but instead seek to poison him. We saw a similar confrontation between saint and *magi* in the story mentioned above (p. 112) about St Columba's well, where no accommodation was possible; the saint simply had to defeat these representatives of the old world in Pictland. The *magi* symbolise what the Church sought to reject from the past; but in this story the well itself also functions as a sign of continuity between the pre-Christian past and the Christian present. Rather than rejecting the well, Columba converts it from a source of disease and death into a healing spring, thus restoring to the water its proper nature – for water is naturally a source of life and healing. Again the pattern is one of grace restoring or perfecting nature.

If the story of Patrick and Dubthach above suggested a Christian blessing on the native poetic tradition, this was only one strand of Christian thinking about poetry. As we have seen in the works of Taliesin and Aneirin, early British poetry was part of the ideological support system for warrior-kings, a celebration of their violent exploits, the slaughter of their enemies and the pillaging of their neighbours. This aspect of poetry inevitably brought criticism from churchmen. Gildas wrote a splendidly vituperative passage about poetry in the service of the 'dragon of the island', a king he regards as violent and corrupt. In addition to his wickedness this king had filled his ears not with praise of God, but with 'empty praises of yourself from the mouths of praise-poets screeching as if at a Bacchanalia, criminals stuffed with lies who are liable to splatter all those near them with foaming phlegm' (DEB § 34). Here is a rather different attitude to poetry, one found in various stories which show poetry – or certain forms of poetry – as problematic because it was so often at the service of violent and oppressive men.

Violence was another area in which churchmen sought to distinguish what was acceptable in the inherited tradition from what was not. In a world where every free man was a warrior and where the status of free men derived in great part from their success in arms, violence was clearly an inescapable reality and the Church had to work out where it stood. Monks and clergy wrote about the wickedness of violent men or 'sons of death', denounced bloodshed, and sought to create peace between rival factions. Churches sought to represent themselves as places of non-violence. In Adomnán's *Life of Columba* the saint is said to have blessed a knife and prayed that 'it will not harm man or beast'. The monks found that this was indeed true, so they melted it down and coated all the other iron tools in the monastery with its metal, thus rendering them all harmless to human or animal flesh (VC ii, 29). The story presents Iona as a place where bloodshed is miraculously kept at bay. The monks' guide, *Aipgitir Chrábaid*, 'an alphabet of devotion' – which has some association with Iona – reveals a monk's view of his world in the late sixth or early seventh century. It includes the warning:

> Four things which the life of violence brings about for people: it shrinks borders, it increases enmity, it destroys life, it prolongs pains.

This Christian rhetoric against violence is found in abundance in our sources. Men of violence either repent or come to a sticky end and go to hell. But there is a counterpoint to this rhetoric. Saints are also presented as supporters of kings in battle, as bringers of victory to their clients. The dream of a peaceable kingdom was a fine one, but monks and clergy recognised that only a strong king (i.e., one capable of defeating his rivals and other disruptive elements) could ensure peace in his territory. In respect of violence, therefore, churchmen tempered their non-violent principles with a realistic assessment of what kind of violence was necessary to keep the peace. Out of this dialectic emerged a quest to direct the behaviour of kings. Kings should use force when necessary for the keeping of the peace, for the enforcement of justice and for the protection of the Church. A good example is found in an Irish text, *Audacht Morainn*, written around AD 700. Here there is a general dissuasion from violence:

> Tell him, let him not redden many fore-courts,
> for bloodshed is the vain destruction of all rule . . .

The author also stresses the role of the king's justice – not the king's violence – in establishing rule within his kingdom:

> It is through the justice of the ruler that he secures
> peace, tranquillity, joy, ease and comfort.

We might ask what the king should do if, in spite of his justice, the peace and tranquillity of his kingdom is disrupted by violent men. The author rather avoids this question in regard to internal disruption, but when there is aggression from outside his kingdom *Audacht Morainn* is more permissive of violence:

> It is through the justice of the ruler that he dispatches
> great battalions to the borders of hostile neighbours.

Audacht Morainn represents one author's working out of the balance between native tradition, the Christian rhetoric of peace-making and love of enemies, and the political and military realities of his time. Others, in various genres of writing, had their own solutions, but it is a constantly repeated theme not only in Gaelic sources, but also in Anglo-Saxon writings. Bede, for example, makes frequent attempts to justify or to condemn particular acts of violence by Anglo-Saxon kings, or to praise their non-violence as in the case of Sigeberht of the East Angles who was slain by his own kinsmen for being too forgiving of his enemies (HE iii, 22).

Another example of pre-Christian practice that was woven – albeit with some difficulty – into the developing Gaelic Christianity was that of *caíned*, the ritual lament or keening for the dead. Some Christian authors had rejected this practice as pagan, but it continued nevertheless and eventually provided a major theme in the work of the eighth-century Gaelic poet Blathmac. In a long poem he places *caíned* at the centre of his account of faith, and he finds salvation (as does the reader) by keening with the Virgin Mary over the dead body of her son. Centuries before the *Stabat Mater* made this a common theme of devotion elsewhere in the west, Blathmac had taken on this previously suspect native tradition and turned it to the service of Gaelic Christian devotion:

> Come to me, loving Mary,
> that I may keen with you your very dear one.

STRUCTURING AUTHORITY

As the Church grew in Scotland, it was never a monolithic insti-tution with a single hierarchical structure. Like its sister churches in other parts of Europe, it comprised many distinct institutions with various arrangements for decision-making and the exercise of authority. In many ways it was this multiplicity of structures and their flexibility that made the Church successful, able to adapt to different circumstances as it spread. At the same time, these multiple institutions with their patchwork of improvised authority structures sought to maintain unity or communion with each other. For present purposes we will highlight two broad kinds of structure: the episcopal and the monastic. The former involves the government of a community of baptised Christians by a bishop; the latter involves the government of a community of monks by an abbot.

Bishops were the topmost level of the ordained clergy. They were pastors: preachers of the Gospel, teachers of faith and morals, celebrants of the sacraments (baptism, confirmation, Eucharist, etc.), and they ordained other clergy to assist in the pastoral work of the Church. They were also judges in legal disputes, managers of Church property, recipients (on behalf of the Church) of gifts and bequests, and directors of poor relief. While continental bishops had jurisdictions defined by the basic secular unit, the *urbs*, or 'city', most parts of Britain and Ireland did not have anything resembling a city. They had bishops, but their units of jurisdiction were defined by the local equivalent of the *urbs*, which in most places meant the petty kingdom, or in the case of higher-level bishops the over-kingdom.

As Christianity moved from being a marginal and sometimes persecuted sect to become the religion of the emperors, with property, income, legal rights and responsibilities, and close ties to the families of secular elites, an ascetic reflex also developed. Men (and some women) sought a 'desert' experience of prayer, simplicity, and contemplation as monks. Though the word 'monk' comes from Greek *monachos*, 'solitary', these monks gathered together under teachers to form communities – the teacher was called their 'father', or *abbas*, whence 'abbot' – and gradually the word 'monk' began to connote not only the one-ness of solitude, but the one-ness of a common life. As Augustine's *Rule for Monks* began: 'The first reason for your gathering together as one is that you should live in one mind in the house, and that you should have one soul and one heart in God.' The monastic movement held these two concepts of 'one-ness' in a creative tension for centuries, nurturing both the solitary ('eremitic') and the community ('coenobitic') forms.

The authority of an abbot was different from that of a bishop. The abbot had an immediate jurisdiction over his monks who, on entering a monastery, surrendered property, family ties, sexual relations and comfort (I should add here that most of what is said here of monks and their abbots is also true of nuns and their abbesses, but we know next to nothing of any nuns in Scotland in our period). But monks as baptised Christians also remained under the authority of the local bishop in respect of those things that related to a bishop's authority – the administration of the sacraments (including the ordination of some monks to the diaconate or priesthood), the consecration of churches, and matters of doctrine and discipline.

In addition, as monasteries acquired a reputation for holiness and scholarship, monks became desirable candidates for vacant bishoprics, and, partly as a result of this, some aspects of the monastic life were introduced into pastoral churches. But the monasticisation of the wider Church was resisted by some. In Sulpicius Severus' *Life of St Martin* we encounter the fourth-century bishops of Roman Gaul, men from powerful families who felt themselves to be 'naturals' in the government of churches. When the ascetic hermit-monk Martin was proposed as the next bishop of Tours the other bishops were horrified: 'They said his person was contemptible, that a man so despicable in countenance was unworthy of the episcopate, that his clothing was dirty and his hair was disgusting' (VSM § 9).

There were also monks who resisted being drawn into the life of the clergy, knowing that their ascetic and contemplative way of life would be compromised by involvement in pastoral care, secular politics and 'family values' – not always a term of praise in a period when the family was a mechanism of political and economic competition, and therefore of violence. This is the background to the observation by the monk John Cassian, who was influential in early Scottish monasticism:

> This is a saying of the Fathers of old which still remains: 'A monk ought by all means to flee women and bishops.' For neither of them, once he has become familiar with them, will allow him to give himself any longer to the quiet of his cell, or to continue in divine contemplation with pure eyes by his understanding of holy things. (*Institutes* xi, 17)

But in spite of such hesitations about the merging of the monastic and clerical vocations, merge they did. Monasticism succeeded throughout the west largely because it was so effectively projected by bishops and popes who had trained as monks at places like Rome, Lérins or Tours. Bishops in the British Isles – Gaelic, British and Anglo-Saxon – succeeded in establishing their churches partly through their successful promotion of monasticism. When Bishop Patrick was church-building in Ireland, many people were baptised by him, and he ordained clergy everywhere (Conf. § 50), but he had particular enthusiasm for those who became 'monks and nuns of Christ' (*monachi et virgines Christi*) (Conf. § 41). The principles of monastic and clerical life may have been different – that is why, for example, monks *qua* monks were forbidden to baptise, because baptising people was a clerical ministry. But many monks were also clergy who did baptise. In Adomnán's *Life of Columba* the saint is seen baptising in Pictland and Dál Riata, not because he is a monk, but because he is also a priest.

It is in the light of this general interweaving of the episcopal and the abbatial, the clerical and the monastic, that we must challenge what has been a popular view which holds (a) that there was such a thing as the 'Celtic Church' in which belief, practice and organisation were different in some consistent way from that of churches elsewhere in early medieval Christendom, and (b) that this Celtic Church was organised along monastic lines, while 'Roman' or continental Christianity was episcopal. Neither of these views is sustainable. There is no evidence that Christians who spoke Celtic languages had a systematically different theology or practice from Anglo-Saxon Christians or from continental Christians, nor that they distinguished themselves from the 'Roman' Church (questions that we shall look at in due course). Far from being an oddity, they were, like churches everywhere else in the west, part of a patchwork of what Peter Brown has called 'micro-Christendoms', local expressions by Christians working out the implications of the Gospel in their own circumstances, improvising responses to different cultural, social and political circumstances, but mostly still looking to Rome as a touchstone of orthodoxy and a sign of unity.

The long-accepted idea that the 'Celtic Church' was unusually monastic is one that has been challenged in recent years. Early Gaelic laws make it very clear, for example, that, no matter how important monasteries might have been, it was the bishop and his clergy who were of fundamental importance to the Christian life of the laity as a whole. This is certainly the church envisioned by Gaelic laws such as the eighth-century *Rule of Patrick*:

> It is on the souls of the men of Ireland from the Testament of Patrick: a chief bishop for every tribe (*túath*), for ordaining their clergy, for consecrating their churches and for soul-friendship with princes and with chiefs, and for sanctifying and blessing their children after baptism.
>
> For any tribe and any kindred which does not have a bishop for these things, the guiding principle of their belief and their faith dies . . . so that there is no limit with anyone to sin, both kinslaying and murder, and fornication and every other kind of evil besides.

The *Rule* requires that all clergy be competent to fulfil the ministerial functions for which they were ordained, and a bishop who ordains an incompetent cleric is heavily censured – he is 'worthy of death'. The *Rule* invokes Patrick's curse on rulers who do not ensure that their clergy function properly, and establishes a contract between the Church and the *túath* in which the clergy offer sacramental ministry and pastoral care, while the *túath* give material support and honour to the clergy.

Likewise, the early eighth-century *Hibernensis* envisaged the structure of the Church as an episcopal and clerical order rather than as a monastic one. The first eleven books in this collection are wholly concerned with the ordained clergy – the bishop, priest, deacon and so on. There is no book *de Abbate*, 'on the abbot'. The thirty-seventh book, *de Principatu*, 'Concerning Rule', includes discussion of the abbot, though *principatus* actually refers to anyone with authority over church property or church personnel and tenants (he may be layman, bishop, abbot or even pope). There is one book, *de Monachis*, 'concerning monks', but the only authority it deals with is that of an abbot over his monks; it is not about the wider government of churches. The *Hibernensis* therefore offers an almost entirely episcopal–clerical view of the government and pastoral care of the Church. Early Gaelic laws likewise, when they describe the social hierarchies of church and *túath*, invariably give pre-eminence to the bishop, usually giving him the same status as the king.

The British Church in Scotland has left us little information as to its character. Carved stones in Kirkmadrine and Peebles commemorate *sacerdotes* who were probably bishops. St Blane is commemorated as the founding bishop of Kingarth on Bute, and as his name is a British one we may assume that he was the head of an originally British Church. Kentigern is not attested until the twelfth century, but when he does appear he appears as a sixth-century bishop, not as an abbot. If it is permissible to see southern British churches as evidence for British church organisation in Scotland, we should note that when Augustine of Canterbury sought a rapprochement between his own Anglo-Saxon Church and the long-established British churches in the early seventh century, he summoned 'the bishops or teachers' (*episcopos siue doctores*) of the neighbouring province of the Britons, and these men agreed that a further conference should be held; when it took place Bede records that it involved 'seven bishops of the Britons and many learned men' (HE ii, 2). The

British Church portrayed by Gildas also seems to be ruled by bishops. Though he lamented that they were 'most learned in the lying tricks of worldly dealings', that is surely because they were the establishment, the churchmen who enjoyed the patronage of the kings or *tyranni* whom Gildas also chastised.

In the ninth century we also hear of an 'archbishop' in the kingdom of Dyfed (southwest Wales), while a certain Elfoddw was called 'archbishop of Gwynedd' (northwest Wales) on his death in AD 809. The existence of archbishops of Welsh kingdoms suggests a pattern similar to that of Ireland, where each kingdom or *túath* had its own bishop, while an over-kingdom had a senior bishop, an 'over-bishop' who might be *archiepiscopus* in Latin. Such an office was presumably held by Cellach *primepscop Fortrenn*, 'the chief bishop of Fortriu', who died in AU 865 and whose title suggests that he probably had local bishops under his leadership, and therefore that a similar pattern existed in Scotland. The *Hibernensis* also suggests a pattern of senior bishops and juniors: 'An established province has ten cities and one king and three lesser rulers ... and one bishop and other lesser ones' (CCH xx, 2). Likewise, the *Hibernensis* directs that when a dispute arises it should be judged by the 'metropolitan bishop', that is, a senior bishop with authority over other bishops (CCH xx, 3), while the 'Irish Canons' mention the offence of refusing hospitality to a 'bishop of bishops' (*episcopus episcoporum*) who presumably represents the same figure.

On the other hand, bishops were encouraged to live in a community. In some cases a bishop was the head of such a community, and the clergy would relate to him rather like monks to their abbot. In other circumstances, the community may have been under the authority of an abbot, in which case two parallel authority structures existed in the same house: the abbot's authority over his monks and the bishop's authority over his clergy in clerical matters and over all the people of his diocese in things concerning all Christians. We catch a glimpse of such interlocking spheres of authority in Bede's autobiographical note: 'In the nineteenth year of my life I was ordained deacon, and in the thirtieth year priest, on both occasions by the ministry of the most reverend Bishop John, at the command of [abbot] Ceolfrith' (HE v, 24).

There is no 'monastically ordered church' as distinct from an 'episcopally ordered church', therefore. In all the churches, 'Celtic' or Anglo-Saxon, we should see a fluid and improvised pattern of overlapping jurisdictions, perhaps sometimes in tension, but often mutually reinforcing. As Bede says of Iona's daughter-house, the church on Lindisfarne, in his *Life of Cuthbert*:

> Let no one be surprised that Lindisfarne, as well as being an episcopal see (which I have already mentioned) is also the home of an abbot and community . . . the episcopal residence and the monastery are one and the same. The abbot, who is elected by the bishop and a council of monks, rules the monastery; the clergy (priests, deacons, cantors, lectors and the rest) live the full monastic life together with the bishop. Blessed Pope Gregory showed himself a great devotee of this way of life. (VSC § 16)

It is significant that Pope Gregory the Great is cited as the exemplar and authority for this way of life. He was a monk who became a bishop; he sent a monk – Augustine – as the first bishop to the Anglo-Saxons, and promoted both the monasticisation of the clerical life and the role of the monastery in the Church's pastoral mission, a model that Bede – monk and priest – enthusiastically promoted.

It seems an obvious question, therefore, to ask why the idea of a distinctively monastic 'Celtic Church' came to dominate historical writing – at least for a period. One reason must surely be Bede's remark about Iona:

> This island, however, is always accustomed to have an abbot priest as its head, to whose authority the whole *prouincia* and even the bishops themselves must be subject, in an unusual arrangement, following the example of their first teacher who was not a bishop, but a priest and a monk. (HE iii, 4)

But note here first that Bede is not describing a general trend of some supposed 'Celtic Church'. He is describing Iona, and in describing this as an 'unusual arrangement' he surely implies that most of the Gaelic-speaking and British-speaking monasteries did not have bishops subject to abbots in this way. Second, Iona's 'unusual arrangement' concerns only one *prouincia* – a term that Bede generally uses for a particular kingdom, or even sub-kingdom. This cannot, therefore, be assumed to represent Iona's domination of the bishops of Ireland and Scotland at large, or even a large part of those territories. Third, Bede does not say what kind of authority the abbot of Iona exercised over bishops, in what field of decision-making the abbots had usurped episcopal authority. Recall that Bede himself had been ordained by a bishop 'at the command' of Abbot Ceolfrith, so the idea of an abbot having authority in regard to some aspects of a bishop's ministry is not one unfamiliar to Bede's own church. It is now impossible to tell from the evidence available exactly what kind of unusual authority the abbot of Iona exercised in his *prouincia*.

Another reason for the belief that the 'Celtic Church' was unusually monastic may lie in the material and financial conditions of the churches in our period. The great majority of the surviving writings from early medieval Scotland are monastic in origin. Monasteries had the resources to support the scholarship necessary for writing, and to maintain *scriptoria* for the creation and copying of documents. Many were large landowning bodies whose identity and corporate wealth continued and increased from generation to generation. They erected daughter-houses, dependent monasteries that sometimes lay at great distances from the mother-house, with their own lands and tenants. They might also possess non-monastic pastoral churches (much as monasteries 'appropriated' parish churches in later medieval Scotland), absorbing their resources and in return supplying clergy to serve the needs of the laity. By contrast, the secular or non-monastic clergy were modestly supported by the laity of the *túath* which they served, as seen in the contract described by the *Rule of Patrick*:

[The ordained man] is entitled to the stipend of his order, i.e., a house and enclosure, and a bed and clothes and sufficient food for him, without hindrance, without neglecting anything that is in the power of the church, i.e., a sack with its condiment, and a milch cow each quarter and the food of feastdays ... a standard day's ploughing every year, with its seed and its arable land, and half the cloth for a cloak or for a shirt or for a tunic. A meal for four people at Christmas and Easter and Pentecost.

This is not the kind of lifestyle – even if higher ranking clergy received a larger stipend than this – that would lead one to expect the secular clergy to leave a large footprint in the historical record. In addition, the property of secular clergy would have been dispersed to their heirs on their deaths, or been consumed by the local church. When an abbot or monk died he might be remembered by his monastery and his good works recorded; this is especially true of founding abbots, about whom many saints' 'Lives' were written. Any wealth a monk brought to the monastery would remain there on his death – he was forbidden to bequeath it to anyone else. When a priest died, by contrast, there were few mechanisms for keeping either his memory or his property intact. Perhaps that is why we know the names of all the abbots of one monastery, Iona, over several centuries, but the names of only a handful of bishops for the whole of Scotland during the same period, and almost none of the ordinary secular priests who cared for the many small churches of the *túatha*.

HALLOWING SPACE AND TIME

The transformation brought to Scotland by Christianity seeped into the most fundamental notions of space and time. The over-arching vision of salvation in Christ was all very well as a general view of things, but believers constantly sought to express this vision in more local and concrete terms. The landscape of Scotland was transformed as new meanings were applied to space, and places were made 'holy'. The *Amra* says that miracles took place at Columba's grave, and a hundred years later Adomnán records that at his tomb God's power continued to be manifest: 'Even today the same heavenly brightness continues to appear in the place where his holy bones rest, together with frequent visits of the holy angels' – clear evidence of a cult around his body (VC iii, 23). New landscapes were created by miracle stories: Columba creates a well miraculously out of a rock, and it is still working miracles in Ardnamurchan; a pagan well is turned into a place of healing (VC ii,10–11). Places of prayer became places of power where a church could give sanctuary to those in danger. The presence of a relic in one place made you present to the body of a holy man or woman which lay many miles away. The grave of a saint joined heaven to earth, dissolving the greatest distance of all, the distance between the living and the dead.

Time also was transformed by the coming of Christianity. As Christ had appeared in time, linear time could be measured in relation to that event: *anno Domini*, 'in the year of the Lord'. Cyclical time was also transformed: the movement of sun, moon and stars had always measured cyclical time, the repeating patterns of days, months and years, but these now became signs of God's saving presence. It was one of the things the *Amra* celebrated about St Columba:

> He read mysteries and distributed Scriptures among the schools,
>   and put together the harmony concerning the course of the
>   moon,
> the course which it ran with the rayed sun,
>   and the course of the sea.
> He could number the stars of heaven . . .

The saint's reading of 'mysteries' included his reading of the skies. According to Genesis, God had created the sun, moon and stars as 'signs', so the movements of sun, moon and stars revealed God's saving action in the world. In monasteries the day was marked by a daily cycle of prayer which sacralised time, collapsing the distance between the past and the present. In the liturgy of Bangor in Ireland, from where monks founded houses in Scotland, the sixth hour of every day was the hour of the crucifixion:

> Almighty eternal God, who has done great things for us, at the sixth hour you mounted the cross and lit up the darkness of the world; so may you deign to enlighten our hearts.

On Easter night the deacon declared 'Haec nox est', 'this is the night', in which our fathers were led out of Egypt; 'this is the night' in which the chains of death are broken and Christ rises as conqueror over death – not some night centuries ago, but 'this night'. Likewise with the days of the week, the seven-day cycle that Christianity inherited from Judaism replaced the native five-day measure. Adomnán recalls the death of his predecessor Columba on a Saturday night, quoting the saint's words concerning the meaning of the day of his death:

> This day is called the 'Sabbath' in the sacred books, which means 'rest'. And truly this day is a Sabbath for me, being for me the last day of this present life, in which after the troubles of my labours I shall go to rest. And at midnight of this following venerable Lord's Day I shall go the way of the fathers ... for now my Lord Jesus Christ deigns to call me. (VC iii, 23)

Here Adomnán is theologising time. On Saturday, the Sabbath and Jewish day of rest, Columba is ceasing from his labours, entering into God's own Sabbath, the rest that God took on the seventh day in the Genesis account of Creation. But by dying at midnight at the beginning of 'the Lord's Day', or Sunday, the first day of the week and the day of Christ's resurrection, he enters not only into God's rest, but into the risen life of Christ, the New Creation – what Augustine calls 'the eternal eighth day' (de Civ. Dei xx, 30).

The Church's calendar of celebration could collapse temporal distance in another way, by celebrating several events on the same day. The Irish Martyrology of Tallaght (which developed partly out of an Iona document) reflected on 25 March, the old Roman spring equinox, that:

> Our Lord Jesus Christ was crucified; and he was conceived; and the world was created ... and the sacrifice of Isaac by his father Abraham on Mount Moriah.

The declaration that all these biblical events took place on the same date made an essential connection between them: the (mercifully aborted) sacrifice of Isaac prefigured the actual death of Christ, a young man climbing a hill carrying the wood on which he was to be slain. Interestingly, Adomnán makes the very same connection between Isaac and Christ in his *De locis sanctis* by observing that the place of Isaac's proposed sacrifice is at Golgotha, the place where Christ died. The *Martyrology* also connects the creation of the world, which began with the words 'let there be light', to the conception of Christ by which the 'true light entered the world', and both of these to the crucifixion by having them all take place on the spring equinox when the hours of light begin to exceed the hours of darkness. So the calendar declared in one moment the triumph of light over dark, of creation over nothingness, and of life over death.

The reckoning of time was not always straightforward, however, and the calculation of the date of Easter in particular caused considerable trouble in the seventh century. It had always been problematic, and as early as AD 314 three bishops from Britain at the Council of Arles were among those who wrote to Pope Silvester:

> In the first place concerning the observance of the Lord's Passover [i.e., Easter Sunday], so that one day and one time should be observed by us all throughout the world, you should send letters to everyone according to custom.

Clearly, it was already a cause for anxiety that different churches were celebrating Easter at different times, undermining the visible unity of the Church. The differences arose from the complexity of the reckoning, requiring as it did the coordination of the weekly seven-day cycle (Easter must be a Sunday), the lunar calendar (counting from the full moon) and the solar calendar (falling after the spring equinox). This was complicated by the fact that Alexandria and the Eastern Churches treated 21 March as the equinox (as we do today), while in Rome the equinox had been fixed on 25 March since 45 BC. Other complications arose from different ways of calculating the lunar calendar (how do you define when the new moon appears?), different views of when a day started (at sunset the previous evening, or at midnight or at sunrise?), and from a variety of ways of trying to reconcile the movements of the moon and the sun in a single reckoning because there are 12.3683 lunar months in a solar year – that is, a lunar year is about eleven days shorter than a solar year. These and other variables gave rise to a number of different 'cycles' – attempts to give a systematic and predictable account of when Easter Sunday would fall in any given year. In the east a nineteen-year cycle emerged as the accepted one, but in fourth-century Rome an eighty-four-year cycle was used and became the norm in the churches of the west. This eighty-four-year cycle was presumably the one that the British bishops at the Council of Arles had expected Pope Silvester to use. But in the mid-fifth century the Roman Church under Pope Leo adopted another calendar devised by Victorius of Aquitaine. The Victorian cycle was not accurate, however, and continued to differ in some years from the Alexandrian; in those years it offered two alternative dates for Easter. In AD 525, Pope John I asked Dionysius, a learned Scythian monk now living in Rome, to create a new Easter table, as a result of which the Roman Church soon began to mark the equinox on 21 March, using an Alexandrian reckoning of the moon, and giving a nineteen-year Easter cycle. The Dionysian table gradually spread thereafter, though for centuries it co-existed with various others, including the old eighty-four-year cycle and the Victorian cycle, which continued to be used by some churches.

This brief and simplified narrative is the background to the arguments that took place in Ireland and Britain about the dating of Easter. Here the churches continued to use an eighty-four-year cycle (which they probably regarded as the traditional Roman one) after Rome had adopted first the cycle of Victorius and then the nineteen-year cycle of Dionysius. In AD 541, a church council at Orleans decreed in the first of its canons:

> That the holy Pasch be celebrated by all priests at one time following the table (laterculus) of Victorius, and that [the date of] this feast is to be announced to the people every year in church on the day of Epiphany.

Around AD 600 Columbanus, a Bangor monk now in northern Italy, sought the support of the pope in his struggle with the

Frankish bishops who were trying to force him to use their Victorian cycle (which Rome had already abandoned when it adopted the Dionysian cycle). About three decades later the clergy of southern Ireland adopted first the Victorian cycle, and then the Dionysian, while the northern part of Ireland and the Gaelic, British and Pictish Churches in Scotland continued to use their old eighty-four-year cycle.

Meanwhile, in the seventh century the Anglo-Saxon invaders of Britain were becoming Christians and were celebrating first the Victorian cycle together with the Frankish Church and then the Dionysian cycle adopted by Rome. But the exile of the pagan sons of Æthelfrith in Scotland and their subsequent return to power as Christian rulers of Northumbria brought a Columban-flavoured Christianity to their territory. It was during the reign of Oswiu (642–70) that complications arose. Oswiu married Eanflæd, daughter of Edwin of Northumbria and granddaughter of Æthelberht king of Kent. Edwin, as we have seen, had been baptised by a missionary bishop from Kent. In such circumstances it was inevitable that a conflict would ensue over the date of Easter: Iona monks followed the eighty-four-year cycle, Kentish clergy followed the nineteen-year cycle of Dionysius. The presence of two traditions with two Easter dates in one kingdom, indeed in one house, could not continue indefinitely, and Oswiu summoned a council at Whitby in AD 664 to resolve the issue. Bede records the debate at Whitby and the king's acceptance there of the nineteen-year cycle promoted by Wilfrid, the English bishop, and the rejection of the eighty-four-year cycle of the Iona monks. As Bede tells the story, the decision was ultimately based on an appeal to papal authority.

But this dispute was not simply about the right way of calculating the date of Easter, nor about papal authority. There were important political implications. Oswiu's overlordship at this point probably extended over both Dál Riata and Pictland, where the eighty-four-year cycle was observed. But his ambitions were more southward-looking. His marital alliance with Kentish royalty lent him political and military weight as he sought over-kingship of other English kingdoms (HE iii, 24). In addition, Oswiu's strength lay in Bernicia. Even though he was married to Eanflæd, the daughter of Edwin of Deira, control of that southern part of Northumbria eluded him for many years of his reign. In AD 651, he had Oswine, king of Deira killed, and his nephew Æthelwald then took power there, but Æthelwald turned against Oswiu and allied himself with Penda of Mercia against his uncle. When Æthelwald was removed c. AD 655, Oswiu's own son, Alhfrith, ruled Deira; but he rebelled against his father at one point (HE iii, 14) and married the daughter of Penda, Oswiu's enemy. The Church in this troublesome kingdom of Deira had its roots not in the Gaelic mission from Iona, but in the Kentish mission of Paulinus. Oswiu's son, as king of Deira, supported the Kentish tradition and gave the church of Ripon to Wilfrid, the intransigent promotor of 'Roman' Easter observance, evicting the monks who followed 'Irish' customs. In this context we may assume that Oswiu's decision for the 'Roman' faction may have been shaped as much by his political ambitions as by theological argument. It is significant that the decision at Whitby was not made by bishops or theologians, but by the king, who then imposed his decision on the Churches of his kingdom.

Bede gives a lengthy account of the argument at Whitby, but his account pays little heed to the political pressures on Oswiu. It is couched in terms of right and wrong Easter calculations, and in the end it was Wilfrid's appeal to papal authority that won the day at Whitby; the 'Roman' party defeated the 'Celtic' monks. There is, of course, a kernel of truth in this view. The need to bring unity to churches divided by their celebrations of Easter was clear throughout the west, not only in Britain. Also, as all the disputants were using the same set of biblical and con-ciliar texts to come to quite different conclusions, unity could be achieved only by appeal to ecclesiastical authority – papal authority.

But an over-reliance on Bede's account has meant that our understanding of the dispute has over-emphasised its 'Celtic-versus-Roman' aspect. We must remember, first, that there was nothing 'Celtic' about the eighty-four-year cycle that the

Columban monks were using. They almost certainly saw it as the old Roman cycle, which they had inherited from their founding fathers. Second, the dispute was not between 'Celts' and 'Romans', but between the monks and clergy of the Columban community (Gaels and Anglo-Saxons alike) and some leading clergy of the Northumbrian Church. The equally 'Celtic' churches of southern Ireland had adopted the nineteen-year 'Roman' cycle more than three decades earlier, and its 'most fierce defender' in Northumbria prior to the council at Whitby was a combative Irishman called Rónán (HE iii, 25).

Finally, although Wilfrid's party used the rhetoric of 'being Roman' to claim superiority over the Columban clergy, this rhetorical claim should not be taken at face value. There are good reasons to believe that the monks of Iona and Lindisfarne also claimed for themselves the *Romanitas* that Wilfrid and Bede denied them. In the *Amra Choluim Chille* the poet describes Columba's Christianity thus:

> *Ro-fess Ruam, ro-fess séiss,*
> *ro- suíthe dó –damtha dëachtae.*

> Rome was known, order was known,
> knowledge of the Godhead was granted to him.

For the poet, the idea of 'Rome' summed up the faith and the godly order and knowledge it brought. Iona's sense of its own *Romanitas* was likewise expressed by its Latin liturgy and its immersion in Latin literature. The Iona-linked *Hibernensis* would direct in the eighth century that disputes that could not be solved locally were to be referred to the 'apostolic see' – to Rome. Likewise, we might look to the views of the Irish monk Columbanus who wrote letters to popes Gregory I and Boniface IV. In the first, *c.* AD 600, he sought the support of Pope Gregory against Frankish bishops who were trying to force him to adopt the Victorian Easter tables (which had already been abandoned by Rome). In the letter he manifests profound respect for his 'Holy Father' who 'lawfully sits on the chair of Peter the apostle', while vigorously criticising the Victorian calculation. When Columbanus wrote to Pope Boniface, in or shortly after

AD 612 (not about Easter, but about a Christological issue), he protested that he and his Irish brethren were as Roman as anyone else:

> For all we Irish, dwellers at the end of the world, are disciples of Saints Peter and Paul and of all the disciples who wrote the sacred Canon by the Holy Spirit, accepting nothing outside the evangelical and apostolic teaching. There has been no heretic, no Judaizer, no schismatic; but the Catholic Faith is held unbroken just as it was first handed on by you, the successors of the apostles. (*Epistola* V, 3)

Bede and Wilfrid claimed that theirs was the 'Roman' way, accusing the Columban monks of being un-Roman, and Wilfrid used the same accusation as part of an attempt to impose his authority over the British, Columban and Pictish Churches. But as we have seen, the Columbans did not accept this designation; nor should we. They were no doubt aware that even in Rome three different Easter cycles had been used within a single century, and that the Frankish and Spanish churches were still using the erroneous Victorian cycle (as they would until the late eighth century). Columban churchmen could therefore deny, not unreasonably, that the Dionysian cycle of the Kentish mission was the defining feature of *Romanitas* or orthodoxy which Wilfrid claimed it was.

The tension between Columban and Northumbrian churchmen continued for decades. Although Adomnán, the ninth abbot of Iona, seems to have accepted the Dionysian cycle in the 680s, as most Irish Churches had, he was unable to persuade many of the monks on Iona to do so, and they continued to use their old eighty-four-year Easter cycle until AU 716. We will return to the implications of this in the next chapter.

4

'The just man will never waver' (Psalm 111:6)
Adomnán and His World

It may seem strange in a book of six chapters, covering nine centuries of Scotland's history, to devote an entire chapter to a study of one man. The man in question, however, happens to be the only individual in that entire period whose personality, biography, interests and ideas can be identified and examined with any confidence at all. Certainly, we hear of other interesting-sounding individuals. There is Calgacus, the eloquent leader of the British resistance to Agricola, but we cannot be certain that Calgacus even existed and, if he did, everything we 'know' about him was written by Tacitus for his own reasons. We also meet warrior kings in the poetry of Aneirin and Taliesin, but these are literary creations that mostly conform to the stereotypes of heroic poetry. Other kings appear in the bare data of annal entries – a battle won, a ruler slain, a patronymic – but these do not emerge as personalities. They remain remote figures in the ceaseless manoeuvring of kingdoms and dynasties. Even a saint like Columba remains an idealised figure created by people writing about him after his death for their own purposes. A few dates and biographical details may emerge, a story here and there, but we encounter such people less as three-dimensional human beings than as the creations of later writers.

In nine centuries of the history of Scotland there is really only one person of whom this is not true. Adomnán mac Rónáin, the abbot of Iona from AD 679 to 704, emerges from his own writings and from writings about him as the one individual in the period of whom we can paint anything like a recognisable human portrait. This in itself would be a good enough reason to examine his life and work in some detail. But in addition it is worth reflecting on the huge influence that Adomnán has had on early medieval historiography. His writings, together with writings that emerged from his monastery, represent the greater part of what survives from Scotland during the first millennium. They have therefore determined much of the way we think about the period. By looking in detail at Adomnán and at the way he saw his world and represented it, we will be in a better position to weigh the significance of his evidence. His work sheds light on many aspects of Scotland's early medieval history: law, kingship, the Easter controversy, the place of women and attitudes to violence.

We may look first at references to him by others which appear in the historical record. His death is recorded in AU 704: 'Adomnán, abbot of Iona dies in the seventy-seventh year of his age'. His feast-day is on 23 September, and as a saint's feast is almost always the day of his or her death we can assume that he died on that day. The reference to his seventy-seventh year implies that he was born between 24 September 627 and 23 September 628.

Adomnán belonged to Cenél Conaill, a kindred of the northern Uí Néill, and on his father's side to a branch known as Síl Sétnae ('the descendants of Sétna'). The eponymous Sétna had been St Columba's uncle. Indeed, almost all of the earliest abbots of Iona were drawn from the Cenél Conaill. There were exceptions to this norm, such as Fergna (d. 623, who was probably a Briton) and Suibne (d. 657), but the expectation was that Columba's kin would rule his monastery whenever suitable candidates could be found. Interestingly, when Adomnán describes Fergna as having become abbot of Iona he says this happened '*deo auctore*', 'by God's authority' (VC iii, 19). This phrase may simply reflect a pious convention, but perhaps Adomnán felt the need to declare Fergna's legitimacy in God's sight even if his abbacy was suspect in the eyes of the world because of his British origin.

Adomnán's mother, Ronnat, came from a group known

as Cenél nÉndai, 'the descendants of Éndae'. The genealogies record Éndae as the brother of the Conall from whom Cenél Conaill and most Iona abbots claimed descent. They occupied the area around Raphoe near the eastern boundary of Cenél Conaill territory.

Adomnán became abbot on the death of his immediate predecessor, Failbe, in AU 679. He may already have been a monk of Iona during Failbe's abbacy, for he claims to have spent time with Failbe (VC i, 1). However, they may have met in Ireland rather than on Iona, since AU 673 records: 'The voyage of Failbe, abbot of Iona, to Ireland', and three years later: 'Failbe returns from Ireland'. Other biographical details emerge in the mid-680s. It seems that Aldfrith son of Oswiu was in exile in Dál Riata when his half-brother Ecgfrith was slain by the Picts at the battle of Nechtansmere in AD 685. It is possible that Aldfrith had studied on Iona under Adomnán during his exile. On Ecgfrith's death (and burial on Iona), Aldfrith obtained the kingship of Northumbria and returned there to rule. The following year Adomnán followed him south, as the *Annals of Ulster* record: 'Adomnán brought back the captives to Ireland.' These were the Irish people captured during Ecgfrith's devastating raid on Brega in AD 684. Adomnán's journey to Northumbria may have had other purposes as well, diplomatic or scholarly, but while there he obtained from Aldfrith the release of these Irish captives and their return home. Adomnán himself points out (VC ii, 46) that he actually visited 'my friend King Aldfrith' again two years later. According to Bede (who only records one of these visits), Adomnán made a gift to Aldfrith of a book he had written, *De locis sanctis*, 'on the Holy Places'. Bede admired the book and wrote an abridged version of it (HE v, 15–16). He also admired Adomnán as a man: 'he was a good and wise man, nobly instructed in the knowledge of the Scriptures' (HE v, 15). Bede reports that his abbot, Ceolfrith, had met Adomnán and recalled: 'He showed wonderful prudence, humility and devotion in his manners and his speech' (HE v, 21).

From Bede we learn that when Adomnán visited Northumbria he became persuaded of the correctness of the nineteen-year

Dionysian Easter cycle which the English Churches were then using. On his return to Iona he urged his own monks to adopt it, but without success. Adomnán may have been persuaded by the Northumbrians, or he may have had other reasons which we will discuss shortly. Whatever his motivation, however, Adomnán failed to persuade his own monks to follow him in the new cycle, which sheds an interesting light on seventh-century notions of monastic obedience: the monks' duty of obedience to their abbot seems to have come second to their sense of what they saw as the authentic tradition of their founder. It was Columba, after all, whose authority they claimed in adhering to the eighty-four-year cycle which the synod of Whitby had rejected in AD 664. Bede claims that, faced with his monks' refusal to change, Adomnán left Iona and went to Ireland to persuade other churches to adopt the Dionysian calendar, only returning to his own monastery in AD 704, the year of his death. This narrative may fit Bede's rhetorical purpose, but, in fact, Adomnán seems to have remained on Iona, though he did visit Ireland in AD 692 and again in AD 697. Furthermore, there is little reason to accept Bede's view that when Adomnán was in Ireland he was there to promote the nineteen-year cycle, or that there was any estrangement between him and the monks of Iona as a result of the Easter dispute.

Finally, there survives an Irish *Life of Adomnán* (*Betha Adomnáin*) written in Kells in Ireland in the tenth century. Given its later date and its concern with miracles and conversations with the devil, it probably gives us little real biographical detail about Adomnán, but it does touch on an issue that we know was of deep concern to Adomnán himself (violence against women), and there are one or two passages that seem to have their origin in Iona traditions about the saint.

THE ABBOT WRITING

In addition to the information provided by other people's writings, we can also explore Adomnán's thought through his own works. Here we encounter his interests and commitments, his theological outlook and his political and pastoral concerns. In what follows we will look at some writings by Adomnán himself and at others that are associated with him, and identify a few of the themes that may be regarded as among his central concerns. These, in turn, will shed light on other aspects of seventh-century Scotland.

The first of his writings that we know of is *De locis sanctis* ('On the holy places'), describing places mostly associated with events in the Bible. As Adomnán gave a copy of this book to his friend Aldfrith on one of his visits to Northumbria, it must have been written before AD 688. Its short preface states that 'Arculf, a holy bishop, a Gaul by race, expert in various far-away places, a truthful informer and quite trustworthy, stayed in the city of Jerusalem for nine months, wandering through the holy places every day.' Adomnán explains that *De locis sanctis* was written using notes that he had written on tablets while interrogating Arculf. Bede gives more detail about Arculf, stating that after a visit to the 'promised land' and other places, he had been thrown up on the west coast of Britain by a storm and eventually came to Adomnán. But we may wonder to what extent Adomnán truly relied on this bishop. Most of the information in *De locis sanctis* would have been available to Adomnán in the extensive library on Iona, and there would have been no need to interrogate Arculf. It has even been suggested that Arculf may have been invented by Adomnán.

Recent scholarship has explored *De locis sanctis* as a work of theology, using information about the holy places of the eastern Mediterranean world to shed light on the events of the Gospel, to answer questions about difficult or obscure passages of the Bible and to explore some of the hidden meanings of scripture. It must also have had profound implications for monastic readers, whose daily performance of the liturgy will have been enriched by the way Adomnán describes the liturgical practices of Jerusalem and Constantinople.

De locis sanctis was Adomnán's chief claim to fame in the Middle Ages, but in more recent centuries it has been his *Vita Columbae*, the 'Life of Columba', that has attracted more interest. Written some time after *De locis sanctis*, it contains two prefaces and three books divided into 119 chapters, almost all being descriptions of miracles performed by the saint. The first book is mostly concerned with his prophetic revelations, the second with his miracles of power, and the third with his angelic visions – though there is some overlap between these categories. Those looking here for chronologically ordered biographical information about Columba will be disappointed. Such information was of little interest in itself to Adomnán, for whom a *Vita* was not meant to be a mere collection of data, but a revelation of the holiness of his patron: how did the power of God manifest itself in this man's life, and what are the implications for 'us' now? The 'us' in question here would be primarily the abbot and monks of Iona and a wide range of people who might need to be convinced of Columba's sanctity. For Adomnán and his readers, the historical Columba, born in Ireland, founder of a monastery in Scotland where he lived, died and was buried, now dwelt in the presence of God as a patron and protector for his clients. For early medieval devotees of the saints these men and women were not 'good examples' to be imitated so much as figures of power, patrons in the heavenly court who could intercede with God for their earthly clients. So when *Vita Columbae* records events that reveal the saint's holiness and power, it is to confirm the trust that his clients have in him. The seventh-century poet Beccán mac Luigdech, possibly a monk on Rum, calls on his heavenly patron Columba to save him:

> The shield of a few, a crowd's shield,
> a fort where all unsafe are safe;
> he is a tight fort – fair prize
> to be in Colum Cille's care.
>
> . . . May he save me from fire – common fight –
> Colum Cille, noble candle,
> his tryst well-famed – he was bright –
> may he bear me to the King who ends evil.

Other poems call on Columba for his powerful *snádud* – his power of protection. In early Gaelic law *snádud* was the power of a free man to grant safe conduct or protection to those of lower status within the boundaries of his territory. Any offence against the protected person became an offence against his protector. The poets borrowed this legal term to express their trust in their saint's power, but here the nature of power was subverted. In secular society the protector had earned his power by his wealth, his high social standing and his ability to use violence to enforce his rights and to defend his honour. In the poetry, however, the saint's power of *snádud* is painted as a deliberate inversion of the legal tradition: now it depends on his embrace of poverty, his monastic meditation, and his rejection of violence:

> He gave up beds, abandoned sleep – finest actions –
> conquered angers, was ecstatic, sleeping little.
>
> He possessed books, renounced fully claims of kinship:
> for love of learning he gave up wars, gave up strongholds.
>
> He left chariots, he loved ships, foe to falsehood;
> sun-like exile, sailing, he left fame's steel bindings.

Columba's power in this subversive sense is central, both in the vernacular poetry and in Adomnán's Latin *Vita Columbae*. But there is another important aspect to the saintly power portrayed in the *Vita*. A saint who founded a church or monastery left a successor, his *comarba*, or 'heir'. The pope, the bishop of Rome, was the *comarba Pheadair*, 'the heir of Peter', and his custodianship of the relics of St Peter was the sign of his authority to lead the Church in Rome as St Peter had. Likewise, the abbot of Iona was the *comarba Choluim Chille*, or 'heir of Columba' and head of the Columban *familia* of monasteries. His authority was an expression of the authority of Columba, and it was expressed and validated, at least in part, by his possession of the relics of the saint. One might almost say that the *comarba* became a kind of virtual presence of the saint himself. So when Adomnán, the ninth abbot of Iona, wrote about the power and authority of Columba, the first abbot of Iona, he was also writing about his own power and authority. When he described Columba's deeds, he was not merely praising his predecessor, but marking out his own claim as Columba's successor. We shall see instances of this pattern later in this chapter.

The *Annals of Ulster* record a major event in the life of the abbot in AD 697: 'Adomnán went to Ireland and gave the *Lex Innocentium* (the 'Law of the Innocents') to the peoples.' The surviving text of this Law, which we will discuss more fully below, contains both the legal material created by Adomnán – or by Iona lawyers working under him – and some interesting tenth-century accretions of a more folkloric character. Adomnán's role as a law-giver may also appear in regulations known as the 'Canons of Adomnán', *Canones Adomnani*. These twenty rules mostly concern dietary restrictions on 'unclean' foodstuffs, but they include two canons on other topics: one canon forbids Christians to accept goods taken in raids, which certainly echoes one of Adomnán's core concerns; another discusses what happens when a woman leaves her husband for another man. It is not certain that all (or any) of these canons were authored or even collected by Adomnán, but they are attributed to him. Another quasi-legal document that may be connected to Adomnán is the *Collectio Canonum Hibernensis*, a collection of authorities offering guidance for the conduct of church and society made by two monks, Ruben of Dairinis and Cú Chuimne of Iona. Ruben died in AU 725, so the collection must have been made before then. As Cú Chuimne was a monk of Iona it is quite possible that he was there compiling this collection during Adomnán's abbacy (AD 679–704).

A good deal of the annalistic record of Scottish history from the sixth century up to about AD 740 is composed of a year-by-year record kept on Iona, usually referred to as the *Iona Chronicle*. The entries written during the twenty-five years of Adomnán's abbacy must reflect something of his worldview and that of his community, even if they were not written by Adomnán himself. This material survives because it was later incorporated into the *Annals of Ulster* and the *Annals of Tigernach*, and to a lesser degree into other Irish annal collections. As the *Iona Chronicle* is the only text of this genre to survive from Scotland during this period, historians are enormously dependent on it, and our understanding of the period is therefore shaped by the view of Adomnán and other abbots of Iona.

Finally, various poems have been attributed to Adomnán. They include some Gaelic poems: *A maccucáin* (addressed to a young lad carrying a bag of relics), three quatrains embedded in the tenth-century *Life of Adomnán*, and a prayer beginning *Columb Cille co Día domm eráil* ('May Colum Cille commend me to God'). None of these can be ascribed to Adomnán with any certainty, but there is a Latin poem that does bear signs of having come from his pen. In a poem beginning *Adiutor laborantium* the poet refers to himself as *'homunculus'*. This is a rare word in early medieval Latin literature, but in spite of its rarity Adomnán uses the word several times in his own writings, together with a related word of the same meaning, *homuncio*. Both *homunculus* and *homuncio* are diminutives of Latin *homo* 'man, person', so *homunculus* means 'little person'. Now Adomnán's own name can be understood as a diminutive form of the Hebrew name Adam, and as the Hebrew name Adam means exactly the same as *homo*, 'person', *homunculus* can be understood as a Latin rendering of the name Adomnán. Indeed, in the Glossary of the scholar Cormac mac Cuilennáin († 908) the name Adomnán was glossed *'homunculus* – a diminutive of the name Adam'. It may be, therefore, that when the poet refers to himself using the uncommon word *homunculus*, he is naming himself as 'Adomnán'. It can be seen as a cryptic 'signature' embedded in the work:

> . . . I beg that me, a little man (*homunculum*),
> trembling and most wretched,
> rowing through the infinite storm of this age,
> Christ may draw after him to the lofty
> most beautiful haven of life.

FATHER OF MONKS

As we have seen, Adomnán as the successor of Columba was keen to promote devotion to his predecessor, and his reverence

for the saint was naturally shared by his entire monastic community, as appears from the opening words of the *Vita Columbae*:
'Wishing to submit to the demands of the brothers, with Christ's
help I shall describe the life of our blessed patron.' At the heart
of the *Vita* is the picture of Columba as an abbot, as the father
of monks, their protector, teacher and guide. He may have been
dead for a century when Adomnán wrote his *Life*, but his death
did not make him a remote figure. On the contrary, Columba
had promised on his death-bed that as long as the brethren loved
one another God would help them, 'and I, dwelling with Him,
will pray for you'. They believed that his continuing closeness to
them would support them in this life, and help them to eternal
happiness in the next (VC iii, 23).

This sense of his closeness to his monks pervades many of the
stories in *Vita Columbae*. A holy monk called Cormac, wanting
to be a hermit or solitary, sought a 'desert in the ocean', but
failed because he had taken with him a monk who had left his
monastery without his abbot's permission (VC i, 6). Seeking
solitude was all very well, but a hermit's holiness could not be
seized by unilateral action, particularly if he tried to do so by
separating himself from his abbot. On another similar voyage,
Cormac landed in the Orkneys, and was protected from mis-
treatment by the local chief because Columba, having miraculously anticipated Cormac's arrival there, asked Bruide, the
Pictish over-king who held Orcadian hostages, to protect him
(VC ii, 42). On a third voyage, the same Cormac was driven
off course by a storm and his boat nearly overwhelmed by
'repulsive and extremely dangerous small creatures ... about
the size of frogs'. Though St Columba was physically far away
(presumably in Iona) he was able to see Cormac's danger and 'in
spirit he was in the boat with Cormac'. Only by the prayers of
Columba and his fellow-monks did Cormac and his companions
survive the attack; the wind changed and Cormac's ship was
brought back to the saint 'to the great wonder of all, and with
great rejoicing' (VC ii, 42). Many other stories show the dependence of all the Columban monks on their founding abbot for
their welfare. Sometimes these take place when Columba is far

away: protection from a great whale at sea (VC i, 19), rest and refection for overworked monks at Durrow (VC i, 29), or relief for exhausted monks on Iona when 'the spirit of Saint Columba met them on the way' (VC i, 37). At other times, he acts for his monks when his is physically present to them: he cures nose-bleeds (VC ii, 18), he heals Diormit of a mortal sickness (ii, 30), and he makes the poison of snakes harmless on his own island (ii, 28). Adomnán's recitation of these miracles would remind his monks of the necessity of remaining close to Columba, and of the saint's continuing care for them.

Columba's patronage embraced not only monks, and Adomnán tells several stories in which lay-folk also benefit from his miraculous concern. But the particular bond between Columba and his monks will have had a special significance for Adomnán. Bearing in mind what we said above about the *comarba* representing the 'presence' of the saint, when Adomnán stresses the founding abbot's closeness to his monks in the sixth century, this implies something about his own relationship to his monks a century later, since he is now the abbot and *comarba Choluim Chille*. We can therefore read in *Vita Columbae* the obligation of Iona monks to remain close to their abbot – not only to Columba, but also to Adomnán. This was of particular importance in the wake of the Synod of Whitby and the ensuing controversy over Easter calculations. The insistence of the Iona monks – or some of them – on following their eighty-four-year cycle was for them an expression of their fidelity to Columba. But their abbot at the end of the seventh century, Adomnán, had accepted the nineteen-year Dionysian Easter cycle after one of his visits to Northumbria.

This must have created something of a crisis of abbatial authority, and parts of the *Vita Columbae* can be read as Adomnán's way of dealing with it. In one chapter Adomnán tells the story of Columba's visit to the monastery of Clonmacnoise in the Irish midlands. It is the only place in the entire *Vita Columbae* where there is any explicit mention of the Easter controversy. At Clonmacnoise Columba prophesied by the rev-elation of the Holy Spirit 'concerning that strife which later arose among the Irish churches concerning the difference of the Easter festival' (VC i, 3). There is no mention here of what Adomnán thought was the 'right' answer to the dispute, though his monks must have known perfectly well what he thought. But they must also have known that Clonmacnoise had accepted the nineteen-year Easter cycle at a synod at Mag Léne in Ireland in about AD 630. And Adomnán's story stresses that the monks of Clonmacnoise welcomed Columba with kisses of great reverence and showed him extraordinary honour. He in turn blessed a boy in their community, Ernéne mac Craséni, and prophesied that he would be a monk of great virtue and wisdom whose tongue would receive from God 'eloquence and healthful doctrine'. Finally, Columba went about identifying places within Clonmacnoise 'which were frequented by angels at that time' – a sign of divine blessing.

Now this description of the mutual admiration between Columba and the monks of Clonmacnoise may have been offered by Adomnán in order to imply Columba's blessing on the nineteen-year cycle. The implicit argument could be understood as follows: Columba had a God-given vision of the holiness of Clonmacnoise, where angels visited; he had also foreseen the Easter controversy while visiting that monastery; and he had foreseen the holiness and sound teaching of Ernéne, who was a senior monk there when Clonmacnoise adopted the new nineteen-year cycle (he died in AU 635). In this chapter, then, we may see Adomnán very gently urging his monks that the nineteen-year cycle accepted by Clonmacnoise could also be accepted by them, because Columba had foreseen it and given its proponents his blessing.

But there is another important reflection on Iona's Easter crisis in *Vita Columbae*. Clare Stancliffe has shown that in the last chapter of the work the final words of the dying saint to his monks contain verbal echoes of a passage in Eusebius' *Ecclesiastical History* (in its Latin translation by Rufinus, c. AD 401). The passage in Eusebius concerns a dispute over the date of Easter between Pope Victor (AD 189–99) and some church leaders from Asia (what is now western Turkey). The pope initially intended to excommunicate the Asians, but he was restrained by Irenaeus of Lyons. Eventually, the pope and the Asians agreed to differ, though remaining in communion with each other: 'they parted from each other in full faith, in complete peace and in steadfast charity'. Adomnán clearly knew from his reading of the *Ecclesiastical History* that it was possible to have different Easter calculations without destroying communion; that the peace and charity that ultimately prevailed between Pope Victor and his Asian opponents were more important than uniformity of practice. The verbal echoes of Eusebius appear in Adomnán's description of Columba's farewell instructions:

> While reclining there he gave his last instructions to the brothers, only his servant hearing him. 'These last words I commend to you, my little sons: that you should have mutual and unfeigned charity among yourselves, with peace. And if you thus follow the examples of the holy fathers, God, who strengthens the good, will help you; and I, dwelling with him, will pray for you'. (VC iii, 23)

Adomnán averted a catastrophic failure in his abbatial role not by making one party give way to the other against its conscience, but by the rhetoric of charity and peace placed into the mouth of their common patron saint, and presumably by his own pursuit of these ideals in practice.

This reassuringly charitable arrangement could not last indefinitely, however. Eventually, the monks of Iona would have to celebrate Easter together on the same day. After Adomnán's death in AD 704, a strangely disjointed sequence of rulers of Iona appears in the annals:

707   Dúnchad assumed the *principatus* of Iona.
710   Conamail son of Failbe, abbot of Iona, rests.
713   Doirbéne obtained the *kathedra* of Iona, and after five months in the primacy he died on Saturday, 28 October.
716   Faelchú, son of Doirbéne took the *kathedra* of Columba.
717   Dúnchad son of Cenn Faelad, abbot of Iona (*abbas Iae*), died.
722   Feidilmid assumed the *principatus* of Iona.

724 Faelchú son of Doirbéne, abbot of Iona, fell asleep. Cilléne the Tall succeeded him in the *principatus* of Iona.

This confusing sequence suggests that for two decades there were two parties in Iona, each electing rival leaders who are sometimes called abbots and sometimes described as holding the *principatus* or the *kathedra*. It is likely that this was the result of the ongoing dispute in Iona after the death of Adomnán over conformity to the nineteen-year Easter cycle. Not until the 720s did it finally settle down, with the death of Faelchú and the accession of Cilléne Fota 'the tall' who seems to have been accepted by both parties.

IONA AND OTHER CHURCHES

Another concern of Adomnán that emerges from the writings associated with him is that of ecclesiastical order, of the relationships between churches, and in particular the position of Iona vis à vis other churches. In *Vita Columbae* we see Iona as the mother-house of a number of dependent communities and churches. In Ireland, there was Durrow, which Adomnán says was founded by Columba himself (VC i, 3) and where the saint gave long-distance spiritual consolation to his overworked monks (VC i, 29) and blessed a fruit tree so that it gave wonderfully sweet fruit (VC ii, 2). In Scotland, there was a monastery on Loch Awe which belonged to Iona: Columba summoned its prior, Cailtán, to Iona, having foreseen that he would shortly die, and wanting to be with him when his life ended (VC i, 31). Another Columban monastery was founded before AD 574 on the island of Hinba, which cannot now be identified. Adomnán portrays it as a place for penitents (VC i, 21), but there was also a hermitage or 'place of anchorites' on the island (VC iii, 23). Another Columban monastery stood on the island of Tiree and was known as Mag Luinge. Like Hinba, it also welcomed penitents (VC ii, 39).

There were other monasteries on Tiree, however, that were not part of the Columban *familia*. Adomnán records 'foul and

very black demons' attacking various monasteries on Tiree. The
Columban monks at Mag Luinge, under their superior Baithéne,
fasted and prayed, so that all but one of them survived the
pestilence which the demons brought, but 'many died of that
plague in the other monasteries of that island' (VC iii, 8). This
story shows that there were at least two non-Columban monasteries on Tiree in addition to the Columban house of Mag
Luinge. But it also suggests a degree of rivalry between the
Columban house and the others. The story suggests that those
churches that were not spiritually obedient to Columba (here
represented by the local superior, Baithéne, who would eventually become Columba's successor as abbot of Iona) were at risk
from demonic attack. Adomnán also remarks that when Britain
and Ireland were being devastated by two great outbreaks of
plague two peoples were spared, 'that is the people of the Picts
and of the *Scotti* of Britain, between whom the mountains of the
Spine of Britain form the boundary'. The argument continues:

> To whom else is this grace granted by God to be attributed except
> to Saint Columba, whose monasteries founded within the territories
> of both peoples are greatly honoured up to the present time by them
> both? But what we are now going to say is, as we judge, not to be
> heard without sorrow: there are many very stupid folk among both
> peoples who ungratefully abuse God's patience, not realising that
> they have been protected from disease by the prayers of the saints.
> (VC ii, 46)

Iona had lost most of its influence in Northumbria with her
defeat at Whitby in AD 664, but here Adomnán defends the
authority of his monastery north of the Forth, in both Gaelic
and Pictish kingdoms. Insisting on the power of his saint to
protect these peoples, protesting that their churches should recognise their debt to Columba, is Adomnán's way of expressing
his expectation that Iona should be honoured in these territories. It is not clear exactly how Adomnán expected this 'honour'
to be expressed. It might have involved the recognition of Iona's
ecclesiastical authority, or acceptance of the abbot of Iona as
the appellate authority in disputed cases, or payment of the

dues that churches and monasteries might pay to their mother-churches. Whatever Adomnán had in mind, it does seem that his claims over both Gaels and Picts were not universally accepted. Some 'very stupid folk' apparently resisted them. As Adomnán was evidently making claims for Iona over other churches in Scotland, it is worth noting that in *Vita Columbae* some important churches in northern Britain that might have challenged Iona's authority are ignored altogether – places such as Lismore, Kingarth, Abernethy and Whithorn. It is hard to know whether his silence about these churches is significant. Does he ignore them because they are rivals? Some of them were episcopal churches: does he ignore them because, during Columba's life-time, one of them may have claimed spiritual authority over Iona, which did not then have a bishop?

Adomnán certainly had an interest in some important churches in Ireland. In *Vita Columbae* we encounter saints associated with the great monasteries of Clonmacnoise, Bangor, Aghaboe, Birr and Clonfert, and these saints honour Columba, recognising his holiness; and Columba in turn reverences them. The pattern is one that suggests a fairly equal and fraternal relationship between Columba and these saints, and so implicitly between Iona and their Irish churches. We have already seen how Columba was honoured by the monks of Clonmacnoise when he visited them, and how he also honoured that monastery (VC i, 3). When Cainnech of Aghaboe arrived on Iona, Columba and his brothers went to meet him and 'received him honourably and hospitably' (VC i, 4), and when Cainnech sailed away leaving his staff on Iona, Columba miraculously sent it back to him across the sea (VC ii, 14) in a gesture of honour towards his fellow saint. When Brendan of Birr died, Columba saw the sky opened, 'and choirs of angels coming down to meet the soul of Saint Brendan' (VC iii, 11). A bishop of Leinster called Colmán is presented as 'Columba's dear friend' (VC iii, 12), while Columba calls his monks 'to help the monks of abbot Comgall (of Bangor) with prayer, for in this hour they have been drowned in the Lake of the Calf' (VC iii, 13).

In these stories we see a vision of fraternal and mutual rec-

ognition between Iona and these Irish churches. But during
Adomnán's lifetime there was a struggle going on among Irish
churches for an island-wide jurisdiction. In the 670s the church
of Kildare was making very expansive claims. Cogitosus wrote
of St Brigit of Kildare:

> she built her monastery in the plains of Mag Lifi on the firm foun-
> dation of faith, as the head of almost all the Irish churches, and
> the eminent summit over all the monasteries of the *Scoti*, whose
> *parochia* is spread over the whole land of Ireland, reaching from
> sea to sea.

But Armagh was also making a claim to be the chief bishopric
of Ireland and head of all the churches. In the 670s or 680s the
Liber Angeli (the 'Book of the Angel') made the case explicitly.
An angel came to St Patrick, the founding bishop of Armagh,
and told him:

> The Lord God has given all the tribes of the Irish as a *paruchia* to
> you, and to this city which in the tongue of the Irish is called *Ardd
> Machae*.

Patrick replied to the angel, giving thanks to God and expressing his universal claim over the Irish churches and his power to
impose tax on them; and 'this right of the ruler of Armagh is
decreed without any doubt to all the monasteries of monks for
ever'. The same work also asserted the rights of Armagh in the
judicial sphere:

> Any very difficult case which should arise, [whose resolution is]
> unknown to the judges of the tribes of the Irish, is rightly to be
> referred to the see of the Archbishop of the Irish, that is of Patrick,
> to be tested by its bishop. If however the dispute in the said case is
> such that it cannot easily be decided there by its wise men, we decree
> that it is to be sent to the apostolic see, that is the see of Peter the
> apostle who has authority over the city of Rome.

By this time Armagh had adopted the new nineteen-year Easter
cycle, and was presenting itself as the 'Irish Rome', claiming
jurisdiction over all the Irish and wielding the relics of Roman
martyrs, including those of Peter and Paul. In this context, the

status and independence of Iona was clearly under threat, and the threat could only have been increased by the fact that the monks of Iona were still using the old eighty-four-year Easter cycle, further undermining their status among the Irish churches. The fact that Adomnán himself (and no doubt some of his brethren) had accepted the Dionysian cycle would have helped to preserve him personally from the taint of irregularity and from accusations of schism or even heresy, but Iona's intransigence made her more vulnerable.

Adomnán makes no direct challenge to Kildare or Armagh, and he does not refer to their expansionist claims, but both of these churches are completely ignored in *Vita Columbae*. Adomnán's picture of the relationship between the great Irish churches probably does not envisage any single over-arching authority, but has multiple centres of authority. This may explain why the *Collectio Canonum Hibernensis*, with its close connection to Iona, expresses itself as it does concerning authority in ecclesiastical disputes:

> If questions should arise in some province and they cannot be settled among the disputing clergy, let them be referred to the major see, and if it cannot be easily settled there let it be adjudicated where a synod is gathered. (CCH xx, 5)

In this context the referral of a disputed question 'to the major see' (*ad maiorem sedem*) would refer to the chief bishop of the province where the dispute had arisen. This is confirmed by the preceding canon which states that a person seeking to have a case settled must not go abroad to look for satisfaction: 'Let it be judged by the metropolitan bishop of his own province' (CCH xx, 3). In this view, each *prouincia* had its own juridical authority – and here we may recall Bede's observation that Iona held sway over a *prouincia*.

Just as *Vita Columbae* is silent on Armagh and its claims, so the *Collectio Canonum Hibernensis* is silent on the role of Armagh in conflict resolution. Having stated that disputes should be referred to the major see of a province, and then to a synod, it identifies the next court of appeal not as Armagh but as Rome: 'If questions arise in this island, they are to be referred to the apostolic see', no particular role being given to Armagh. This contrast between Armagh's claims and Iona's view of jurisdiction is also echoed by their respective hagiographies. Early Lives of St Patrick present him as the founder of many named churches across Ireland, implying that Patrick's successor at Armagh had the right to rule over them. Adomnán tells of no such grand church-founding expeditions by Columba, and the stories he does tell seem to imply a more diffuse arrangement of authority.

CREATING KINGS

The difference between Armagh and Iona may be manifested in another aspect of Adomnán's work. In his seventh-century account of St Patrick, the pro-Armagh writer Tírechán sought to portray the saint as a latter-day Moses, who of course was Israel's law-giver. Tírechán expresses it in this way:

> Patrick was like Moses in four things:
> (i)   first he heard an angel [speaking] out of a thorn-bush;
> (ii) he fasted for forty days and forty nights;
> (iii) he passed one hundred and twenty years in this present life;
> (iv) nobody knows where his bones are.

Elsewhere Tírechán notes that Patrick fasted on a mountain 'following the example of Moses, Elijah and Christ'. It may be in response to Armagh's presentation of Patrick as Moses that Adomnán presents Columba as a latter-day Samuel. Samuel appears in the Old Testament as God's prophet charged with the creation of the kingship of Israel as an institution (1 Samuel 8) and as the one responsible for electing and anointing kings, and with instructing them about how to behave (1 Samuel 10). Samuel also prayed and prophesied to obtain victory in battle for his chosen ones, and he anointed the young shepherd boy David (1 Samuel 16:6–13), who would become Israel's greatest king, at God's command. Also occurring in the Samuel story is the idea that kings, anointed by God, are sacred figures who enjoy divine protection: 'Who can raise his hand against the Lord's anointed and be guiltless?' (1 Samuel 26:9). Adomnán uses all these motifs in his portrait of Columba as a latter-day Samuel. In the first chapter of *Vita Columbae* he gives a general picture of the saint's powers in respect of kings:

> In the terrible crashing of battles he obtained from God by the power of his prayers that some kings were conquered and other rulers were made conquerors. This special privilege was granted by God, who honours all the saints, not only in this present changing life, but also after his departure from the flesh, as to a victorious and mighty champion. (VC i, 1)

Adomnán goes on to give one impressive example of the exercise of this special power: the post-mortem involvement of St Columba in the victory of Oswald of Northumbria. The day before Oswald fought the British king Cadwallon he was sleeping in his tent when he had a vision of Columba. The saint was 'shining, in angelic form, whose great stature seemed to touch the clouds with its head ... Standing in the midst of the camp he covered that camp with his shining clothing, except for a small part at the edge.' (The covering of a saint's clients with his clothing as a sign of his protective power is a gesture we will encounter again in due course.) Columba promised Oswald that if he marched into battle he would defeat his enemies and return to his kingdom to rule happily. On hearing of Oswald's dream, his men promised that they would accept baptism after the battle, and they went on to defeat Cadwallon.

Several other stories in *Vita Columbae* confirm the saint's power to affect the outcome of battles in which the victors become kings, or to bless men and prophesy that they will acquire kingship, or to prophesy that a king will lose his power (VC i, 7–15). In one case, Columba is portrayed not only blessing a man who subsequently becomes king, but actually making him king in a rite of inauguration. In this story an angel gives Columba 'a glass book of the ordination of kings', commanding him to ordain Áedán mac Gabráin as king. The saint refuses, preferring Áedán's brother Iógenán, and he is struck by the angel – leaving him with a livid scar for the rest of his life. Eventually, Columba submits to God's will:

> He sailed to the island of Iona and there, as he had been commanded, he ordained Áedán as king, who arrived about that time . . . And laying his hand on his head, ordaining him, he blessed him. (VC iii, 5)

The story establishes Columba – and by implication his successors, including Adomnán – as the instrument of God's will in the election and inauguration of kings, at least of the kings of Dál Riata. Not only does the saint elect the king, he is forced by God to choose a candidate contrary to his own inclination, perhaps implying that in the future the one who is chosen by the abbot has really been chosen by God, rather than being simply the abbot's favourite candidate. The abbot not only has the power to choose the king on behalf of God, but has the power to 'ordain' the king, to perform the rite that actually elevates the chosen one to kingship. There had been older native rites of royal inauguration, of course, but in this story we may see the partial displacement of the older rite by a new Christian ritual, and the displacement, or at least relegation to a secondary role, of the people who were traditionally involved in the rite: poets and genealogists who recited the king's genealogy and qualifications, the leaders of the noble kindreds and perhaps *magi*. From now on the abbot of Iona is to be the key figure, and the channel of God's grace. As the *Hibernensis* recalls concerning the ordination of the king by the prophet Samuel:

> Samuel took a vial of oil and poured it over the head of Saul, and he kissed him and said, 'Behold, God has anointed you as ruler over his people.' (CCH xxv, 1)

The claim that it was God who anointed the king (although Samuel actually poured the oil) corresponds to claims made by Adomnán about some kings in *Vita Columbae*: Oswald was 'ordained by God as emperor of the whole of Britain' (VC i, 1); and Diarmait mac Cerbaill had been 'ordained by God's will as ruler of all Ireland' (VC i, 36).

Such an insistence on God's will in the creation of kings must have undermined native ideology to some extent. Traditional Gaelic laws concerning kingship treated it as a contract between the king and the people. In the picture painted by Adomnán and the *Hibernensis*, the people are not given a role. Of course, traditional processes of king-making did not disappear in the wake of this new theology of kingship. The recitation of genealogies to establish the right of a man to become king, for example, continued for centuries. It is certain that the leading men of a *túath* continued to have a say in who would become king, and other aspects of the pre-Christian rite may have continued (the presentation of a rod or staff, and a symbolic marriage between king and territory). But Adomnán and the *Hibernensis* together weave a new understanding of what kingship involves. In place of a contract between king and people in which each fulfils their obligation to the other, the image is of a relationship between God and the king, mediated by the abbot. God chooses and sustains the king through the church's anointing, while the king must in return ensure justice for the people (according to the Church's conception of justice). This is why the book '*de Regno*', 'on kingship', in the *Hibernensis* moves directly from questions of the ordination of the king to questions of his justice or injustice:

> This indeed is the justice of the just king. To judge no one unjustly; to be the defender of strangers and widows and orphans; to restrain theft; to punish adultery; not to maintain shameless people and fools; not to promote the wicked, but to get rid of the wicked from the land; not to allow parricides and perjurers to live; to defend churches; to feed the poor with alms; to set just men over the affairs of the kingdom; to have the advice of mature, wise and sober counsellors . . . (CCH xxv, 4)

The *Hibernensis* also outlines the catastrophe that will result from the rule of an unjust king. The consequences of royal injustice are not only social (political disorder, criminality and violence), but are cosmic in scope:

> It brings stormy winds, it prevents the fertility of the earth and the sea; it produces lightning, it destroys the flowers of the trees, it casts down their unripe fruit . . . (CCH xxv, 3)

The notion that unjust rule brings natural catastrophes, and that just rule brings natural wellbeing and prosperity, is a regular motif in Gaelic literature – it is also a biblical one. Adomnán proposes the centrality of justice to the rule of the king, but draws the notion of the king's justice into a theological world-view, away from the old legal one of the contract between king and people. For Adomnán justice is an obligation placed on both king and people by God.

ADOMNÁN'S LAW

It is Adomnán's concern for justice – in particular, justice for the poor and the powerless – that gives rise to one of the most remarkable aspects of his life: his work as a law-maker. Seeking to give shape to his notion of justice, and to give it divine authority, he placed a handful of miracle stories in *Vita Columbae* about how the saint protected the powerless from abuse by violent and powerful men and brought 'terrible vengeance on his enemies' (VC ii, 25). These stories appear as a cluster in the middle of the second book of the *Vita*, the book concerned with Columba's acts of power rather than his prophecies or visions. Following an assortment of life-enhancing miracles (water turned to wine, healing of injuries and diseases, increasing food production, protection of travellers in danger and feeding the poor), the cluster begins with Ioan, 'an oppressor of good men', being punished for his repeated robbery of a poor man; as Ioan sails away after another raid, Columba prays, and Ioan and his fellow robbers are sunk and drowned by a sudden squall (VC ii, 22). The second story in the cluster describes how Columba entrusted a Pictish exile called Tarain to the protection of a certain Feradach on the island of Islay. Feradach had the exile slain, and Columba declared that, 'This wretched little man has lied not to me but to God', and uttered a prophecy of his death and damnation which was rapidly fulfilled (VC ii, 23). A 'persecutor of churches' tried to kill one of Columba's monks with a spear, but the monk was wearing Columba's cowl, which miraculously saved him; the persecutor himself was slain a year later by a spear that had been 'thrown in the name of St Columba' (VC ii, 24).

In the sequence of miracles performed against violent men, the final story is headed, 'Concerning yet another persecutor of the innocents' (VC ii, 25):

> When the blessed man was still a young deacon, living in Leinster and studying divine wisdom, it happened one day that a certain man, a pitiless and cruel persecutor of the innocents, was pursuing a young girl as she fled across the level plain. When she saw Gemmán, the elderly teacher of the aforesaid young deacon, reading on the plain, she fled straight towards him as fast as she could. Alarmed by this sudden event he called Columba, who was reading some way off, so that together they might defend this girl from her pursuer in so far as they could. But when he came on them he showed them no reverence but with his spear he slew the girl as she hid under their robes, and leaving her dead at their feet he turned away and began to depart.
>
> Then the old man, deeply saddened, turned to Columba. 'How long, holy boy Columba,' he said, 'will God the just judge allow this crime and our dishonour to go unpunished?'
>
> In response the saint pronounced this sentence on that wicked man: 'In the same hour in which the soul of the girl killed by him rises to heaven, let the soul of her killer descend to hell.' And quicker than speech, at that word, like Ananias before Peter [Acts 5:5], that killer of innocents fell dead in that same spot before the eyes of the holy youth. The report of this sudden and dreadful punishment was immediately spread throughout many provinces of Ireland, with the wonderful renown of the holy deacon.

The injustice and violence of the 'persecutor' are obvious, and the story broadly represents his death as a straightforward act of divine retribution. But the details are important. First, the girl hides under the clothing of Columba and Gemmán, seeking their protection. As we have already seen, Columba's clothing was a sign of his protective power.

Second, the girl's murder is described as 'this crime and our dishonour'. That is to say, the offence is twofold: it is a crime against the girl, of course, but it is also an offence to the honour of the saints. When someone sought and obtained the protection of someone else, any attack on the person being protected was an offence against their protector. By hiding the powerless girl under their robes the saints elevated a crime against her into a crime against them and against their honour. Third, we may note that the punishment of the murderer is achieved by the utterance of the saint, the future abbot of Iona.

We should see this cluster of miracle stories about the saint protecting the poor or powerless as a kind of manifesto, Adomnán using stories about St Columba to assert his understanding of his own role, and that of his monastery. This is particularly apparent in the story about the murdered girl. As we have seen, in AU 697 Adomnán 'went to Ireland and gave the Law of the Innocents to the peoples'. The law was also known as *Cáin Adomnáin*, 'Adomnán's Law'. Promulgated by Adomnán at a synod in Birr (Co. Offaly), it was designed to protect clergy, women and children from violence. These three classes of people were 'innocent' not in some general moral sense, but in the sense of being harmless, for they did not carry weapons. The law also protected churches and their sanctuaries and relics from violation. It was an attempt to reduce the scope of violence in a society where it was all too common, creating what in a later age would be called 'non-combatant immunity'.

Just as the murder of the girl hiding under their robes was an offence against the saint, so the 'Law of the Innocents' makes violence against women, children and clergy an offence against the abbot and community of Iona. The Law required offenders to pay, in addition to the compensation due to victims and their kindred as prescribed in traditional laws, heavy extra fines which were payable to the community of Adomnán. The Law also gave the community of Adomnán the right to appoint judges 'in every church and in every tribe', and established the necessary financial and practical support for those administering and enforcing the Law in each place. The Law therefore simultaneously depended on the power and prestige of Iona as its underlying authority, and reinforced Iona's power and prestige by giving Adomnán and successive abbots the right to obtain revenues from its enforcement and the right to appoint officials in all the many territories where the Law was enforceable.

And the territories where the Law ran were very widespread indeed. The text of the Law begins thus:

> This is the enactment of the Cáin of Adomnán of Iona. At Birr this enactment was imposed on the men of Ireland and Britain as an everlasting law until Doom, a proclamation of the nobles, the clerics and the laity: the rulers and their chief poets, their bishops and their wise men and their soul-friends.

There follows a list of ninety-one guarantors of the Law, all of them ecclesiastical and secular rulers. It begins with Fland Febla, 'learned bishop of Armagh', who is followed by thirty-nine clerics and monks. Loingsech mac Óengusso, 'king of Ireland', heads the section of secular rulers, which includes men from all over Ireland and Dál Riata, and even Bruide mac Der-Ile, king of the Picts. Parallel to Bruide, the clerical list includes Curetán, who was probably the bishop of Ross among the northern Picts or Fortriu. Adomnán's achievement in garnering the necessary support from all these disparate churches and polities was partly a matter of timing. The year AD 697 was the centenary of Columba's death, and this may have had some bearing on the promotion of the law in this year. But more significant was surely that Adomnán's Cenél Conaill kindred had been excluded from the kingship of Tara from AD 658 until the death of Fínsnechtae Fledach in 695, when the high kingship returned to the control of Cenél Conaill in the person of Loingsech mac Óengusso. Loingsech belonged to the same branch of Cenél Conaill as Adomnán, so now the abbot of Iona and his royal kinsman could act in concert: the king would strengthen and support the monastery, and the monastery would enhance the status of the Cenél Conaill king. This coincidence of interests would enable Adomnán to promote his law over a wide territory.

One further important feature of *Cáin Adomnáin* is that it represented an increase in royal power. Generally speaking, in the old Gaelic legal tradition (and in the British and Anglo-

Saxon worlds, too, for that matter) kings were not true legisla-
tors. Law consisted of a large corpus of precedents, judgments,
decisions, arguments, poetry and proverbs which grew organi-
cally out of the work of a more or less independent legal profes-
sion. The king may have had a role in judicial processes, but not
usually in legislation as such. In this context, *Cáin Adomnáin*
represented a clear innovation in royal power, giving kings – in
collaboration with church synods – the power to create new law
or *rechtge*. As stated by *Críth Gablach*, a tract on the law of
status, around AD 700:

> There are three *rechtgai* which it is proper for a king to bind on
> his peoples: the *rechtge* for driving out foreign kindreds, i.e., the
> Saxons; a *rechtge* for the cultivation of crops; and a *rechtge* for
> kindling faith, as in the case of the law of Adomnán.

The first two of these three 'laws' are not really laws in the
usual sense. They represent executive orders given at a particular time, perhaps in an emergency: one summoning a host
to repel invaders and one mandating agricultural labour at
a particular time – for manuring or harvesting? – perhaps in
response to a crisis. But the third is a genuine legislative act by
the king, the promulgation of a long-term legally binding act
which he was committed to enforcing. *Críth Gablach* not only
gives kings the power to legislate, but cites the *Cáin Adomnáin*
as an example of such legislation, perhaps even as a precedent.
We have seen that Adomnán is concerned with the process of
king-making; here we see him helping to redefine kingship,
establishing a new kind of law whose enactment extends royal
power at the same time as helping him in his own quest to
restrain violence.

The inclusion of one Pictish king and a Pictish bishop in
the list of guarantors of *Cáin Adomnáin* is also remarkable.
Although it was written in the language of the native Gaelic laws
of Ireland and Dál Riata, *Cáin Adomnáin* was also deemed to be
enforceable among people with different laws. Nothing survives
of any Pictish law, but the fact that the Pictish king Bruide guaranteed the enactment and enforcement of *Cáin Adomnáin* in his

territory suggests that there must have been some kind of basic compatibility between the two systems.

The terms of the Law indicate that Iona appointed judges and administrators of *Cáin Adomnáin* within Pictland and obtained revenues from Pictland through the mechanisms of the Law – which can perhaps be seen as an ecclesiastical and legal dimension of the Gaelicisation of Pictland which we discussed in Chapter 2. Thirty-four years after Iona's defeat at Whitby, her influence in Northumbria may have waned, but in Pictland she was still able to draw a powerful Pictish king into her ecclesiastical jurisdiction and to take control of legal and fiscal mechanisms in his kingdom.

It is worth recalling here Adomnán's remark that his patron saint Columba was held in great honour by both the Gaels and the Picts in the territories where Columban monasteries had been founded, but also his concern that many 'very stupid people' among them failed to recognise that Columba had protected them from the plague (VC ii, 46). It is hard to know how to read these two statements. Exactly what balance are we to imagine between the honouring of the saint by some and his neglect by others? Were there some provinces or sub-kingdoms in Pictland where Columba was not held in honour, where perhaps another saint was preferred? If so, it seems likely that Adomnán had enough influence with Bruide mac Derile, king of the Picts and apparently overking of all the Pictish provinces, to induce him to support the *Cáin Adomnáin* and to enforce it even over the 'very stupid' folk. Although the Law had dozens of guarantors from the kingdoms and provinces of the fissiparous Gaelic world, only one Pictish king appears on the list: *Nechtan mac Derile*. As we suggested above (p. 106), this appears to indicate a degree of political centralisation in Pictland in which one king could act on behalf of, and with authority over, all the lesser kingdoms or *provinciae* under his control. Whatever doubts some of the Picts may have had about Columba's sanctity and power, their overking was in a position to commit them to the support of Adomnán's Law.

MONK AND SCHOLAR

The preceding discussion of Adomnán's life and work has focused on his activism: his law-making, the way he used *Vita Columbae* to promote his monastery in relation to other churches, his views of abbatial authority and ecclesiastical organisation, his interest in law and kingship, and so on. But such a perspective omits a central aspect of the man's identity: the fact that he was a monk. Much of his life was spent in performing the *opus Dei*, the round of shared prayers, readings and psalms that occupied much of a monk's waking time. In addition to this, private prayer and study were integral to the monastic life, and Adomnán was an accomplished scholar. His description of Columba's regime can reasonably be read as his account of how he sought to live his own life: 'Living for thirty-four years as an island soldier, he could not let even the space of one hour go past in which he did not apply himself to either prayer or reading or writing, or to some other work' (VC, second preface). From Adomnán's own writings we know that he had read works by the key figures of the western tradition: several works by Augustine, Jerome's biblical commentaries, Gregory the Great's *Dialogi*, the monastic classics of John Cassian, Cassiodorus' commentary on the Psalms, the historical and encyclopaedic works of Isidore of Seville, Eusebius' *Church History*, Athanasius' *Vita Antonii* (a foundational text of monastic spirituality), sermons by Pope Leo the Great, and more. Adomnán was also familiar with Virgil's *Eclogues*, and continental manuscripts contain commentaries on Virgil in which *Adannanus*, probably our Adomnán, is cited as an authority. It seems that Adomnán was lecturing on Virgil in Iona, or perhaps at another Columban monastery before he became abbot. In addition, there must also have been in his library the *Acta* of various Church councils and legal works, as these formed an important part of the *Hibernensis*. There were also, of course, Bibles and books containing what was needed for the liturgy.

Biblical scholarship of a high standard seems to have been practised at Iona from the very beginning. There survives a partial copy of the Psalter which has been treated for centuries as a relic of St Columba, as a manuscript made by his own hand. Palaeographic evidence makes this perfectly plausible, and its name, the *Cathach*, or 'battler', reflects its use in invoking that saint to protect armies before battle. The text of the Psalms in this manuscript has symbols known as asterisks and *obeli* marking points where two versions of the Latin psalms have been compared with each other and differed. Where one version lacked something that another version had, one of these symbols was used to mark the difference. This shows that critical work on the biblical text was being carried out on Iona in the sixth century, and in this context we should note that the *Amra*'s praise of Columba includes the observation that 'he fixed the Psalms'. A later medieval gloss on this line interprets it: *ro-glinnig na salmu fo obil ocus astrisc*, 'he fixed the Psalms under *obelus* and asterisk'.

The Psalms were therefore both the material of prayer and devotion and the object of scholarly study, and we find other areas where scholarship and prayer were interwoven. In *De locis sanctis* Adomnán shows a particular interest in the cult of biblical relics, the material objects that provide a tactile bridge between the modern community of believers and the primordial events of human salvation: there in Jerusalem one can see or touch the sepulchre where Christ's body lay and the stone that closed it, the cup that Jesus used at the Last Supper, the lance that pierced his side and the *sudarium* or shroud that covered his body in the tomb. In Constantinople is the Holy Cross itself, and Adomnán describes in detail the choreography of its veneration on the three successive days of the Easter Triduum. This material would have been of interest to the scholar, but it would also have inspired the monk. The cult of relics was a feature of the monastic life on Iona, and Adomnán must have looked towards such cults in Jerusalem and Constantinople as a validation of the cult of relics in Iona. He also describes the hereditary stewardship of a relic within a particular family, passed down from father to son. He may have seen here a parallel with the emerging custom in Scotland of families of *deòraidh*, or stewards, holding relics 'by hereditary right' (*hereditario iure*) in his words.

De locis sanctis, in its preface and three books, immerses the reader in the geography of the Mediterranean. The first book deals with Jerusalem and its immediate environs; the second book explores Bethlehem and other sites in the Holy Land further from Jerusalem, as well as Damascus, Tyre and Alexandria; and the third book deals with Constantinople and, in its final chapter, the island of Vulcan off the coast of Sicily. Thus, its structure echoes the last words spoken by the risen Christ to his disciples before he was taken from their sight: 'You shall be my witnesses in Jerusalem, and in all Judaea and Samaria, and to the ends of the earth' (Acts 1:8). By beginning with Jerusalem and then moving further afield, *De locis sanctis* re-enacts the spread of the Gospel, its movement from the centre towards 'the ends of the earth'. At the same time it draws the minds and hearts of his readers back to Jerusalem, the source and origin of their faith, the place of Christ's death and resurrection.

All churches did this, of course, quite consciously. The Church itself was the sacrament of the 'new Jerusalem', and Christians singing the Psalms were constantly referred to Jerusalem or its temple, 'Mount Zion', as their point of reference:

> I rejoiced when I heard them say, 'Let us go to God's house'.
> Now our feet are standing in your gates, O Jerusalem.

When Christians sang this Psalm in church, they collapsed the distance between Jerusalem and their own building. They were in Jerusalem. When they celebrated the Eucharist, they were in the upper room in Jerusalem where Christ took bread and gave it to his disciples saying, 'Take this, all of you, and eat it.'

An important model for this collapsing of distance was the Church in Rome, which had long ago devised a way of making Jerusalem present: the Lateran Basilica in Rome represented the Jerusalem Temple, and objects plundered by Romans from the Temple were believed to have been given by Helena, the mother of Constantine, to the Lateran. Likewise the church of Santa Croce in Rome became Golgotha, the place of the crucifixion; relics of Christ's passion and death had been placed there by Helena, including a piece of the Holy Cross. By the late seventh century, this relic was venerated every Good Friday, much as it had been in Jerusalem in the fourth century and, later, in Constantinople. Indeed, when a seventh-century pope walked barefoot on Good Friday from the Lateran to Santa Croce (otherwise known as *Hierusalem*) accompanied by a relic of the Cross, he was reproducing the Good Friday procession of the Patriarch of Jerusalem. The geography of Jerusalem was transposed to Rome, and likewise to every local church where the same ritual of processing and venerating the Cross was carried out on Good Friday.

For Adomnán, then, his descriptions in *De locis sanctis* of the places and the cult that was celebrated around them were not of mere scholarly interest, a matter of geographical curiosity. They were an invitation to his fellow monks and other readers to 'find themselves' in the liturgy – to find themselves at the Last Supper, at the foot of the Cross, at the empty tomb, so that what they did in the church on seventh-century Iona made them present to the events that took place in first-century Jerusalem.

There may also have been a wider and more political concern underlying *De locis sanctis*. In the wake of Iona's defeat at Whitby, the rhetoric of their opponents must have rankled with Adomnán and his monks. At that synod, Wilfrid, for the party of the nineteen-year cycle, had spoken to his Columban opponents with apparent contempt. When Colmán, an Iona monk and now bishop of Lindisfarne, had argued that Iona monks followed the Easter practice of Columba, who was a saint, Wilfrid had replied:

> Even though your fathers were holy men, do you think that this fragment in one corner of a remote island is to be preferred to the universal Church of Christ which extends throughout the world? (HE iii, 25)

A similar argument from remoteness had been made by the Irish writer Cummian in a letter to Abbot Ségéne of Iona and a hermit called Beccán, probably in AD 631. Cummian urged the Iona monks to follow the southern Irish churches in adopting the nineteen-year Easter cycle. He contrasts 'the universal Church' with 'a tiny party of Britons and *Scotti* who are almost at the end of the earth and, if I may say so, mere pimples on the face of the earth'.

The monks of Iona may well have felt aggrieved by such attributions of remoteness and implied insignificance, but Adomnán accepts this geographical description and incorporates it into his writing. He shows that far from having a negative value, remoteness can be a motif which enables him to demonstrate the sanctity of Columba:

> Although he lived in this small and remote island of the Britannic ocean, he merited that his name should be brilliantly renowned not only throughout our *Scotia*, and throughout Britain, the greatest of all the islands of the whole world, but that it should reach even as far as three-cornered Spain and Gaul, and Italy, lying beyond the pennine Alps, and to the Roman city itself, which is the head of all the cities. (VC iii, 23)

In this argument Iona's very remoteness, coupled with the spread of Columba's reputation, now serves to demonstrate just how holy he was. In *Vita Columbae* Adomnán demonstrated how personal sanctity could defeat the distance between Iona and Rome. In *De locis sanctis* he showed how scholarship, liturgy and the cult of relics could also bridge the gulf between Iona, Rome and Jerusalem. This message may have been in Adomnán's mind when he gave a copy of *De locis sanctis* to his friend King Aldfrith of Northumbria in AD 686 or 688: a subtle reminder that the sanctity of Columba and his monastery made mere geographical distance irrelevant.

COLUMBA AFTER ADOMNÁN

During the century after Adomnán's death Iona faced continuing difficulties. As we have seen, the monks were divided for years over the Easter question. It was finally settled in AU 716 when the annals report that 'Easter is changed in the *ciuitas* of Iona'.

According to Bede, this was engineered by the English bishop Ecgberht, who finally managed to achieve what Adomnán had tried and failed to do. This change, however, was not so much a triumph of Northumbrian or 'Roman' Christianity over Iona as a post-mortem triumph for Adomnán, and a triumph for his successor Dúnchad, the abbot who presided over the change and died a year later.

Around AD 713, Nechtan king of the Picts had received a letter from Abbot Ceolfrith in answer to his own enquiries about Easter and the tonsure. According to Bede, Nechtan had already been persuaded of the correctness of the nineteen-year cycle and the crown-shaped tonsure, and was seeking Northumbrian support to enforce them throughout his kingdom. It is likely that he had been brought to this position by the arguments of Adomnán's party of reforming Iona monks. This would explain why Ceolfrith's letter did not urge Nechtan to reject the Iona *familia*. On the contrary, as we have seen, he praised Adomnán's holiness of life and manners. Such remarks about Adomnán cannot be construed as damaging to Iona's interests.

Nevertheless, in the same year as Dúnchad's death, AU 717, we read of 'the expulsion of the *familia* of Iona beyond *Dorsum Brittanie* [Druim Alban, the Spine of Britain] by Nechtan the king'. It is not clear what this expulsion involved. It cannot have been designed to oust a recalcitrant conservative Iona clergy whose old Easter cycle Nechtan had rejected, since by this time Iona had already accepted the new nineteen-year cycle. Recalling that there were still two rival abbots at the time in Iona, we might suspect that it involved the removal of the leaders of the conservative faction. But we might also see the expulsion as a move by Nechtan to re-align ecclesiastical politics and authority in his kingdom. No ruler would want the churches of his own kingdom to regard a monastery in another kingdom as their head.

In spite of the expulsion, Iona saints were still culted in Pictland, and Iona clergy continued to work there. The church at Kilduncan in Fife was probably named in honour of Abbot Dúnchad, as perhaps was nearby Kilconquhar. Churches in

Atholl were dedicated to Adomnán and Céti, abbot and bishop
of Iona, respectively. As we have seen, in the eighth century
Pictish military and political power pushed westwards at the
expense of Dál Riata, and the position of Iona changed. It was
becoming part of a Pictish *imperium*; perhaps we should even
regard it as becoming in some sense a Pictish monastery. The
Pictish élite was now able to profit from the spiritual capital
of Columba and his monastery, and it is perhaps no accident
that the mid- to late eighth century marks the high-point of
Iona's artistic output: a flowering of sculpture with the erection
of high crosses and perhaps building work too in the shape
of the stone shrine-chapel, which may have been built for the
remains of Columba and Adomnán – two stone cists underlie
its modern wooden floor. We may suspect that Pictish patronage lies behind much of this outburst of creativity. The *Book of
Kells*, now thought to have been made on Iona at the end of the
eighth century, shows signs of Pictish influence, and its sheer
magnificence testifies to an enormous level of investment in the
visual arts.

If the *Book of Kells* was made in the 'Pictish monastery' of
Iona, however we construe that term, it testifies to the patrons'
continued devotion to Columba. The illustration on the cover of
this volume – the book now in your hand – is a detail from one
folio of the *Book of Kells*. It shows the upper half of a man's
body attached to what seems to be the lower part of a fish. In
fact, the text within which the figure is embedded tells us who
this figure is – or at least how we might begin to understand it.
The text is the genealogy of Christ in Luke's gospel. It tells us
that 'Jesus was the son, as was supposed, of Joseph, who was the
son of Heli, who was the son of Levi', and so on back to 'Adam
who was the son of God'. The figure on our cover has his hand
attached to the word *fuit* in the phrase '*qui fuit Iona*', 'who was
[the son] of Jonah'. Clearly, the scribe has conflated two biblical figures with the same name: Jonah, who was an ancestor of
Jesus, and Jonah, the prophet who was swallowed by a great
fish. This figure is not a strange man–fish combination, therefore, but a man being eaten by a fish.

But why was Jonah highlighted by the scribe in this way? It cannot have been because the name *Iona* was the name of his monastery. The island now called Iona would not get that name for several centuries to come, and when it did it was by a scribal *n*-for-*u* misreading of its proper name, *Ioua Insula*. But the illuminator probably knew that Adomnán had reflected on the significance of the name *Iona*:

> There was a man of venerable life and blessed memory . . . who received the same name as the prophet Jonah . . . For what is pronounced *Iona* in Hebrew, and which Greek calls *peristera*, in the Latin language is called *Columba* [i.e., 'dove']; it means one and the same thing. (VC second preface)

The highlighting of Iona in the genealogy may therefore be a reference to Columba, 'the dove', which Adomnán notes is also used as a sign in the sacred books 'to mystically signify the Holy Spirit'. It was also a sign of simplicity and innocence (Matthew 10:16), as Adomnán points out while discussing the names Columba and Iona, and he adds that in Columba 'a simple and innocent man was rightly called by this name, who by his dovelike way of life gave a dwelling within himself to the Holy Spirit.'

The highlighting of the name *Iona* also refers to Christ himself, who said of his own generation, 'No sign shall be given to it except the sign of Jonah' (Matthew 16:4), referring to his own death and resurrection. Just as Jonah spent three days in the belly of a great fish before being spat out on dry land, so Christ would spend three days in the tomb before rising from the dead. The Jonah symbolism of death and resurrection, not only for Christ but for all believers, led to early Christian burial monuments being inscribed with images from the Jonah story as reminders that as all Christians died in Christ, so they would also rise in him.

The strangely positioned arms of 'Jonah' in *Kells*, crossed over at an absurdly uncomfortable angle, also connect him to Christ, for they form the Greek letter χ, the first letter of Χρίστος (*Christos*), which is regularly used in the *Book of Kells* to denote

Christ himself. The colouring of the man's body is also significant. It is painted in the bright yellow pigment called orpiment, used here to represent gold – the word 'orpiment' comes from Latin *auripigmentum*, 'gold-colouring'. Gold, bright, shining and incorruptible, often had connotations of divinity.

In this rich complex of visual and verbal allusions, two centuries after the death of Columba, and a century after Adomnán played on the names Jonah and Columba, the monks of the 'Pictish' monastery of Iona were still offering to the discerning reader images of the special sanctity of their founding saint.

5

'Justice and Peace have embraced'
(Psalm 84: 11)

Laws and Societies

Adomnán gives an account of St Columba visiting a man called Nesán in the territory of Lochaber, and describes the man as being 'very poor' (*ualde inops*), having only five cows. In spite of his poverty he joyfully welcomed and cared for the saint, and Columba blessed him, his wife and children so that they prospered thereafter (VC ii, 20). Adomnán's purpose in telling this story is to show how the saint would bless those who loved him – which meant, of course, that they should love Adomnán too, as Columba's successor. But for the social historian the story also reveals that in seventh-century Dál Riata a family with only five cows could be thought of as 'very poor'. At about the same time, the Gaelic law text *Críth Gablach* indicated that seven cows were the requisite of the *ócaire*, the lowest grade of free adult whom Gaelic laws regarded as a full 'person'. This was a world in which the reckoning of wealth was largely in cattle. So important was cattle ownership to notions of one's worth that in early Gaelic laws the word *ambue*, whose etymology indicates someone 'lacking in cows', came to refer to a person without legal standing in a community, someone with no legal protection who could be injured or killed with impunity. Nesán with his five cows is not as desperate as that, but he is poor enough to be dependent and vulnerable, and fails to make the grade as an *ócaire*.

In this chapter we will look at some aspects of the texture of life in Scotland during our period. How did people organise their families and communities, and how did they understand

and express the relationships in which they stood? How did people experience power and wealth? How was law used to create and regulate people's relationships with each other? As we have just seen, the 'Lives' of saints can provide some information to help us answer these questions. Likewise, poetry and wisdom texts may be useful sources of information. But perhaps most important are the surviving laws of early medieval Insular communities. These texts are the residue of centuries of legal activity: the living practice of law in its daily use, and professional or scholarly reflection on those practices. They also reveal something about the lives of people who are almost invisible in sources such as annals, histories, saints' 'Lives' and poetry: what was the experience of women, of children, of slaves? Many narrative histories of this period have been written in which women are almost entirely absent, because they are absent from most of the sources. Where they do appear they do so because, like Edwin's sister, Acha, they have been taken to wife by some powerful king, or they have some walk-on part in the drama of a man's life. It is the laws that help us sense the presence and meaning of these 'lesser lives' and the experience of the communities in which they were lived.

A significant objection to the use of such laws in a history of Scotland is the fact that very little of the surviving material can be shown to have originated in Scotland itself. The only law text during the whole of our period that we can securely connect to somewhere in Scotland is *Cáin Adomnáin*, which we discussed in the previous chapter. As a law promulgated by the abbot of Iona, it is the oldest law to have its roots in Scottish soil. It represents, however, a single legal act within a tradition that in most respects was Irish, produced in an island monastery which was an eastern outpost of Irish legal culture. It was not, therefore, distinctively 'Scottish'. But the fact that a seventh-century law originating in western Scotland was in effect an eastern manifestation of Irish law encourages us to regard Irish laws as evidence for life in the Gaelic-speaking western parts of Scotland. Indeed, a legal tradition that was produced and used by Gaels in both Ireland and Scotland should really be regarded as 'Gaelic law'. The term 'Irish law', for present purposes, is rather misleading.

There survives a large corpus of Gaelic law texts reflecting the work of generations of lawyers, judges and commentators, beginning in the seventh and eighth centuries. But this represents only one legal tradition in early medieval Scotland. The Picts had their own laws, but not a word of Pictish law has survived. The only surviving law that we know to have been current among the Picts is *Cáin Adomnáin*, which was essentially a Gaelic law. However, the fact that it was guaranteed by a Pictish king and a Pictish bishop – Bruide mac Derile and Curetán – indicates that it was in force (whatever exactly that meant) in Pictland from AD 697, and it also suggests that there was some compatibility between the structures of the Irish and Pictish legal systems, making possible the promulgation, enforcement and administration of a Gaelic law in Pictish territory.

No early Anglo-Saxon law survives from Scotland, but a good deal of material survives from Northumbria and other parts of England, and there is no good reason to believe that the laws in Northumbrian southern Scotland differed radically from the laws in English Northumbria. We must be more cautious in using laws from elsewhere in England, but it is surely legitimate to use the material as evidence for the culture and society of Anglo-Saxon communities in southern Scotland.

The British-speaking peoples of southern Scotland have likewise left little legal writing to modern scholars. Nevertheless, it is likely that their laws were akin to those of the British communities further south which form part of the background to medieval Welsh law. The Welsh vernacular legal tradition known as *Cyfraith Hywel*, 'the Law of Hywel', survives in manuscripts dating from the thirteenth century and later. Though at some level it purports to be law created by Hywel Dda, a powerful Welsh king of the first half of the tenth century, it is better seen as the gathering of a legal tradition. Much of this law is likely to be of great antiquity, while some is of tenth-century or later date. One of the indications of antiquity in some of the Welsh laws is the fact that their terminology (and therefore some of their legal content) is clearly related to that of some seventh- and eighth-century Gaelic laws.

Old Welsh	Old Gaelic	
adauel	*athgabail*	'distraint, seizure'
adneiu	*aithne*	'deposit'
mach	*macc*	'surety'
nawdd	*snádud*	'protection'
rhaith	*ráth*	'compurgator' and 'surety'

The use of such cognate terms for similar legal concepts encourages us to see the medieval Welsh laws as embodying an earlier British legal tradition that bore some similarity to early Gaelic laws.

Although no Scottish charters survive from before AD 900, later charters, such as those in the *Book of Deer*, sometimes contain elements whose origins lie in the Gaelic laws of our period. Surviving Welsh charters are also useful: some date back to the early medieval period and attest to the workings of Welsh law. Even if none of these relate to anywhere in Scotland, they may shed light on the social history of early British communities north of the Tweed. A similar argument may be adduced for the usefulness of early Anglo-Saxon charters with regard to parts of Scotland under Northumbrian rule.

A warning is in order here, however. Though we may talk of a legal tradition as 'Gaelic law', we should not imagine that this is some simple and static corpus of material. Gaelic law contained various tensions and oppositions, as well as differences from one region or school of thought to another. It also underwent change over the centuries as these tensions worked themselves out, and as it came under the influence of Roman and Christian ideas of law. Much the same could be said of British and Anglo-Saxon laws. What follows in this chapter should therefore be regarded as a series of significant snapshots rather than a coherent and comprehensive picture of nine centuries of Scottish life and four different legal traditions. If this chapter offers glimpses of societies very different from our own, in which men and women behaved in ways that we can begin to understand and even empathise with, then it will have done its job.

We will examine Gaelic material in more detail than that of neighbouring traditions, partly because the corpus of surviving early Gaelic law texts is larger than those of the others, but also because the emerging kingdom of Scotia worked with laws from that tradition, eventually incorporating strands of Gaelic law into its own legal framework.

PAYING THE PRICE OF PEACE

For most people in the modern world our sense of identity and belonging and our sense of social obligation are to a great extent informed by the fact that we are citizens. Our lives are structured by laws that have been promulgated and enforced by the authority of the state – its legislature, police force and courts. Criminal law prohibits and punishes certain kinds of behaviour, such as violence and theft. Other laws make fiscal demands on us, requiring us to pay tax and insure our motor vehicles. Another class of law governs relationships between citizens: it protects contracts between buyer and seller, grants rights to divorcing spouses, and obtains compensation for a citizen who has been injured by someone else's neglect. These relations between citizens are also governed by laws and courts operating in the name of the state.

But early medieval Scotland – like many other parts of Europe – had no state that could operate in this way. There had been something of the sort in the Roman Empire: legislatures with the power to issue publicly binding laws, an imperial army with policing functions, government functionaries, courts and public administration. But little of this sort existed in early medieval Scotland. How was social order maintained, therefore, in the absence of such an over-arching structure? What social bonds and obligations maintained peace and cohesion in the absence of a state? The key to answering these questions is to consider law as a set of accepted rules and practices through which members of a community negotiated with each other under the watchful eye of a professional caste of lawyers. Where a legal dispute occurred, it was not between an individual and 'the state', but rather between one individual and another, or one family and another. People owed each other certain duties, and when those duties were violated the way to make peace was for the offender to pay compensation to the offended person.

The so-called '*Welsh Canons*' – a sixth-century text in the British legal tradition, though perhaps written by Britons in Armorica – is partly a list of the payments made for various offences:

> If someone in a quarrel has injured a person's hand or eye or foot, let him learn that he shall pay one female or male slave.
> If someone cuts off the thumb of someone's hand, we command that he pay half that compensation.
> If someone should strike a person with a spear or a sword, and [one] can see the inner parts [of his body], he shall pay three pounds of silver.
> If someone should inflict a blow with the open hand on another, but neither blood nor bruise appears, let him pay five silver solidi.
> If someone should strike another with an open-handed blow to the face, so that blood or bruise appear, let him learn that he shall pay one female slave.

Gaelic law texts likewise list the levels of compensation required to make peace following offences of varying seriousness. The analysis of physical injuries is detailed and precise in *Bretha Déin Chécht*:

> [Compensation for] any wound that is round is divided in two aspects: half for its depth, and the other half for the width of its opening. If it be irregular it is divided in three: one third for its length, one third for its depth, and one third for its width.
> . . . For breaking a bone, two ounces of silver [are the penalty], one of them for the physician and the other for him on whom the groaning wound has been inflicted.
> . . . An eye or an ear, if it is one of them, half the penalty for the head is paid; if it be both of them it is the full *éraic* [a fixed penalty], that is their price.

The text goes on to discuss various injuries in great detail, including broken bones, injuries which may or may not leave a lump or discoloration, which shed or do not shed blood, which require or do not require sick-maintenance, or which 'bring shame on the countenance'. Facial wounds are distinguished according to whether they are between the brows and the hair, in the nose, in the chin, above the eyelash, 'in the hollow between the two jawbones', or between ear and hair, and other body parts and their injuries are carefully enumerated and valued.

The *Laws of Æthelberht of Kent* († 616), the earliest Anglo-Saxon law text, likewise define the level of compensation or *bot* to be paid for physical injuries of a range of severity:

> If a shoulder be lamed, let bot be made with thirty shillings.
> If an ear be struck off, let bot be made with twelve shillings.
> If the other ear hear not, let bot be made with twenty-five shillings.
> If an ear be pierced, let bot be made with three shillings.
> If an ear be mutilated, let bot be made with six shillings.
> If an eye be [struck] out, let bot be made with fifty shillings.
> If the mouth or an eye be injured, let bot be made with twelve shillings.
> If the nose be pierced, let bot be made with nine shillings.

In all the above examples the compensation paid to victims was related to the extent of physical injury. But offences against property were also dealt with through a system of compensation payments, as were breaches of contract. In addition, Gaelic law treated offences against someone's 'honour' as violations of their person. Mockery, satirising someone or telling lies about them were severely punished, for such behaviour dishonoured them and – as we shall see – a person's honour was vital to their legal and social standing. *Cáin Adomnáin* discusses this in regard to women:

> If it is making a good woman blush, by [accusing her of] lust or by denying her children's paternity, seven *cumals* is the fine for it down to [but not including] the wife of an ordinary lord. Seven half-*cumals* if she is the wife of an ordinary lord. From there down to the wife of a *muire*, seven ounces. (*Cáin Adomnáin* § 51)

The most serious crime in Gaelic laws, as might be expected, was that of unlawful killing. It should be remembered, of course, that there were various killings that were not unlawful and therefore resulted in no legal process and required no compensatory payment. These included killing in self-defence or during a battle, killing a thief caught in the act, or killing a captive criminal (*cimbid*) whose kin were unwilling or unable to pay the compensation for his crime. With unlawful killing, serious though it was, the social disruption it caused could still generally be settled by payment of compensation. A killer made peace with his victim's kin (who were otherwise expected to take revenge on the killer) by paying them two types of fine. The first was a fixed fine of seven *cumals* for the murder of a free man (we will return in due course to the *cumal* or 'female slave' as a unit of value). The fixed payment was sometimes also called *cró*, originally 'slaughter' and by extension 'compensation for killing'. The second payment that must be made to the victim's kin – *lóg n-enech*, or 'price of the face' or 'honour price' – varied according to their status and according to how closely they were related to the victim. The higher the kinsman's honour price and the nearer his relationship, the higher the payment of *lóg n-enech* that must be paid to him. All this meant that the killing of a high-status person would be very costly for the murderer and his kindred (who would be required to support him with payments of their own). The killing of a lower-status person would clearly entail much less of a burden.

In a gradually Christianised society, making peace after unlawful killing did not always require payment alone. In the sixth century the *Penitential of Finnian* treated homicide as both a sin and a crime, and so required two things of a cleric for this offence. For murder considered as a sin he must repent, going into exile for ten years, doing penance for seven years, and doing a great deal of fasting and abstaining from wine and meat. But for murder considered as a crime he must make redress to the victim's kin in accordance with native law:

> If he has done [the penance] well . . . let him be taken back into his own country and let him make satisfaction to the friends of him

whom he killed. And let him offer recompense to [the victim's] father and mother, if they are still alive, and say, 'Lo, I will be for you in place of your son; whatever you say to me I will do.' If he does not make satisfaction, however, let him never be brought back.

It is hard for the modern citizen to imagine that the parents of a murdered son could be in some way 'satisfied' by having their son's killer serve them in place of their own son, or even find such an arrangement tolerable. But arrangements of this sort continued for centuries as part of the process of making peace after outbreaks of violence. In early modern Scotland it was accepted practice for a killer to make peace by paying compensation, or *assythment*, to his victim's kindred in return for which he received a 'letter of slanis' – effectively a pardon which made him immune to criminal prosecution. But the killer might also have to perform other services. In 1554, William Chalmer of Drumlochy murdered George Drummond of Blair and his son. As *assythment* of this offence he offered to pay 1,000 marks and marry his own son to his victim's daughter, and his cousin to the slain man's sister. It is hard to imagine what 'satisfaction' a woman might have found in marrying the son of her father's killer, but such early medieval practices survived for a surprisingly long time in the Scottish legal system.

In early British laws the compensatory principle was likewise the means of restoring the peace following murder. An echo of British legal practice in Scotland appears in the thirteenth-century 'Berne Manuscript' in a text later known in a Latin translation as *Leges inter Brettos et Scottos* ('the laws between the Britons and the Gaels'), which was evidently intended to accommodate their two legal traditions. The text defines the levels of compensation to be paid for violence against men of different ranks. It does so using the traditional Gaelic terms *cró* and *enech*, but also the British term *galanas*, the price of a man's life based on his status and payable to his kin (a woman's *galanas* was calculated as half her brother's). It was a key element of medieval Welsh laws. *Galanas* also appears in the fourteenth-century Scottish text *Regiam Majestatem* as the payment made by a horseman who causes death by trampling on someone in the middle of a town or village: 'he shall pay *cró* and *galanas* for the dead man slain in this manner, as if he had killed him with his own hands'. Lesser offences in Welsh laws were also dealt with by compensation. The victim of an offence was dishonoured by it, and peace was restored by the payment of *sarhaed* – a word that meant both the 'dishonour' caused by an offence and the payment made to resolve it. *Sarhaed* was paid according to the status of the victim, being calculated as a proportion of that person's *galanas*.

In Anglo-Saxon laws, likewise, offenders had to pay *wergeld* (literally 'man-gold') to their victim's kin following unlawful killing of a free man. The killing of a slave entailed no such payment, but the lord of the slave had to be compensated for his loss.

In all three legal traditions one particular kind of killing was regarded as particularly catastrophic because compensation was impossible. When a man killed a close kinsman the usual practice of one kindred compensating another could not work, since both killer and victim belonged to the same kindred. Neither could the victim's kin take revenge on the killer, since he was also their kinsman. This was therefore a crime of particular horror. The Anglo-Saxon poem *Beowulf* records the disaster that befell King Hreðel when one of his sons, Hæthcyn, killed his brother Herebeald with an arrow. In Seamus Heaney's fine translation:

For the eldest, Herebeald, an unexpected
deathbed was laid out, through a brother's doing,
when Hæthcyn bent his horn-tipped bow
and loosed the arrow that destroyed his life.
He shot wide and buried a shaft
in the flesh and blood of his own brother.
That offence was beyond redress, a wrongfooting
of the heart's affections; for who could avenge
the prince's life or pay his death-price?
. . . [Hreðel] was helplessly placed
to set to rights the wrong of the murder,
could not punish the killer in accordance with the law

of the blood-feud, although he felt no love for him.
Heartsore, wearied, he turned away
from life's joys, chose God's light
and departed . . .

In Gaelic laws also the response to kinslaying, or *fingal*, differentiated it from other forms of killing. One text required the
kin-slayer to be set adrift in a boat so that his kin need not be
responsible for harming him directly. He may survive the experience and settle in the territory where he landed as a *fuidir*, a
low-level tenant whose status is discussed below.

It should be recognised, however, that in spite of the horror
that kin-slaying induced in early medieval societies, it was far
from unknown, especially amongst royal kindreds and warrior
aristocracies. A man acquired power to a great extent by virtue
of his position within a kindred. But if his position in the kindred
made him a candidate for a position of power, it would do the
same for his brothers and his cousins. As only one candidate
could normally succeed to a particular kingship or lordship, and
as his principal rivals often included his close relations, violence
might well ensue: 'a man's enemies will be those of his own
household'.

HIERARCHY AND STATUS

As already indicated in some of the law texts mentioned above,
compensation varied not only according to the degree of injury,
but also according to the status of the person injured. Thus,
'making a good woman blush' in *Cáin Adomnáin* required
varying levels of compensation depending on her social status or
rank, and her rank was determined by that of the man to whom
she was married. In this text only three levels are identified: the
wife of the highest rank down to but not including an *aire deso*
(the lowest grade of lord); the wife of an *aire deso*; and the wife
of a lower-class of person. But some Gaelic laws offer a far more
elaborate and finely graded view of social hierarchy, and they
consistently make the same connection between the status of the
injured party and the quantity of compensation paid to them. A

law governing the support due to those who have been injured, *Bretha Crólige* ('judgements about blood-lying') declares, 'the sick-maintenance of everyone is increased according to his rank'.

A similar connection between social rank and the level of compensation paid for injury is found in the Anglo-Saxon 'North People's Law':

> The North people's king's geld is thirty thousand thrymsas ...
> An archbishop's and an aetheling's wergeld is fifteen thousand thrymsas.
> A bishop's and an ealdorman's, eight thousand thrymsas.
> A hold's and a king's high-reeves, four thousand thrymsas.
> A ceorl's wergeld is two hundred and sixty-six thrymsas, that is two hundred shillings by Mercian law.
> And if a Welsh-man thrive so that he have a hide of land, and can bring forth the king's *gafol*, then his wergeld is one hundred and ten shillings. And if he thrive only to half a hide, then let his wer be eighty shillings.
> If he have not any land, and yet be free, let him be paid for with seventy shillings.

Similar texts in the Welsh legal tradition survive, describing levels of compensation that varied according to the social status or honour of the person injured.

The traditional laws of all these societies – Gaelic, Welsh and Anglo-Saxon – reflect their profoundly hierarchical structures. In Gaelic law the wealthy and noble were protected to a great extent by their honour price or *lóg n-enech*. To offend a person of high rank and high honour price was to risk being obliged to pay crippling compensation, and those who could not pay the amount required may be enslaved or killed. The risks involved in injuring a lower-class person were correspondingly less.

In this world, the idea that all individuals were equal before the law was a foreign one, but it was an idea that was known and understood, largely because it appears to have been part of the Church's thinking. *Bretha Crólige* gives a nod towards the idea of equality of *díre* for all, 'king and subject, free and unfree, weak and strong' as found 'in the books' (*hi lebruib*), but it also asserts the native Gaelic tradition, or *fénechas*, that their honour price is unequal. 'The books' in this reference are ecclesiastical books, so the author clearly saw the tension in this area as lying between book-law (i.e., ecclesiastical or Roman law) and the native tradition. For this reason the very ecclesiastical *Collectio Canonum Hibernensis* gives very little support to the notion that a person is protected by a high status.

In the native laws, one's rank determined not only levels of compensation; it also affected one's ability to swear an oath. Oath-swearing was a central aspect of the law, and the outcome of a legal dispute over property or a contract, and even over a person's criminal guilt, would depend on the oaths sworn by the parties and their witnesses. In such contexts a person with a high honour price could 'over-swear' a person of lower rank, effectively reducing them to silence. As the Gaelic text *Di Astud Chirt ⁊ Dligid* puts it:

> Every grade which is lower than another is oversworn; every grade which is higher than another overswears.

Similar inequalities can be found in English laws where, for example, 'the oath of a twelve-hynde man is equivalent to the oaths of six ceorls'.

Another legal inequality in Gaelic laws relates to the ability to enter into contracts. No one could validly enter into a contract for anything of greater value than his own honour price. This meant that people lower in the social order could make only modest contracts. Contracts must also be supported by sureties, that is, people swearing to fulfil the terms of the contract if the party for whom they stood surety defaulted. Again, no one could stand surety for a contract of higher value than his honour price – though a party could engage two people whose two honour prices added up to the value of the contract to act as joint sureties.

The hierarchy of status was a complex feature of early Gaelic society. There were, in fact, several distinct hierarchies: those of secular rule and lordship, ecclesiastical orders, and the *áes dána*, or 'people of the arts' (a group which itself was subdivided into categories of people such as poets, jurists and craftsmen). The law tracts do not allow us to create a single coherent map of the relative positions of all the people in all these different groups, as there are significant variations among the texts themselves. In principle, however, people could be treated as being of the same rank if they had the same honour price, whichever group they belonged to, though other indicators of rank were relevant too, as we shall see. In some cases, we can see parity fairly clearly. Kings and bishops of a single *túath* are given equal status, for example, in terms of honour price. But *Críth Gablach*, a tract on status composed *c.* AD 700, though apparently assuming their equality in strictly legal terms, seeks to give the bishop a slight edge in terms of protocol.

> Which of them is more venerable (*sruithiu*), the king or the bishop? A bishop is more venerable, because the king rises [before the bishop] on account of the faith; a bishop, however, raises his knee before a king.

Another indication of the status of a man is the number of people he may have in his retinue (*dám*) as he travelled around exercising his office. At such times, the *túath* is required to entertain him and his retinue with bed and board – a service known in Old Gaelic as *coinnmed* (a term that survived in later medieval Scottish law as *conveth*, a payment in lieu of the service). In *Críth Gablach* a king and a bishop are both allowed to have twelve men in their retinue. The same tract also permits a retinue of twelve men to a scholar, or *suí*, a senior member of the learned class.

Of course, just as there were various ranks of kings, ranging from the *rí túaithe*, 'king of a single petty kingdom', to over-kings and provincial kings, so there were various ranks of bishops, ranging from the bishop of one see (which would normally be co-terminus with a single *túath*) to what we might call 'over-bishops'. Thus, in *Uraicecht Becc*, or 'little primer', the king of Munster, who is the over-king of many lesser rulers, has the same status as an *ollam úasalepscop*, 'a chief noble bishop'. This latter is the senior bishop of a province with its many lesser bishops, each ministering to a *túath*. We may suppose that he has the same status as the person referred to in the *Canones Hibernenses* as *episcopus episcoporum*, 'a bishop of bishops', who ranks higher than a mere *episcopus*.

The examples given above refer to individuals at the summit of the hierarchy – kings, bishops and scholars. But the hierarchical scheme of honour price embraced the whole of early medieval Gaelic society. Rulers or lords had a status that depended largely on the number of clients they had, but also on the number of armed men on whom they could call and the number of hostages they held as guarantors of the good behaviour of their subjects or clients. In *Críth Gablach* the lowest grade of lord, the *aire déso*, is expected to have ten clients – five base clients and five free clients. The base client, or *dóer-chéle* (otherwise known as *céle gíallnae*, 'client of submission'), received a grant (*rath*) from his lord – typically of cattle, but maybe of other animals or of land – with which he would farm and from which he paid his lord a fixed annual food tribute whose quantity depended on the size of the initial *rath*. The base client must also render various kinds of labour for his lord: working on his harvest, building his fort, fighting for him when required and digging his grave-mound when he died. In addition to any land granted in *rath* by the lord, the base client may also have a share in the *fintiu*, or 'kin-land', of his kindred, which he held separately from the contractual relationship he had with his lord. When he first became a base client of his lord he also received an initial payment of his own honour price, and, in return for this, the lord acquired a right to part of any fine that his client might receive in compensation for injury. This meant, of course, that it would be in the lord's interest to support his base client in any legal dispute that he entered into; only if the client was successful in law would his lord profit from any fines he was awarded.

The free client, or *sóer-chéle*, also received a grant or *rath* from his lord, but in return he had to make a higher payment than the base client. However, after seven years of this relationship the free client obtained proprietorial rights over the whole *rath* and ceased to be a client of the lord – unless he decided to enter into a new contract of clientship. Furthermore, while the base client must simply pay his food-render to his lord, losing sight of it so to speak, the free client was in a more honourable position. He sat with his lord as an honourable guest in his house, eating and drinking with him, attending on him and sharing in his counsel – a closer and more personal relationship with the lord than that of the base client. He may also be part of the lord's *dám*, or retinue, when he moved around his territory, sharing with him the entertainment that was the lord's due in each house. Unlike the *dóer-chéle*, the *sóer-chéle* received in full any payment made in respect of injuries done to him.

The status of the various ranks of free men also depended on the size and value of their farms and stock. Some law tracts, such as *Críth Gablach*, go into great detail about the distinguishing marks of different ranks in society: their honour price, the extent of their land, the weight of their oaths, the amount of their render, the size of their houses, their diet and the number of men in their retinues.

Beneath the 'free man' was the *fuidir*, a 'semi-servile' tenant whose obligations to his lord were not fixed, but who must do whatever his lord requires of him. He is unable to enter into any kind of contract without the permission of his lord, and injuries done to him entailed compensation that was paid not to him, but to the lord. If three generations of men live on a lord's land as *fuidirs*, then their descendant is tied to the soil as a *senchléithe* and cannot leave the lord or his farm – rather like a serf in other parts of Europe. If the lord disposes of his land, the *senchléithe* must stay on it under his new lord.

Similar structures of status applied to other social groups. Skilled craftsmen and scholars had a status that depended largely on their professional skills, but there was also an hereditary element determined by the status of their father and grandfather. Thus, *Uraicecht na Ríar* – a text about the various ranks or grades of poets – discusses the highest rank of poet, the *ollam*, whose honour price is seven cumals, the same as that of a king (*rí túaithe*) or a bishop:

He is a poet whose qualifications are complete and genuine, who is not found to be perplexed in the mass of his craft; through his *nath* (a kind of poetry), through his *laíd* (a metrical composition), through his poetic faculty, through his purity he illuminates nobility; and he is the son of a poet, and the grandson of another. If he is not the son of a poet, however, or a grandson, only half honour-price goes to him, as Irish law says: 'Only half honour-price goes to scholars if they were not born into a family [of scholars].'

This passage neatly illustrates the dependence of status both on kinship and on personal qualifications. Among those personal qualifications were not only the skill someone achieved in poetic craft, but also his honourable and righteous conduct of the craft, for a poet was in a position of power. A poet might make a satire on another person, which would be an attack on his honour. Satire was therefore feared, since it damaged the target's social standing and was even thought to have physical consequences, such as facial blemishes or death. Fear of being satirised was thus a powerful motive for people to behave well. But a poet could not satirise someone without good cause, and if he did so he would himself suffer a loss of status as well as having to pay the honour price of the person he had unjustly satirised.

In the above discussion we see that a poet's qualifications for status are related to his family tree, his competence and his justice in pursuing his craft. Analogous qualifications applied to others – physicians, lawyers, craftsmen and musicians. Kings also depended on kinship, competence and justice for their status, and so for the continuation of their rule. The law texts and other sources constantly stress the *fír flathemon*, 'the ruler's truth or justice', as a vital part of the public good. If a king ruled well, nature would repay him and his people with fertility, good weather and healthy children. If he ruled badly, all kinds of catastrophe would fall on his people. A seventh-century Irish Latin text, 'On the Twelve Abuses of the World' (*de Duodecim Abusiuis Saeculi*), describes the consequences of the king's injustice in terms found in several texts throughout the period:

Whoever does not govern his kingdom according to this law will certainly suffer many adversities to his rule. For on that account the peace of the people is often breached; hindrances appear in the kingdom; the fruits of the earth decrease; the services of the people are hampered; many and various sorrows mar the prosperity of the kingdom; the death of loved ones and children brings sadness; invasions of enemies destroy the provinces everywhere; wild beasts tear to pieces herds of cattle and domestic animals; wintry and windy storms prevent the fertility of the land and the service of the sea, and when lightning strikes it burns up cornfields, the flowers of the trees and the shoots of the vines.

Such dire warnings served to stress the importance of the king's justice. All kinds of leverage were also exercised to achieve this end, but particularly the threat of loss of honour. A king lost his honour price for acts of injustice, such as defaulting on an oath, giving unjust judgements, sheltering someone fleeing from the law or in other ways tolerating criminality. He could also lose his honour price by failing to look or behave like a king: having a physical blemish, travelling without his retinue, doing manual labour (if he is found holding the handle of a mallet, an axe or a spade), not having hostages in chains to guarantee the good behaviour of their kin, lacking courage in battle, or failing to enforce payment of tribute or fines.

What was true for a king was also true of other ranks of secular persons: they must behave according to the requirements of their station. It was also true of the clergy. Their status normally allowed them to overswear many others, but if they or their church failed to live up to the expectations of their people by bad behaviour or by failing to maintain the proper services they lost their honour and could be oversworn. To enjoy its full honour a church should have, according to *Bretha Nemed Toísech*:

The shrine of a righteous man, the relics of saints, divine scripture, a sinless superior, devout monks, seven gifts of the Holy Spirit . . . Let it not accept the gifts of the unjust, let it not take away anything which is the property of another.

Parallel to this were the conditions under which a church lost its honour:

> Being without baptism, without communion, without mass, without praying for the dead, without preaching, without penitents ... reddening it with blood, putting it under a secular lord, going to it after plundering.

The clergy of such a dishonoured church lost their own honour and harmed their community:

> [Such a church] does not over-swear a righteous one; a righteous one overswears it. He who is not in complete innocence does not take complete honour-price. Their disqualifications detract from the innocence of those who do not have a lawful shepherd with his due good qualifications.

Honour was therefore a fragile thing for all men of any status, and required constant nurturing by proper behaviour and by sheer hard work in maintaining the standards expected. In the small and closely intertwined community of the *túath*, the constant watchfulness of one's neighbours and kin combined with the risk of dishonour to discourage misbehaviour.

SLAVERY

Below the extended hierarchy of rulers and their subjects, each with their different *wergeld*, *galanas* or *lóg n-enech* (depending on the legal tradition of their community), were slaves. These men and women ranked so low as to be scarcely members of society at all. People might become slaves having been captured in raids; Patrick says that he was one of many thousands of Britons captured by Irish raiders. He also protested, as we have seen, against Coroticus over the enslavement of recently baptised Irish people by British and Pictish raiders (see p. 63, above). One could also become a slave if one injured someone and found oneself unable to pay the fine. A woman in Adomnán's *Life of Columba* expresses just this fear. The saint had given her husband a miraculous sharp stake on which an edible animal impaled itself every day, enabling him to feed his family. But she warned him, 'Take the spike out of the ground. For if people or cattle die on it, you yourself and I with our children will either be put to death or led into slavery.' Other people were simply born into slavery, inheriting the servile state of their parents. People might also become slaves in time of famine, selling themselves or their children into slavery in order to survive the period of want. Theodore's *Penitential* envisages such a situation in an Anglo-Saxon society:

> If he is compelled by necessity, a father has the power to sell his son of seven years of age into slavery; after that he has not the right to sell him without his consent.

It is likely that this kind of enslavement as a survival strategy also took place in Gaelic and British communities.

In principle the slave had no rights, no protection against violence or abuse by his or her master. In the Gaelic laws an injury done to a slave was an offence not against him but against the master. This was also true in Welsh law where the slave was effectively treated as part of his owner's livestock: 'There is no *galanas* for him, but only the payment of his value to his master, like the value of a beast.' Anglo-Saxon laws about slaves likewise deny them legal protection. As an aside we might note that one Anglo-Saxon word for 'slave', *wealh*, is the same word as that meaning 'foreigner', but usually applied to British people. This feature of the language sheds light on the relations between Anglo-Saxon incomers and their defeated British neighbours.

In the Gaelic laws there are different words for male and female slaves: *mug* for a male slave, *cumal* for a female. The latter word *cumal* also became a word for a unit of value and exchange. Thus, the honour price of a bishop, a king or a chief poet was seven *cumals* as noted above. The slave was a unit of value in British communities too. In the sixth-century *Canones Wallici*, or 'Welsh Canons' (actually legal material used by a British community in Armorica), the female slave (*ancilla*) and the male slave (*seruus*) are mentioned as units of value in the payment of fines or compensation:

If someone commits intentional homicide, let him pay three female slaves and three male slaves, and he shall receive immunity.

If someone murders a man in a quarrel, or cuts off his hand or his foot, or his eye, let him know that he must pay one female or male slave.

If he cuts off the thumb of his hand, let him pay half a female slave, that is half of the price, or half of a male slave.

This last sentence with its 'half-slaves' makes it clear that the 'slave' as a unit of value for exchange was not being reckoned here as an actual living person, but had been transmuted into material goods of equivalent value – and we know that payments were made in gold, silver, copper, cattle and other valuable objects. The same process was clearly happening in the Gaelic world where payment in cumals was made in objects of equivalent value. The value of seven cumals was expressed thus in the Irish Canons (*Canones Hibernenses*):

The blood of a bishop, a high ruler or a scribe which is shed on the ground, if it requires a dressing, wise men judge that he who shed it is to be crucified [probably meaning 'hanged'] or pay seven female slaves (*ancellas*). If [payment is made] in kind, he shall pay a third part in silver, and an amount of gold equal to the size of the top of the head, and likewise a precious stone the size of an eye ... Whoever strikes or pushes a bishop without shedding [his blood] shall pay half the price of seven female slaves.

The fact that the word *cumal* came to be used as a unit of value for buying and selling in the marketplace and for compensation in law is significant. It suggests that there was a thriving market for slaves, especially female slaves. This may have arisen in part from the method of acquiring slaves in British and Gaelic circles, where raiders went from their own territory to another, fought with the menfolk and killed many of them, and then took the women as captives. Women slaves may have been more valuable because they could be sexually exploited as well as providing their labour, and perhaps they were also less likely to cause trouble to their owners by escaping or offering any kind of violence. Concern for female slaves underlies at least part of

Patrick's protest over Coroticus' raid and capture of recently baptised members of Patrick's community: 'You hand over the members of Christ as though to a brothel' (*Epistola* § 14). We may imagine that similar concerns underlie Adomnán's story about a visit by St Columba to Pictland:

> At that time the venerable man asked Broichan, a magician, to release a certain Irish slave-girl (*seruam*) for the sake of human kindness. When he, with a hard and stubborn mind, kept hold of her, the saint addressed him and spoke thus: 'Know, Broichan, that if you will not release for me this captive pilgrim before I leave this province, you will swiftly die.' (VC ii, 33)

Having fallen ill and lying close to death, Broichan relented and the slave-girl was freed and handed over to the saint's safe-keeping. The story is partly about the power of the saint's malediction, of course. But the moral context is one in which the Church sought to alleviate at least some of the suffering of those who were captured and enslaved. This is the kind of operation Patrick commended among the Christians of Gaul: 'They send holy and worthy men to the Franks and other nations with so many thousand *solidi* to redeem baptized captives' (*Epistola* § 14). The sixth-century penitential associated with St Finnian, who was St Columba's teacher, also deals with the redemption of captives, though here it identifies an abuse of the practice:

> If any cleric under the false pretence of the redemption of captives is found to be despoiling churches and monasteries, he shall be reprimanded until he is confounded ... We command and urge contributing for the redemption of captives.

The Church did not seek to undermine or even criticise slavery as an institution. Indeed, there were slaves on church estates. That was simply the way things were, almost a force of nature. But given the existence of the institution, churchmen also sought to moderate the treatment of captives, to protect Christian slaves from pagan owners, and to encourage the freeing of slaves as an act of Christian mercy. Thus, a woman called Geatfled in the north of England had several slaves 'whose head she took in return for their food in those evil days' – that is to say, people had bowed their heads before her, becoming her slaves, whom she then fed in a time of famine. In the document of their manumission in Durham she declares that 'she has given [them] freedom for the love of God and for the sake of her soul'. Similarly, in the Gaelic world freeing a slave was an act of Christian merit. According to the *Collectio Canonum Hibernensis*, the bishop as the agent of his church was obliged to redeem captives – part of a programme that included: 'to care for the poor, to feed the hungry, to clothe the naked, to welcome strangers, to redeem captives and to protect widows and orphans' (CCH i, 8).

FAMILY VALUES

In the absence of a state or public policing, it was the family that offered people the best legal protection. If you were unlawfully killed, your family would demand heavy compensation from the killer and his kin, and pursue a blood-feud against them if they did not pay. This provided some disincentive to anyone tempted to use violence against you. If you were injured in some other way, your family would support you in your struggle for legal redress.

In Gaelic law members of your family should also act as your sureties to enforce contracts to which you were a party. The chief man of a kindred (*cenn fine*, 'head of kin') in particular might act as a surety, having a higher social and legal standing and therefore lending more weight to any claim you had. For this reason, he was also called the *aire coisring*, or 'lord of obligation'. This was something of a two-edged sword: you might call on him to make sure that your debtors paid what they owed to you, but your creditors might also call on him to make sure that you paid what you owed to them. He and your other kinsmen had an interest in making sure that you honoured your obligations, for the honour of the family and of its individual members was dependent on the community's recognition of their integrity. The kindred was also jointly responsible for payment of compensation for its members' crimes. In the first instance, in the Gaelic laws, if a criminal defaulted, his son or father would be responsible, but failing them the whole kin had to take responsibility. If they failed to make satisfaction, their cattle or other livestock were subject to distraint – the legal process in which a plaintiff seized and impounded the defendant's property (or that of his kin) to force him to accept his responsibilities and pay what he owed. A family would therefore bring great pressure to bear on a delinquent member whose behaviour might otherwise cost them dear. They had numerous ways of making a family member conform to their collective requirements, including expulsion from the kindred as a last resort. And an expelled man was a nobody, unable to act in most legal contexts, and lacking all kinds of protection. After all, if the deterrent to killing a man was the threat of having to pay heavy compensation to his family, if he had no family he could be abused or even killed with impunity.

In this context we should understand 'the family' not simply as the domestic household, the nuclear family with its affective bonds, its care and tenderness, conflict and play. These are vital aspects of family life, but we glimpse them only occasionally in our sources. In the law texts and for our present purposes, 'family' refers rather to a legally defined group of people. In Gaelic laws the relevant group was usually the *derbfine*, or 'true kindred', whose members were all descendants through the male line of a single great-grandfather (though the family was sometimes more broadly or more narrowly defined for different purposes). It is this legally defined family to whom an offender usually paid compensation for an offence against one of its members, and which was collectively responsible for payment for its members' crimes.

Kinship was also of central importance in the Gaelic laws governing land. Most farmland was 'kin-land', or *fintiu*, collectively owned by the *derbfine* and divided among them, each competent adult male farming his own share with his wife, children and servants or slaves. This sharing out of the *fintiu* did not make each man autonomous with respect to his land, however. Each remained responsible to the whole kindred for his custody of his share. This meant that an individual could not sell 'his' share of land as if it were simply his personal property. If a man tried to dispose of his share in the *fintiu* his male kin had the power to stop him. A successful farmer might acquire other land that was not part of the *fintiu*, and if he did so he had power over it and could sell it or treat it as he wished, but he may not do so with *fintiu*. *Fintiu* was the ground, both literally and metaphorically, on which the kindred stood together. It also united the kindred across the boundary of death: when a man died, his share in the *fintiu* remained in the common possession of his kindred after him.

The possession of the *fintiu* by a particular kindred, beyond the deaths of individual members of that kindred, sheds light on some interesting practices in the Gaelic world. The *fintiu* was believed to be protected by the dead bodies of members of the kindred which had rights over it. In the seventh-century *Life of St Patrick* by Tírechán, the saint goes to meet the pagan king Loíguire at Tara in Ireland. The king tells him:

> My father Níall did not allow me to believe [in Christ], but [said] that I should be buried in the ridges of Tara, I the son of Níall, and the sons of Dúnlang in Maistiu in the plain of Liffey, face to face like men armed for war until the day of *erdathe*, as the magicians call it, that is the day of the Lord's judgement. For the pagans are accustomed to be armed in their tombs, with weapons ready. This is on account of the bitterness of [our] hatred.

Here the bodies of the dead are imagined as being placed in the ground at the edges of a territory, defending it against hostile neighbours. The implication was that the grave-mounds ('ridges', here in Latin, *cacuminibus*) of the ancestral dead make it difficult for anyone but their descendants to enter and occupy the *fintiu*. While this story breathes the atmosphere of ancestral myth, its depiction of burials as a form of boundary protection is rooted in the actual custom and practice of early medieval society. Recent archaeological exploration has shown that many Irish burial mounds appear to be boundary markers. Though often prehistoric in origin, they were re-used centuries later for burial of the dead – or of some of the dead – well into the Christian period. It appears that ancient monuments in the landscape were imagined by early medieval people to be the *fertae*, or burial mounds, of their own ancestors, and treated as boundary markers of their farms or territories. They may have buried their own more recent dead in these mounds as a way of reinforcing the kindred's connection with the land and with that ancestral protection. This was perfectly acceptable to churchmen as late as the eighth century. The *Collectio Canonum Hibernensis* cites authorities for the burial of a layman *in paterno sepulcro*, 'in the ancestral tomb', and even cites a curse for those who are not so buried: 'Cursed is every man who is not buried in the tomb of his fathers' (CCH xviii, 2).

The power of an ancestor's *fert* to protect the kin-land of his supposed descendants underlies a fascinating legal–ritual process in Gaelic law by which someone took possession of land. When someone believed he (it is normally a 'he') had a legal claim to a piece of land that was currently occupied by someone else, the law described the process by which he might take possession of it. This process, known as *tellach*, involved the claimant taking gradually increasing numbers of horses across the *fert* or *fertae* on the boundary of the territory, over a period of several days and in the presence of a growing number of witnesses. At various points during this process, the current occupier of the land could submit the matter to a judge's decision. If he failed to do so, the claimant made a final entry over the *fert*, occupied the house, lit a fire and spent the night there. The land was now legally his. The fact that the disputed land was claimed by driving animals over the ancestral burial mounds represents a belief that the dead people interred in them were somehow acknowledging their kinship with the claimant, accepting his kin-based claim to the land, and allowing him to enter and settle there.

Territorial boundaries were marked not only by burial mounds, but also by inscribed stones. Many of the surviving *ogham*-inscribed stones in early medieval Ireland were placed on or near boundaries. It may be that the individuals commemorated in the *ogham* inscriptions were, or were thought to be, buried nearby. In that case, the stones may simply have advertised the kin-based protection that those ancestors continued to provide on the boundaries of their kin-land. If so, we do not need to choose between regarding these stones as grave-markers or as boundary-markers – some earlier discussions of the monuments assume they were either one or the other. If burial mounds mark boundaries, then such stones may be boundary markers because they are burial markers. It may be, however, that some of the *ogham* inscriptions served as a substitute for ancestral burials, a name permanently chiselled into a stone pillar symbolising the continued protection of the ancestor and the claim of his kindred, even in the absence of a body. Given the boundary significance of such stones in Ireland, we might assume that they had much the same significance in Scotland, where the use of *ogham* spread from Ireland, particularly in the eastern part of the country. We might also recall that many of the surviving stones carved with Pictish symbols in Scotland are situated on or near to boundaries, as are some early historic cemeteries. It may be that these cemeteries had some territory-marking or even protective function like those of Ireland, and that Pictish symbols – like *ogham*, and like sub-Roman Latin inscriptions in southern Scotland – were also related to kinship and territory.

The Welsh legal tradition envisaged a kin-based entitlement to occupy land rather like that of the Gaelic laws. It also had restrictions on the disposal of kin-land by members of a kindred, and we can assume a similar situation among the British communities of Scotland.

Most of the above discussion has related to the patrilineal kindred of the *derbfine*, the male descendants of one great-grandfather, and similarly patrilineal arrangements in Anglo-Saxon and British areas. This is the view of kinship taken by legal texts. Likewise, the genealogical records for early medieval Scotland are also almost entirely patrilineal, while men (and occasionally women) named in saints' 'Lives' or in the annals are almost always described as offspring of their fathers, rather than of their mothers. There are interesting exceptions to this as we shall see in due course, but patriliny is clearly the norm.

CREATING KINSHIP

The foregoing account of family identity represents only part of how it was understood in the early medieval world. First, there were forms of kinship that were not biological: marriage and fosterage, for example, and sponsorship at baptism, all created new forms of kinship between individuals, and therefore between kindreds, as a result of contracts or agreements. Second, although laws and other literature stress patrilineal kinship, this does not mean that descent through the female line was unimportant. In the Gaelic laws, when a woman married she normally entered the kindred of her husband, lived with him and bore children who would be regarded as members of his kindred. There were important exceptions to this pattern, however, such as when a woman married a man from overseas – a *cú glas*, literally a 'grey dog'. Such a man would be absorbed into his wife's *túath* and kindred, and had some limited rights that were dependent on hers. But even the normal form of marriage did not put an end to a woman's legal membership of her own birth-kin. In Gaelic law the family of a *cétmuinter* or lawful wife would receive a third of any *éraic* paid for injuries committed against her, and on her death her male kin would receive a third of her inheritance (her sons getting the other two-thirds). Her birth-kin also remained responsible for paying one-third of any compensation entailed by her unlawful actions, her husband's kin paying the other two-thirds. Such a wife was in these respects more fully connected to her husband's kindred than she was to her own birth-kin. For a wife who had not been given to her husband by her kin, however, a different expression of kinship applied: her own kin would receive two-thirds of her inheritance, and they would be obliged to pay two-thirds of her debts. In some cases, where the rights of a woman's family had actually been violated by a man – as when he had abducted his wife against their wishes – all her inheritance reverted to her own male kin, while her abductor was liable for any debts she incurred. Here we see a ranking of different qualities of marriage, each with its own implications for the woman's continuing relationship to her birth-kin. The highest and most formal and fully consensual union (this referred to the consent of the wife's kindred), was a marriage in which both partners contributed equally to the union and each used or disposed of that property with the consent of the other. Other forms of marriage deviated from this form in various ways: one or other of the couple did not contribute so much property to the union, for example. In other unions, there was a lack of full commitment to the union (the woman stayed with her kindred), or there was no consent by her kindred. The lowest unions involved rape (*lánamnus ecne*, 'union of violent seizure') and the union of two insane people (*lánamnus genaige*, 'union of mockery'). All these indicators of kinship are primarily fiscal, of course; they tell us a good deal about the legal view of women, marriage and kinship, but say little about the affective relationships of those involved.

In Anglo-Saxon and Welsh laws we see similar expressions of the continued involvement of the wife's male kin after her marriage. In a case of murder in Anglo-Saxon law, *wergeld* was paid to the victim's kin by the killer and his kin: two-thirds were paid by the killer's paternal kin (*faedren maegth*), one-third by his maternal kin (*mêdren maegth*). And among the victim's kindred who received the *wergeld* from the slayer, his paternal kin received two-thirds and his maternal kin one-third. Likewise, in the Welsh laws concerning the payment of *galanas*, two-thirds were paid to the victim's father's family, and one-third to his mother's family. In all these legal systems, marriage created a bond between two kindreds which were defined more strongly by patrilineal descent, but in which matriliny also played a significant role.

The continuing connection of married women to their own birth-kindred, briefly explored above, raises the vexed question of 'Pictish matriliny'. It has been supposed by many historians of the period that there was something peculiar about the Picts, that, unlike their British, Gaelic and Anglo-Saxon neighbours, they were a matrilineal society and in particular that royal status was inherited by men from their mothers rather than from their fathers. There are a number of reasons that people have seen the Picts in this way. One is that the 'Pictish king-lists' record successive kings of the Picts from one rule to the next in which each king is named as 'X son of Y'. As the record does not usually mention the 'Y' in this formula as having been a previous king, it has been assumed that kings did not inherit their right to kingship from their fathers. Given that assumption, the conclusion was drawn that they must have inherited it from their mothers. Another reason for positing Pictish matriliny is that Bede says in his origin legend of the Picts that 'The Picts had no wives, and they sought them from the *Scotti*, and they agreed to give them on one condition: that when the matter [of succession] should come into doubt, [the Picts] should choose for themselves a king from the female royal line rather than the male. And this continues to be observed among the Picts until today' (EH i, 1).

Scholars in recent years have increasingly doubted these two arguments. In the first place, the Pictish king-lists are not contemporary records but the result of later medieval historical reflection, and they are shaped by the ideological needs of their authors. Furthermore, we cannot treat 'the Picts' as a single political entity with one king at any given time. People whom we now see as Picts were probably ruled by over-kings and under-kings whose shifting dynasties made claims and counterclaims about their respective ancestries to justify their own positions and to undermine their rivals. A list of kings with their respective patronymics need not represent the sequence of rulers of a single Pictish monarchy; it may include under-kings who ruled at the same time in different parts of Pictland. The character of the Pictish king-lists as they now stand need not be evidence of matrilineal succession. In addition, we must wonder, if matrilineal descent were a vital part of royal succession, why would the Pictish king-lists and the annals almost entirely ignore the mothers of the men who became kings, naming only their fathers?

Furthermore, Bede's testimony, sometimes cited as evidence of general matrilineal succession among the Picts, is better read as implying the opposite. He says that matrilineal succession for kings is resorted to 'when the matter should come into doubt'. The clear implication of this is that the succession of Pictish kings was normally dependent on patrilineal claims; but when a succession crisis occurred and no single claimant emerged as victor on patrilineal claims alone, then matriliny was taken into account. As was the case with their neighbours, a claim to royal power in Pictland probably depended on a number of factors. Being descended from a royal father or grandfather may have made you a potential king, whose equivalent among the Gaels was known as *rígdamnae*, 'king material'. But such descent would not have distinguished you from many of your close male kin who also had a patrilineal claim. The successful candidate could not always be distinguished by patrilineal right alone, and his success would depend on his wealth, his age and experience, his reputation, his ability to call on numbers of armed men, and his support among kindreds who were not his rivals. This last factor would include the support he got from his matrilineal kin (who may not have had any patrilineal claim to royal power) and his foster-kin (we will discuss these in due course).

Bede's account fits fairly well with such a process: 'when the matter should come into doubt' the candidate's maternal kin will be one of the factors that shape the outcome of a power-struggle. This does not radically distinguish the Picts from other Insular communities in our period. We may recall, for example, that Oswald ruled the united kingdoms of Bernicia and Deira in the seventh century (see above, p. 90), although by patrilineal descent his qualifications lay only in Bernicia. But his Bernician father Æthelfrith had earlier driven Edwin of Deira from his throne, taking control of the southern kingdom and marrying Edwin's sister Acha, daughter of King Aelle of Deira, who would become Oswald's mother. Bede accounts for the situation thus:

> By the industry of this king [Oswald] the kingdoms of the Deirans and the Bernicians, which until then had been at strife with each other, were joined in single peace and, as it were, as a single people. For he was the nephew of King Edwin through his sister Acha, and

it was fitting that so great a predecessor should have such a kinsman as his heir in religion and in kingship. (HE iii, 6)

For Bede there was something 'fitting' about Deira being ruled by a man whose matrilineal kin – his maternal grandfather and his mother's brother – had been kings of Deira.

One final thing to observe about Bede's witness to 'Pictish matriliny' is that the kings of the Picts between AD 697 and 729 were two brothers, Bruide and Nechtan. Their mother was a Pictish woman called Der-Ile, but their father was from the royal family of Cenél Comgaill in Dál Riata. In spite of their apparent lack of patrilineal entitlement to rule in Pictland, they did so for thirty-two years between them – not without opposition it has to be said. Of these two brothers Nechtan in particular was the object of Bede's admiration and approval. It was he who had made the decision to align all the Pictish churches with the religious observance of the Northumbrian church, seeking their help and guidance in a letter to Ceolfrith, the abbot of Bede's own monastery. Having received Ceolfrith's reply, Nechtan 'rose in the midst of his assembled nobles and bent his knees to the ground, giving thanks to God that he had been made worthy to receive such a gift from the land of the English' (HE v, 21). For Bede this made Nechtan as nearly a saint as it was possible for a king to be without actually undergoing martyrdom. He had brought the fullness of the Gospel (for Bede this meant Christianity in a Northumbrian flavour) to his people, and had enforced it by royal decree. Nechtan's reign had been disrupted by violence as others contended for power in Pictland, and it is quite likely that his enemies had used his lack of patrilineal right against him. Bede, his great admirer, therefore found it useful to tell a story that validated Nechtan's rule by explaining why matrilineal succession was acceptable.

Marriage was not the only way in which non-biological kinship could be created. Another important way of connecting biological families to each other was by the fosterage of children – a widespread practice in Gaelic and British societies. Fosterage involved members of one family taking over the care and education of a child from another family. Like marriage, fosterage created lasting bonds of friendship and alliance between the families involved. There was an important educational role, too: children were expected to learn the skills appropriate to their station during their fosterage, under the direction of their foster-parents.

There were Gaelic laws governing the formal arrangements of fosterage. These included, for some children, the payment of a fee to the foster-family by both the paternal and maternal kin of the child (again showing the continuing significance of matrilineal connections in the child's life). In the laws, fosterage created a new network of kinship for a child which brought with it a kind of belonging that would endure for a lifetime. Long after leaving his foster-home a man could call on his foster-kin for support in times of trouble. If a fosterling was unlawfully killed his foster-father and foster-brothers had a right to compensation along with his biological kin. And a grown-up fosterling was obliged to support his foster-parents if they became impoverished, or if they needed support in their old age.

Fosterage was also practised in British society, though the Welsh laws are less explicit about the nature of the contract and what the various parties might expect of each other. They do, however, show that foster-children were treated as heirs of their foster-parents when it came to inheriting property or land, and that they were expected to support their elderly foster-parents if they were in need.

The institution of fosterage existed in the Anglo-Saxon world, too, and, as in Gaelic society, it could be undertaken for love or for a fee. High-status families sent their sons to be fostered in the halls of other high-status or royal kindreds; there is much less Anglo-Saxon evidence for fosterage further down the social scale than there is for Gaels or Britons. But here again fosterage created new kinships, strengthened political friendships, and gave one's children protection and educational opportunity. It also gave boys an entry into the social and military world of the king or the lord, preparing them to serve as part of his inner circle.

The picture of fosterage found in legal sources generally describes a system of legal rights and obligations, as one might expect. But occasionally we catch a glimpse of the human warmth that might exist between foster-parents and their charges, as in the poem *Beowulf*:

> At seven I was fostered out by my father,
> left in the charge of my people's lord.
> King Hrethel kept me and took care of me,
> was open-handed, behaved like a kinsman.
> While I was his ward, he treated me no worse
> as a wean about the place than one of his own boys,

The Gaelic tradition also hints at the affection and warmth in foster-relationships, with the words for foster-mother (*muimme*) and foster-father (*aite*) being intimate words for parents, like 'mum' and 'dad' in English, rather than the more formal *mathair* and *athair*.

With the growing role of the Church in the Insular world, another form of fosterage emerged in which children and youths were fostered by monks or clergymen. Adomnán tells us that 'the priest Cruithnechán, a man of admirable life' had been St Columba's foster-father (*nutritor*) when he was a boy, while Columba himself is described as having been the *nutritor* of Baithéne, his cousin and his immediate successor as abbot of Iona. There is also some evidence to suggest that the Anglo-Saxon monk Aldhelm had been fostered on Iona during the 660s. It is noteworthy that these young men who had been fostered by churchmen all entered monastic or clerical life themselves. Perhaps youths were fostered in churches in the hope that they would become clergy, monks or nuns when they were older; but even if they returned to secular life their experience of church-fosterage and education would sustain links thereafter between churches and secular kindreds. It might also have cultivated values in those young people which differed from those of the warrior aristocracy. We find references to powerful Anglo-Saxon families seeking to foster their children in churches in the *Life of Bishop Wilfrid*:

Secular rulers too, noble men, gave him their sons for the sake of learning, so that they might serve God if they chose, or if they preferred he might hand them over to the king as adults to be warriors. (§ 21)

Christianity also brought another form of kinship to the Insular world: the relationship between a godparent and the person being baptised. This seems to have been a more important relationship in the Anglo-Saxon world than it was among Britons and Gaels. In the Anglo-Saxon community, the *godfaeder* or *godmoder* acted as sponsor to a candidate of the same sex at his or her baptism and received their godchild from the font following the baptism. This established an important relationship between the godparent and the person baptised, the latter becoming the godparent's 'spiritual child' (*filius* or *filia spiritualis*). The relationship may have been 'spiritual', but it had legal implications, too. In the seventh-century *Laws of Ine*, a godfather was entitled to compensation on the killing of his godson, and a godson entitled to compensation on the killing of his godfather. A godparent might also be asked to support a godchild in court, and having a royal or episcopal godfather could increase a godson's *wergeld*. Among kings and lords baptismal sponsorship also became an expression of political alliance; a king might act as sponsor at the baptism of a defeated enemy or his child. The ritual around the font became a place where kinship, religious faith and political negotiation met, and new relationships and obligations were formed.

A WOMAN'S PLACE

Much of our discussion has so far been rather male-oriented, with an emphasis on patrilineal kinship, on men and their status, their clients and their farms. Women have not featured to such a great extent. The reason for this is that we have obtained a view of this period largely from the laws, and the laws treat the free adult male as the paradigm in their account of human affairs. Indeed, not only is the free adult male the paradigm, but women are in many instances specifically excluded from central aspects of social life – especially in the Gaelic legal tradition. This was a society that understood itself to a great extent as an intertwining of sworn contracts between its members. Individuals swore oaths supported by their kinsmen and strengthened by the sworn participation of witnesses and sureties. But in most circumstances a woman was not able to enter contracts independently of her 'head' (*cenn*) or male guardian, for she was regarded as *báeth* – 'senseless, lacking legal capacity' – and her contracts were invalid, as were those of others regarded as *báeth*: 'the contract of a slave without his lord, the contract of a monk without his abbot, the contract of a son of a living father without his father, the contract of a fool or a mad woman . . .' The inability of a woman to act without her 'head' is reflected in a Gaelic tract on *díre* 'payment of honour-price':

> The worst of transactions are the contracts of women. For a woman cannot sell anything without [the consent of] one of her 'heads' (*oen a cenn*). For her father prevents her when she is a girl. Her husband prevents her when she is a wife. Her sons prevent her when she is a woman with children [after the death of her husband]. The kindred prevents her when she is a woman of the kindred [i.e., when she has no father, husband or sons, and so is reliant on other male kin].

Likewise the capacity of a woman to act as a witness was rejected as a general rule, for this would require her to give sworn evidence, something that the Gaelic legal tradition did not normally permit. This native Gaelic rejection of women's evidence was given a most peculiar twist by the clerical authors of *Collectio Canonum Hibernensis*:

> The evidence of a woman is not accepted, because the apostles did not accept the evidence of women concerning the resurrection of Christ. (CCH xvi, 3)

The fact that the women who were witnesses to the resurrection of Christ were right and the apostles completely wrong does not seem to have given the legal theorists pause for thought.

Another major incapacity for women in the Gaelic laws was their general inability to own or inherit property within the *fintiu.* When a man died his daughter could inherit some of his moveable goods, but his land would be divided among his sons; his daughter would get none of it. There were some exceptions to this general rule, however. If a woman had married a foreigner, a *cú glas*, then she might inherit a limited right to *fintiu* which she could pass on to her own sons. A more commonly occurring exception was when a man died with a daughter and no sons; then the daughter could become a female heir, or *banchomarbae*, and inherit land up to a value of fourteen cumals. But in such circumstances she inherited only a life-interest in the land, and could not normally pass on this inheritance to either her husband or her sons. On her death it reverted to the male kindred on whose behalf she had held it during her lifetime. Of course, if she had married a near kinsman and borne him sons, then her sons might inherit some right in the land on her death, but they would do so as members of their father's male kindred, not as her sons. However, the exception that allowed women to inherit a life-interest in land meant that other legal exceptions had to be made as well, for if the *banchomarbae* held land she had to be able to act in some ways as a man: to buy and sell, to make contracts with other farmers over shared ploughing, to give evidence and swear oaths, and to distrain others. Once a *banchomarbae* had a claim to *fintiu* she might also have to be able to reclaim it from another occupant by the ritual of *tellach* which was discussed above, and a special rite of *bantellach*, 'a woman's taking possession', was devised for this purpose, so that a *banchomarbae* could act legally to regain her land. And this involved her going to law, swearing oaths and getting other women to be her witnesses – all things normally beyond women's capacity.

There were other exceptions to women's general legal incapacity. A woman could swear an oath in regard to gynaecological issues: the paternity of her children, the timing of her fertile period, whether or not her marriage had been consummated and such like. The reason *Críth Gablach* gives that a king should not travel on his own is that on that day a woman might swear that he had fathered a child on her, and she needed no one else to swear in support of her. Another exception was that a woman in some kinds of marital union also maintained the right to some independent action if she had contributed half or more of the couple's joint wealth. A married woman could also impugn her husband's contracts if they were disadvantageous to their joint prosperity. But these were exceptions to a general pattern of legal incapacity.

Women under the Welsh laws shared many of the incapacities of their Gaelic sisters. A woman could not normally inherit a share of her father's land, though 'if an owner of land have no other heir than a daughter, the daughter is to be heiress of the whole land'. This was only a life-interest, however, as in the Gaelic laws. Another exception was in the case when a daughter was given in marriage by her father and brothers to a foreigner, or *alltud*; then her sons might inherit land through her, her male kin being understood to have consented to this by virtue of giving her in marriage. Again, this exception is like that in the Gaelic laws where a woman married to a *cú glas* could inherit land and bequeath it to her sons.

Welsh laws also limited a woman's ability to enter into contracts (again there were exceptions) and connected to this was the guiding principle: 'No woman is competent to act as a surety or witness against a man.' She was also extremely limited in what she could give away: a noble woman could give away clothing, food and drink, but the wife of a *tayauc*, or 'commoner', could not give away anything except her own headgear, nor lend anything 'except her sieve, and that only as far as her voice may be heard from the dunghill calling for it to be brought home.'

In comparison with the general incapacity of women found in both Gaelic and Welsh laws, Anglo-Saxon women enjoyed a wider range of rights and liberties. We can see the difference in several aspects of the early Anglo-Saxon laws, and in other documents that record the behaviour of women. They were oathworthy, able to swear independently of men and even against men, and able to grant land and receive grants on their own account. They were also able to inherit estates even when they had brothers, and to pass them on to their sons and daughters, or bequeath them to churches, servants or friends, as numerous Anglo-Saxon wills testify. Nothing of this sort has been found in a Gaelic legal context of the period.

While in Gaelic and Welsh laws most crimes committed against women required the offender to pay compensation to the woman's male guardian, Anglo-Saxon law made compensation payable to the woman herself. Likewise, where Gaelic law dealt with offences committed by a woman by requiring her male kin to pay compensation on her behalf, Anglo-Saxon law treated a woman as a responsible subject in her own right: she must pay for her own crimes.

The most striking example of the status of Anglo-Saxon women is surely that of Æthelflæd, a daughter of King Alfred who married King Æthelræd of Mercia in the ninth century. As her husband became ill and incapacitated she increasingly acted on his behalf, and on his death she became 'Lady of the Mercians' (*Myrcna hlæfdige*) and ruled on her own. She governed Mercia in close collaboration with her brother, Edward king of Wessex; she built fortifications, made war on Viking armies and made pacts with Viking settlers, granting lands to nobles in return for military service. Most extraordinary of all, on her death in AD 918 Æthelflæd was succeeded by her own daughter, Ælfwynn, as ruler of Mercia, though that only lasted for a few months. No woman with anything like this authority and independence appears in the Gaelic or British annals.

The position of Anglo-Saxon women is seen not only in the sphere of secular lordship, inheritance and law. Throughout Europe at this time women found a degree of autonomy in monasteries which offered independence of father or husband, and sometimes fulfilment in monastic life and scholarship. It seems that the relatively advanced position of Anglo-Saxon women was apparent in this context, too. There are surprisingly few women's monasteries in the British- and Gaelic-speaking churches, and those that existed seem to have been short-lived and poorly resourced in comparison with male communities. This may relate to the inability of women in those cultures to inherit more than a life-interest in land, and the reluctance of male-dominated kindreds to alienate their kin-land to women's monasteries. In sharp contrast, considerable numbers of women's monasteries were founded in Anglo-Saxon areas, some of them double monasteries where an abbess ruled over both men and women. Aldhelm's letters to the nuns of Barking in the seventh century record his admiration for these scholarly women who were evidently immersed in the study of scripture, history, grammar and poetry. Anglo-Saxon nunneries also had their own *scriptoria* where books were copied both for their own use and for distribution to others. At the Minster in Thanet in the 730s, Abbess Eadburg sent books to Boniface in Germany, who expressed his gratitude to his 'dearest sister'. Such nunneries could not have undertaken scholarship or scribal work without resources, and they were supported by generous grants of land. In the seventh century one such grant reads:

> I, Ædelmod . . . for the relief of my soul, grant to you, Beorngyð, venerable abbess, and to Folcburg, and through you to your monastery, 20 hides by the river Cherwell . . . that you may hold it by right and your authority.

In this context it is remarkable that we have good early medieval evidence for only one monastery of women in all of Scotland for the whole period under study in this book: it is the Anglo-Saxon monastery of Coldingham where both men and women served under the founding abbess Æbbe.

This chapter has relied largely on legal sources to paint a picture of life in the various communities of early medieval Scotland. While poetry and stories may sometimes offer us more vivid glimpses of someone's life, the laws provide the background against which those glimpses make sense, revealing in detail the internal workings of their respective communities, and allowing us to understand something of the motives and perceptions of the agents in those stories.

6

'Gird your sword upon your thigh'
(Psalm 44: 3)

Vikings and the Formation of Scotia

In the year 793 the *Anglo-Saxon Chronicle* recorded death and destruction at the church of Lindisfarne, the great church of Bernicia originally founded from Iona:

> In this year terrible portents appeared over Northumbria and miserably afflicted the inhabitants. These were exceptional flashes of lightning; and fiery dragons were seen in the air. A great famine soon followed. And a little after that, in the same year, on 8 January, the heathens' harrying miserably destroyed God's church in Lindisfarne by rapine and slaughter.

This is the first record, and probably a roughly contemporary one, of an attack on Britain by Scandinavian pirates or Vikings. The chronicler highlights the violent drama of the attack by citing natural disasters that preceded it. For him and his community the natural world was charged with signs that spoke to them about human affairs, about history and its meaning. In spite of Lindisfarne's close historical connection to Iona, the *Annals of Ulster* do not record this attack. Perhaps news did not reach the scribes of the chronicle, who by this time were working in Ireland rather than Iona. But the Gaels certainly began to pay attention when Norsemen turned up on their own shores in Scotland and Ireland. In the following year the *Annals of Ulster* record: 'Devastation of all the islands of Britain by heathens.' This must refer to the islands around the northern part of Britain, the Northern Isles and the Hebrides. In 795 the *Annals of Innisfallen* record further attacks in Scotland and

Ireland: 'The plundering of Iona, and of Inis Muiredaig and of Inis Bó Finne.' In the same year in the *Annals of Ulster* we find 'the burning of Rechru by the heathens, and its reliquary was broken up and despoiled' – *Rechru* represents either Lambay Island near Dublin or Rathlin off the coast of Antrim. In AU 798 an attack is recorded on another island near Dublin:

> The burning of Inis Pátraic by the heathens, and they took the cattle tribute of the territory and broke the shrine of Do-Chonna, and also made great devastations both in Ireland and in Britain.

The records lay some stress on attacks on churches. That may simply reflect the fact that the records were kept by monks and clergy who were more likely to notice raids on churches; there must have been many other attacks on farms and secular settlements which went unrecorded. It may also be that the Norse raiders saw churches as particularly profitable places to raid. The breaking up of shrines is noted in two of the above references; these contained the relics of saints which would have been decorated with precious metals and jewels, making them valuable and easily portable plunder.

It is worth considering whether attacks on churches were also motivated by a specifically anti-Christian element in Viking culture. The eastward expansion of Charlemagne's Frankish empire in the 780s and 790s, especially his devastating conquest of Saxony, had been accompanied by forced baptisms of the defeated people (in spite of the protests of leading churchmen such as the Northumbrian Alcuin). Southern Scandinavian people who saw Charlemagne's armies as an ever-growing threat must have associated Christianity with that threat, urging a particular hostility to churches and churchmen.

In addition to material plunder, these Viking raiders took captives: men and women who might be kept or sold as slaves, or held to ransom by their captors and released in return for payments of gold or silver. When Lindisfarne was raided in 793, Alcuin, now at the court of Charlemagne in Francia, wrote a letter to console the community there, promising to ask the emperor for help 'regarding the youths who have been taken into captivity', presumably intending that they should be ransomed.

These initial Viking attacks on Britain and Ireland may have begun as mere freebooting piracy by wealthy Norsemen, opportunistic raids on coastal settlements by Norse shipowners. In other circumstances they might perhaps have come as traders as they did elsewhere. At Ribe in western Denmark, for example, Norsemen were trading some seventy years before they started raiding in Britain. During such mercantile voyages they developed the maritime skills and technology for long-distance journeys which later enabled their raiding activity in Britain, Ireland and Francia.

What began as an improvised and fairly haphazard series of attacks on British coastal areas by wealthy Norsemen (the kind of men who could afford to build and man a warship) soon became an overwhelming campaign. The monastery of Iona was attacked at least five times over three decades in the earlier part of the Viking invasion, including in:

AU 793, 'all the islands of Britain' were harried;

795, according to the *Annals of Innisfallen*, perhaps by the same raiding party which burned the island church of Rechru in that year (AU);

AU 802, it was 'burned by the heathens';

AU 806, 'the community of Iona, to the number of sixty-eight, was slain by the heathens';

AU 825, the monk Blathmac was killed along with several other monks in an attack that was vividly described by the contemporary German monk Walafrid (he may have got his information from Iona monks who had migrated to Germany).

Such Viking raids were a way of obtaining moveable wealth rapidly. With the technical superiority of their longboats, able to attack scantily defended coastal sites at will, and also able to penetrate inland using lochs and rivers, they overwhelmed some areas and seized control. In Shetland and Orkney, and likewise in the Western Isles and some coastal areas of the mainland, they appear to have eliminated native communities – either by massacre and enslavement, or by putting local people to flight. Having colonised these territories, Norsemen used their island and coastal settlements in Scotland as bases for conducting raids elsewhere in Scotland and in Ireland and even further afield. An attack on the Isle of Man in AD 798 and a further raid the following year in Aquitaine on the Atlantic coast of Frankish territory are likely to have been launched ultimately – if not directly – from Viking bases in the Hebrides, and during the following years the whole Irish Sea area seems to have been reduced to a pillaging zone for Norsemen with bases in Scotland. During the first decades of the ninth century the annals frequently mention both Viking raids and native resistance in Scotland and Ireland, reaching a crescendo in the 830s and 840s. The chronicles usually contain only brief references to some fighting or destruction, or a note as to who defeated whom. Sometimes an entry sheds light on the outcome of the raid – the removal of a valuable shrine, as mentioned above, or the taking of captives, as in AU 821: 'Étar was plundered by the heathens, and they carried off a great number of women.' While large numbers of captives were taken from various places, women were a particularly valuable commodity to Norse raiders, partly because widespread female infanticide in Scandinavia meant that women were in short supply there, and partly because these were men who had sailed far from home in what must usually have been all-male companies.

The targets of Norse attacks on Scotland lay not only in the Irish Sea area. In AU 839 'the heathens won a battle against the men of Fortriu, and Eóganán son of Óengus, Bran son of Óengus, Áed son of Boanta, and others almost innumerable fell'. The Pictish names of the slain have been Gaelicised by the annalist, but we can recognise here Uuen, king of Fortriu, and his brother Bran as the two sons of Unust son of Uurgust (*Óengus mac Fergusso* in Gaelic) who had been an earlier king of the Picts.

Áed son of Boanta who fell in the same battle was the king of Dál Riata, probably ruling as an under-king of the Pictish

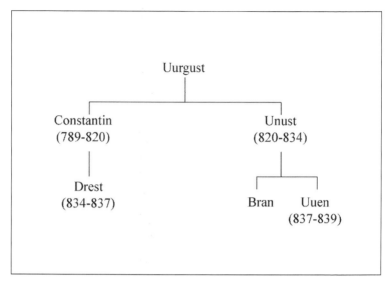

Descendants of Uurgust

ruler, Uuen, and therefore fighting for him. This catastrophic
battle should be seen as the culmination of a sustained Norse
attack on Pictish territory in the 830s. We do not know where
the slaughter took place, but the fact that the men of Fortriu
had assembled a large army – 'almost innumerable' according
to the annalist – suggests that they were prepared for a Norse
attack and had gathered to defend their territory, and that it was
probably somewhere in Fortriu, in the north or north-east of
Scotland. This defeat of the royal house of Uurgust, which had
ruled Pictland for fifty years, had a transforming effect on the
whole of northern Britain, as we shall see in due course.

But as Norsemen continued to travel 'west over sea' to Britain
and Ireland, they found more long-term and sustainable ways of
exploiting the territories they encountered. Within a few decades
of the first raids, Viking settlements in Scotland seem to have
consolidated into a regional power. There is a short but telling
entry in the *Annals of St Bertin* for the year 847, at which point
the annals were being kept by Bishop Prudentius of Troyes. By
this time there were numerous influential *Scotti* in Francia, so

it is no surprise that a Frankish chronicler should have been interested in this event:

> The *Scotti*, who for several years had been attacked by the Northmen, were made into tribute-payers. And [the Northmen] also took possession of the surrounding islands and dwelt there, with no one offering resistance.

The word *Scotti* here simply means 'Gaels', and at this stage it could refer to Irish people or to Gaels in Scotland. But the area of which the Northmen took possession, 'the surrounding islands', should be understood as being the Hebrides, the islands that lay in the midst of ninth-century *Scotia*, between Ireland and Gaelic Scotland. By 847, then, the Norse had taken possession of these islands and were in a sufficiently powerful position to extract tribute from at least some of the surrounding Gaelic population.

The annal of 847 raises an important question about the Norse settlers: what exactly does their 'taking possession' of the islands imply? We know that raiding and some degree of Norse occupation had been going on for five decades in the Hebrides, but what marked out the events of 847 as different from the immediately preceding years? Why would the annalist identify this particular year as the moment when they began to dwell there 'with no one offering resistance'? The most natural explanation is that some political settlement had taken place whereby the Gaelic kingdoms of Dál Riata, and probably their Pictish overlords in the east, had ceded control of the islands to the Norse. This would not be surprising following the massive defeat of Fortriu in 839, when Norsemen had slain the kings of Pictland and Dál Riata, and there were no doubt numerous other attacks of which no records survive. It would have been a rational response by the Pictish rulers in the east and their Gaelic under-kings in Dál Riata to accept the loss of the Western Isles in return for some hope of relief from the Norse threat. A similar tactic had been adopted by the Frankish emperor Louis the Pious (814–34). In the 820s he dealt with Scandinavian threats in the northeast of his empire by appointing a Scandinavian king, Harald, to rule in a kind of buffer-state on the far side of the Elbe – the Elbe being at that time the border of his empire. Harald became a Christian and an ally of Louis, and agreed to protect the empire from raids by other Scandinavians. Such a precedent may have found an echo two decades later in a Pictish concession of the Hebrides to the Norse. This might have involved a treaty between Norse and Pictish rulers, and perhaps even the baptism of some leading Norsemen. The arrangement would subsequently be reflected in the Gaelic names for the coastal area of the mainland, *Airer Gáidel*, or 'coastland of the Gaels' (whence the modern name of Argyll), and for the Hebrides, *Innsi Gall*, 'islands of the foreigners', that is, of the Norse.

The picture of a stable Norse polity in the Hebrides may be given further support by the record of events six years later in AU 853:

> Amlaíb (Old Norse Ólafr) the son of the king of *Laithlinde* came to Ireland, and the Norsemen of Ireland submitted to him, and he took tribute from the Gaels.

Laithlind (or *Lochlann* as it is later found, among its many and varied spellings) at this early date has traditionally been understood to refer to Norway or part of Norway, but Ó Corráin has recently suggested that it was the name of some or all of the Norse-dominated territories in Scotland – the Northern and Western Isles together with Sutherland and Caithness and parts of the west coast. If he is right, the first remarkable thing about this entry is that there was already a 'king of Laithlind' in the mid-ninth century – that is to say, a Norseman ruling Scottish territory as a king, implying that the Norse occupation and settlement of these parts of Scotland had acquired a degree of political stability. This would support the suggestion made above that Picts and Norse had come to some political settlement concerning the rule of some of the Hebridean islands.

The record of AU 853 also shows two distinct political outcomes for Amlaíb's expedition to Ireland. One is that the 'Norsemen of Ireland' (*gaill Erenn*) simply 'submitted' to him (the verb *ro giallsat* implies that they gave hostages or sureties), acknowledging their incorporation into the Norse kingship or over-kingship of Laithlind. This had probably already happened in some form in AU 849 when 'a naval expedition of seven score ships of the people of the king of the foreigners came to impose [his] authority over the Norsemen who were in Ireland before them . . .' Here we see the early signs of a politically integrated Norse polity on both sides of the Irish Sea (though no doubt there were some groups of Vikings who continued to operate independently).

The second outcome of the expedition of 853 was one that affected the native Irish, the Gaels: they were reduced to paying tribute, giving them an inferior status to that of the 'Norsemen of Ireland'. They were essentially buying off the Norse in the face of threatened violence, paying tribute without being incorporated into the ruling structures of Norse power. This condition no doubt applied only to a few parts of Ireland (and no doubt to parts of Scotland, too), in those areas where the new Norse rulers were able to enforce such an arrangement.

The advent of Amlaíb in Ireland in the mid-ninth century, together with his two brothers Ímar and Auisle, marked a new development. Viking raids launched from Scotland, which were essentially a summer-time activity, had gradually given way to Norsemen over-wintering in Ireland in the 840s, and the occupation of Irish sites now gave new opportunities for further raiding. There was an encampment of Norsemen at Dublin, *Áth Cliath*, in AU 845. As the occupation of parts of Ireland grew more stable during the 850s and 860s, the sons of the king of Laithlind, Amlaíb and his two brothers, moved their centre of operations from the Hebrides to Ireland. Henceforth, it would be Dublin, not the Scottish islands, that would be the heart of Norse politics in the Irish Sea. And these new rulers of Dublin began to play a significant role in wider Irish politics, forming occasional alliances with other Irish kings against Máel Sechnaill, 'king of all Ireland' (d. 862), as we shall see.

Following their settlement of Dublin, the sons of the king of Laithlind dominated the Norsemen in Ireland and Britain, and made war with some success on neighbouring Gaels and Picts. But the British kingdom centred on Alclud, now called Dumbarton Rock, also suffered a most dramatic blow at their hands. The entry in AU 870 begins the account:

> The siege of *Ail Cluaithe* by the Norsemen: that is Amlaíb and Ímar, the two kings of the Norsemen, besieged that stronghold and at the end of four months they destroyed the fortress and plundered it.

And the following year:

> Amlaíb and Ímar returned to Dublin from *Alba* with two hundred ships, bringing away with them in captivity to Ireland a huge prey of human beings – Angles and Britons and Picts.

The fact that it took four months to capture this place is testimony to the strength of the fortress on Clyde Rock. It was a place of great strategic importance. As the power centre of the northern British kingdom around the Clyde, it dominated the firthlands, standing near the confluence of the Clyde and the Leven. From here men in boats had access to Loch Lomond and the Lennox, but more importantly they could use the Clyde to go deep into the central lowlands and further upstream into the southern uplands.

The siege is also testimony to the power of the Dublin Norse in 870. Its four-month duration is itself remarkable and gives some idea of the scale of the action, as does the size of the fleet with at least two hundred ships. The fact that the Norsemen were able to fill these ships with not only British captives from the kingdom on the Clyde, but also with Picts and Angles, suggests that the fighting men of this large besieging army were not all sitting patiently at the bottom of the Clyde Rock for four months; they must also have been ravaging both in Pictland and in areas of Anglian settlement – perhaps the Lothians or Kyle and the southwest – to collect all these captives.

Following the siege, the British kingdom appears to have been weakened, probably placed under tribute to the Dublin Norse. Clyde Rock ceased to be its royal *caput* and Govan, twelve miles upstream, became the new main power centre. After the disaster of 870–1 the British kingdom emerged with a new name, referred to in the records now as Strathclyde (from British *Ystrad Glud*, 'valley of the Clyde'). The name first appears in AU 872, when Artgal 'king of the Britons of Strathclyde was killed on the advice of Constantín son of Cináed', king of the Picts. We can see Artgal, therefore, as the last king of Clyde Rock or Dumbarton and the first king of Strathclyde. Why Constantín should have sought his assassination is not clear, but it is surely significant that Constantín's sister was married to Artgal's son, Rhun. It may be that Artgal had selected one of his other sons to be his successor and that by having Artgal killed Constantín hoped to ensure the succession of his own brother-in-law to the kingship of Strathclyde. The British kingdom continued hereafter, its centre now apparently spanning the Clyde at Govan and Partick; perhaps we should see this as a bipartite power centre with a royal fortress or palace on the north side of the river and a royal church and burial ground on the south bank. Govan was not a new foundation in the 870s, for early Christian burials in the churchyard have been carbon-dated to the fifth or sixth century, but it must have enjoyed a rising status with the collapse of Clyde Rock and a new investment of royal patronage at Govan.

Two years after Artgal's assassination, the *Anglo-Saxon Chronicle* records the 'great heathen army', another Scandinavian group, moving northwards through England in the 860s and 870s, entering Northumbria, taking York, and, in 874, moving even further north, taking quarters on the River Tyne, and 'making frequent raids on the Picts and Strathclyde Britons'. It is likely that the defeat of Clyde Rock and the pressure of this new Norse threat from the south forced Strathclyde into an accommodation or alliance with a now Norse-dominated Northumbria. Part of the evidence for this is that, in spite of the devastation of Dumbarton in 870–1, it seems that the British kingdom of Strathclyde (also known as Cumbria, a Latinisation of British, *Cymru*, 'Britain', in modern Welsh 'Wales') enjoyed a revival during the later ninth and early tenth centuries, expanding far to the south, reoccupying former territory that had been

British but had been conquered by Anglo-Saxon Northumbria. This expansion is implied in English accounts of a royal meeting in AD 927 at which various kings accepted Æthelstan of Wessex as their overlord. By combining two different accounts of the event we obtain a picture of which rulers were there with Æthelestan: Constantin king of Scots, Owain of Gwent, Owain of Strathclyde and Ealdred lord of Bamburgh (acting as the ruler of Northumbria under Æthelstan's over-kingship). The meeting took place on the River Eamont, which flows through Penrith and Brougham, close to the line of Hadrian's Wall, and it is likely that this was seen as a boundary place, between Strathclyde and Northumbria. The expansion of Strathclyde so far south would hardly have happened if Norse armies had been continually attacking and weakening Strathclyde, and it is likely that following the destruction of Clyde Rock the Strathclyde Britons were allied with Viking power in Northumbria and Ireland, and so were permitted to expand southwards. Such an alliance would explain the cultural influence of Viking York at the highest levels of Strathclyde society, as witnessed by the presence of 'hogback' stones in southern Scotland. This is a kind of carved stone monument very much associated with Norse culture in Britain, and there are several of them in the kingdom of Strathclyde – five at Govan, one across the Clyde in Partick (now lost) and others at Luss on Loch Lomond and at Dalserf further up the Clyde. The presence of another five hogbacks in the Tweed basin (at Stobo, Ancrum, Bedrule, Nisbet and Lempitlaw) suggests that the River Clyde and the River Tweed, whose headwaters are only about five miles apart at the 'Biggar gap', may have formed an important routeway connecting the kingdoms of York and Govan.

A PATCHWORK OF POLITIES

Our discussion of the Vikings in Scotland so far has largely explored the trajectory of the most successful: they took the islands around *Scotia* in AD 847, and reduced the *Scotti* to tribute-payers; they were regarded as having a king – perhaps in Scotland – whose sons then established their own rule in Dublin from where they dominated significant parts of Ireland and Britain. But there is no reason to suppose that Norsemen acted as a single block drawn together by some kind of ethnic solidarity. Not all Norsemen formed communities strong enough to eliminate or subjugate the native population in the territories where they settled. Some settled in less powerful communities which had to negotiate with their native neighbours – Britons, Gaels or Picts – improvising different strategies for their advancement. Part of the evidence for this is found in Norse place names. If we map the distribution of the common Old Norse place-name element *dalr*, 'valley', we begin to get a picture of where Norsemen settled in Scotland and stayed long enough to plant names on their landscape. Though *dalr* is a topographical element, referring to a landscape feature, in fact, a great many of these *dalr*-names belong to farms or settlements. It is, in fact, a characteristic of the earliest settlement names that they often contain topographical elements like *dalr* or Old Norse *vík*, 'bay'.

The distribution of Scottish *dalr*-names shows a concentration largely in the Northern Isles and the Hebrides, and along the west coast of the mainland, as well as, less densely, in Sutherland and Caithness and Easter Ross. Many of the islands would in later centuries become, from a church point of view, part of the diocese of the Isles, which was a kind of ecclesiastical echo of the Norse kingdom of the Isles around AD 1100. But some of the distribution on the Argyll coast and in the Clyde firthlands is perhaps a bit surprising. After all, these areas would not become part of the diocese of the Isles. This means that there was Norse settlement in these areas in the early period of invasion, but these people either disappeared from their settlements or, more likely, became assimilated to native Gaelic society. Such an observation is supported by another set of place-name data. The Old Norse word *bólstaðr*, 'farm', is a term that seems not to have been used of primary settlements in the initial phase of occupation, but was used of secondary settlements, probably within a hundred years or so of the initial Norse occupation of an area.

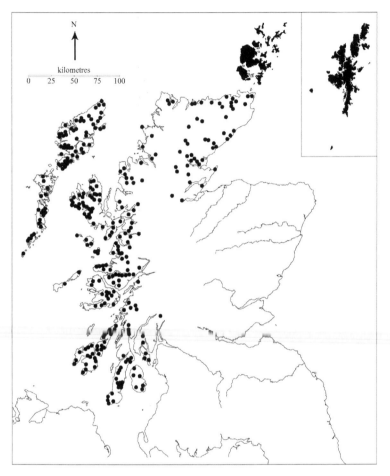

Scottish place names in dalr

The distribution of names in *bólstaðr* is in some ways similar to that of *dalr* names, but it is significantly reduced. There are no place names in *bólstaðr* southeast of the cluster on Islay, so that the whole of Knapdale, Kintyre, Arran, Bute and Cowal are free of those names. Furthermore, along the west coast of the mainland in several areas where *dalr*-names are present there is an almost complete lack of *bólstaðr*-names. Recent scholarship has suggested

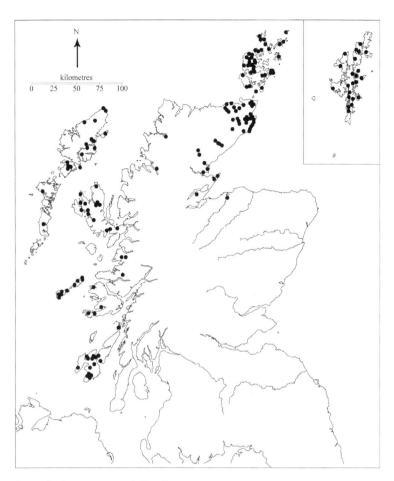

Scottish place names in bólstaðr

that in such places there was indeed Norse settlement, but it did not displace local Gaelic lordships or, if it did, those Gaelic lordships re-asserted themselves. This meant that by the time *bólstaðr* was being used in the Western Isles and the Northern Isles the descendants of Norse settlers in other places were already speaking Gaelic, assimilating to the local culture, and probably in many cases being knitted into existing native lordships.

This assimilation to local culture may have included in some cases a turning to Christianity. This idea has already been suggested in respect of those who had seized control of the islands around *Scotia* in AD 847, and who may have agreed to undergo baptism as part of a treaty with the Picts. Evidence of early Norse conversion may also be found in a discovery in the sand dunes above Kiloran Bay on Colonsay. A burial uncovered in 1882 contained a man buried in the sand within a setting of stone slabs and underneath an upturned boat. His body was laid out in a crouched position on its side, accompanied by a set of weights, some coins, an iron sword, a spear-head, an axe-head and a horse's harness. There was a horse buried beside the grave. This is clearly a Viking burial, but the setting of grave-stones was oriented east–west, as Christian burials were, and the grave was marked by two stones bearing roughly carved crosses. This is the body of a Christian, or at least those who buried him wanted him to have a Christian burial and this was what they thought it should look like. The Anglo-Saxon coins in the grave are dateable – one to between 808 and 841, the other to between 831 and 854. We cannot tell how old the coins were when they were buried, but this looks very like a Christian Viking burial of the mid- to late ninth century.

It is in such circumstances of cultural adaptation that we should locate the emerging ethnic group known to their contemporaries as *Gallgoídil* (in modern Gaelic *Gall-Ghàidheil*), a name which means 'foreign Gaels'. We should understand them as Norsemen who had improvised in the face of the threats and opportunities offered by native communities, and had adopted some aspects of Gaelic culture – notably, but not only, the Gaelic language. Perhaps they also included Gaels who had adopted aspects of Norse culture. The presence of bands of armed Norsemen had for decades provided both threats and opportunities to native rulers. The threats are obvious enough; but Norse warriors also represented a source of military power to any native ruler who was able to harness it. Such interactions between native and Norse will have often involved cultural, linguistic and religious change, and the Gallgoídil should be understood as the outcome of such change.

The Gallgoídil first appear in the annals in the mid-ninth century, when they are taking part in the power struggles of Irish and Norse rulers. In AU 856:

> Great warfare between the heathens and Máel Sechnaill supported by the Gallgoídil.

Máel Sechnaill was at this point the king of Mide, but the following year he would become king of Tara, or 'high king of Ireland'. In this annal entry we see part of the process by which he did so: a power struggle between himself, as one of the most powerful rulers in Ireland, and his 'heathen' Viking enemies, the Dublin Norse under the rule of Amlaíb and his brothers. What is striking here is, first, that Máel Sechnaill is allied with Gallgoídil and, second, that these Gallgoídil are seen as different from the 'heathen' (*gennti*). The most obvious interpretation of this passage is that the Gallgoídil were not heathen and were therefore Christians. Other annal references to this ethnic group in the mid-ninth century continue to place them in Ireland, usually taking part in military action in alliance with the Irish king Máel Sechnaill.

But the fact that these Gallgoídil were operating in Ireland does not imply that they had their origin there. In fact, the earliest non-annalistic reference to Gallgoídil gives us a very accurate location for their territory. An entry in the *Martyrology of Tallaght*, probably made in the late ninth or early tenth century, celebrates the feast of St Blane on 20 August thus: 'Blane, the bishop of Kingarth among the Gallgoídil.' Here we have a record of the Gallgoídil, not much later than the annal records, that places them in an area that includes Kingarth on the Isle of Bute, on an island where *dalr*-names are present (Roscadale, Birgidale, Burgidale), but *bólstaðr*-names are absent, suggesting a Norse population that was rapidly Gaelicised. We cannot be certain that the Gallgoídil mentioned in the annals came from precisely the place mentioned in the *Martyrology of Tallaght*. It is possible that Gallgoídil referred not to a single group, but to a number of different bands of rapidly Gaelicised Norsemen, some of whom were from the Clyde or southern Hebrides, others of whom may have emerged in Ireland. But it is a tantalising possibility that the Gallgoídil of the Clyde area were sufficiently enmeshed in Gaelic politics and warfare by the mid-ninth century to form an alliance with the high king of Ireland against the Dublin Norse.

SCANDINAVIAN IONA

As we saw above, between AD 795 and 825 Iona was raided five times by Vikings, and there may have been other unrecorded attacks. But after AD 825 no further raids on Iona are recorded for 160 years. (In AU 986, 'Iona of Colum Cille was plundered by the Danes on Christmas night, and they killed the abbot and fifteen elders of the monastery', but this was not a return to the bad old days of Viking raiding; it was rather one of several incidents in which rival rulers – both Norse and Irish – attacked each other's monasteries as a way of inflicting harm on each other.) We may ask why Viking raids on Iona ceased after AD 825. Writers have sometimes assumed that in the early ninth century there was a collapse of monastic life on Iona, so does the disappearance or near-disappearance of the monastery explain the cessation of raiding? In AU 807 we find 'the building of the new *civitas* (monastery) of Colum Cille at Kells', and it has sometimes been supposed that Kells was being constructed in the Irish midlands as a replacement, a place of safety to which the Iona monks could flee from Viking violence. In AU 814, 'Cellach, abbot of Iona, when the construction of the temple of Kells was finished, resigned the office of superior, and Diarmait the fosterling of Daigre was appointed in his place'.

The fact that it took seven years to finish the construction of the monastery may shed light on the kind of buildings which Kells had in the ninth century. These were not wattle-and-daub huts hastily erected for monastic refugees from Iona, but a collection of buildings substantial enough to require seven years for their construction. But although Kells was built at a time of crisis in Iona, it was not intended to replace its mother-house. When Cellach of Iona retired to Kells, Diarmait was appointed in his place to rule Iona. Clearly, Iona was still a going concern in 814, in spite of the threat of Viking violence. It also seems that the abbot of Iona continued to have authority not only over his own monastery, but over the whole Columban *familia*, as the 'heir of Columba'.

The building of a new monastery at Kells may nevertheless have provided some relief for the monks of Iona during the Viking attacks. Some of the monks must have gone there, and if it was seen as a less vulnerable place than Iona perhaps some of the monastery's treasures were taken there, too. But the foundation of Kells should be seen in a wider context in which Iona's place in the world was changing for several other reasons. Part of this context is the drift of the Iona leadership towards new Irish alliances for reasons quite unrelated to the Viking threat. One of these reasons was the collapsing power of the Cenél Conaill, St Columba's own kindred and the traditional supporters of Iona. From the 730s they had been eclipsed by another section of the northern Uí Néill, the Cenél nEógain whose devotion was not towards St Columba and Iona, but towards St Patrick and Armagh – a Church that was seeking to establish its own metropolitan authority over the whole of Ireland. In AD 734, Flaithbertach of the Cenél Conaill had been high king, but he was deposed in that year by Áed Allán of Cenél nEógain and forced to retire into a monastery. From that time Cenél Conaill would provide no further high king.

In addition to the rise of Cenél nEógain, another shift in power was taking place in Ireland. Flaithbertach's deposition had been accomplished by the Cenél nEógain, but their king Áed Allán was in turn slain in AU 743 by Domnall mac Murchada, king of the Clann Cholmáin, a dynasty of the southern Uí Néill. Interestingly, the battle seems to have been fought, at least according to a later addition to the annals, at Kells. Having slain Áed, Domnall was king of Tara for twenty years. On Domnall's death in AU 763, the high kingship returned to Cenél nEógain, and thereafter for three centuries there was an alternating sequence of Cenél nEógain and Clann Cholmáin kings of Tara. In this context, it is hardly surprising that Iona and the Columban monks would seek to associate themselves with the Clann Cholmáin kings. If Cenél Conaill could no longer offer Iona the support she wanted, and Cenél nEógain favoured Armagh, then Clann Cholmáin was now the natural choice. It is clear that Iona and its *familia* of churches were already building a relationship with Clann Cholmáin as early as the reign of Domnall himself, who promulgated 'the Law of Colum Cille' (*Lex Colum Cille*) in AU 753; and on his death in 763 he seems to have been buried in the monastery of Durrow, one of the earliest Columban foundations.

There may have been other reasons for Iona re-directing her attention to Clann Cholmáin in the Irish midlands during the eighth and early ninth centuries. What had been the impact of the *percutio*, or 'hammering', of Dál Riata by Unust son of Uurgust, king of the Picts, in AU 741? The long-term consequences of this dramatic event are yet to be fully explored, but it seems that Dál Riata was thereafter dominated by Pictish rulers. We should therefore see Iona as in some sense a Pictish monastery from the 740s onwards, or at least a Gaelic monastery under Pictish royal patronage. Pictish overlordship of Dál Riata may have contributed to the Columban monks' desire to restore their fortunes in Ireland by building a relationship with Clann Cholmáin.

Since Iona had been drawn into Clann Cholmáin's sphere of influence for more than sixty years by the time a new monastery was erected at Kells – which lay in territory controlled by Clann Cholmáin – we should not assume that its construction was entirely motivated by the need to escape from Viking raids on Iona, nor that Kells displaced Iona as the centre of power for the Columban *familia*. The relics of Columba remained on Iona, providing saintly backing to the abbot's claim of authority, and the abbots of Iona continued for some time to be heads of the Columban *familia*. The fact that Viking raids on Iona ceased after AD 825 therefore suggests that Iona, still an important church ruled by a powerful abbot, was developing a relationship with its new Norse overlords; perhaps they could see an advantage to themselves in having control of this significant ecclesiastical centre. Such a development makes sense in a mid- to late ninth-century context where, as suggested above, some Norsemen in western Scotland were already adopting Christianity as witnessed by the Christian–Viking burial on Colonsay. Henceforth, the cult of St Columba and the monastery of Iona would serve as symbols of a gradually Christianising Norse culture and lordship in the Isles and more generally in the Irish Sea world.

A PICTISH EMPEROR

The arrival of the Vikings meant that new identities were emerging in western Scotland, as we have seen. Norsemen first raided and then settled in areas of hitherto Gaelic, Pictish and British culture, transforming those areas in some respects while at the same time adapting themselves to local cultures. In eastern Scotland, too, changing identities and cultures can be traced. But in this case the transformation had less to do with the immediate impact of the Norse than with a long-term infiltration into Pictish society of Gaelic culture and Gaelic kindreds from the west. We discussed this process at some length in Chapter 2, including the observation that Gaelic-speaking clergy were at the core of the administrative and legal class who were essential to the management of kingship, and also provided the intellectual resources for its legitimation. There are other indicators of Gaelic Church influence in Pictland, such as the fact that the *Cáin Adomnáin*, or 'Law of the Innocents', gained support in AD 697 not only from the Gaels of Ireland and Britain, but also from the Pictish king Bruide and Bishop Curetán, apparently the bishop at Rosemarkie in Easter Ross. We should not underestimate the significance of this law as a step towards the creation of a Gaelic Scotland. It represents the subjection of a Pictish kingdom and its rulers to a Gaelic law and to a Gaelic monastery's administration of that law.

Since the 730s, the Gaels of the west had to a great degree become subject to Pictish overlordship, with the devastation of Dál Riata and the seizure of Dunadd in AU 736, and the 'hammering' of Dál Riata in AU 741, as we saw above. Sporadic bouts of resistance are recorded – a battle in AU 768, for example, and during the reign of Pictish king Constantin son of Uurgust (789–820) – but Pictish control of the Gaelic west seems to have been fairly stable. It was stable enough for Constantin to impose his own son, Domnall, as king of Dál Riata from 811 to 835. This Pictish overlordship in the west explains otherwise strange references in the ninth century to parts of western Scotland as 'Pictish'. Walafrid Strabo's account of the Vikings' murder of Blathmac on Iona in AD 825, written only a few years later, refers to Iona as 'a certain island on the shores of the Picts' (*insula Pictorum quaedam . . . in oris*). Similarly, Loch Lomond appears in the *Historia Brittonum* (written around AD 830) as lying 'in the region of the Picts' (*in regione Pictorum*). It is possible that these two texts are simply confused in their geography, but a better assumption would be that they reflect the westward expansion of Pictish rule at the time.

There is little sign of Dál Riata breaking free of Pictish control during the reigns of Unust (729–61) and his successors. Pictland was a powerful and confident polity, with a strong dynasty at its heart. The expansion of Pictish interests during this period is also attested in their relations with Anglo-Saxon kingdoms and the Britons of Clyde Rock. We know that at least two Northumbrian kings were deposed and exiled to Pictland in the eighth century, Alhred in 774 and Osbald in 796. Pictish rulers must have been only too ready to play whatever cards they held to maximise their influence in Northumbria, and building links with royal exiles was one way to do this. Another way of expanding influence was by patronage of churches. The names of three Pictish kings appear in the *Liber Vitae* of the great Northumbrian church of Durham. This 'book of life' contains the names of benefactors for whom her monks were obliged to pray. The earliest benefactors may actually have made their gifts to the church of St Cuthbert on Lindisfarne, but they were remembered later when the Lindisfarne community was put to flight by Viking raids and ended up in Durham where they had carried the body of their patron saint. The *Liber Vitae* begins with a list of royal benefactors, and it includes Unust,

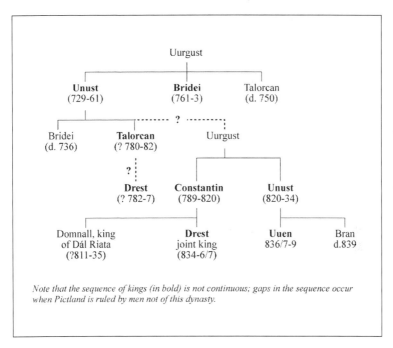

A conjectured Pictish dynasty: the descendants of Uurgust

his probable grandson Custantin (789–820) and great-grandson Uoenen (the Uuen who died in AU 839). The appearance of this powerful Pictish dynasty in Durham's book points to a southward-looking Pictland, with rulers keen to build links with Northumbrian churches, and so to extend their power in that territory.

It seems that we also have glimpses of Unust acting in alliance with the ruler of Mercia in the English Midlands. Bede's *Continuator* notes in AD 740 that 'Æthelbald king of the Mercians, by wicked trickery, laid waste part of Northumbria while their king Eadberht was busy with his army against the Picts.' This could be seen as a military collaboration between Unust and Æthelbald, with the Picts and Mercians acting in concert against Northumbria. It would be unwise to read too much into this record on its own, but an alliance between Unust and Æthelbald is also indicated by the *Continuator*'s entry for AD 750: 'Cuthred, king of the West Saxons, rose against Æthelbald and Unust.' According to Bede himself, Æthelbald held overlordship over all the English kingdoms south of the River Humber, including the West Saxons (HE v, 23), so there is nothing surprising about a West Saxon king rebelling against him. But the idea that a West Saxon king could have 'risen' against both Æthelbald and Unust implies that these two rulers were presenting themselves as joint *imperatores* of, respectively, southern and northern Britain. This represents a huge claim on the part of Unust, and for a while this king of the Picts does seem to have been the most powerful ruler in northern Britain.

This *imperium* may have been sustainable in respect of his power over Dál Riata, but it would not last in respect of the Dumbarton Britons. AU 750 records 'a battle between the Picts and the Britons, in which fell Talorgan son of Uurgust, the brother of King Unust'. The *Annales Cambriae* add the detail 'that is the battle of *Mocetauc*', which probably locates the battle at Mugdock (NS558768), in what must have been a boundary area between Pictish and British territories. We may presume from the death of his brother that Unust was defeated in the battle at Mugdock. Meanwhile, Bede's *Continuator* records King Eadberht of Northumbria pushing northwards against the Britons and conquering 'the Plain of Kyle' (*campum Cyil*) in what is now Ayrshire. Where Unust was losing power over the Britons, Eadberht found success. This must explain the entry in AU 750, 'The ebbing of the power of Unust.' Unable to dominate the Britons on his southwestern flank, and with Northumbria gaining some of their territory, Unust could no longer present himself as *imperator* of northern Britain. The ebbing of Unust's power did not bring his kingship to an end, however. He formed an alliance with King Eadberht of Northumbria, according to Symeon of Durham, in AD 756, marching on the British citadel of Clyde Rock, obtaining their submission there (an expedition which ended in disaster for Eadberht, whose army was slaughtered ten days later on their journey from *Ouania*, which is possibly Govan, to *Newanbirig*). And Unust was still *rex*

Pictorum when he died in AU 761. During the thirty-two years of his reign he had dominated northern politics, and even after his 'ebbing' his Pictish kingdom was still dynamically engaged with Northumbrian power.

The engagement with Northumbria during Unust's reign is also manifested in cultural exchange. It seems likely that this Unust was the founder of the church of St Andrews and that the eighth-century sarcophagus that survives there was carved and erected for his entombment in the church he had founded. The carving of its panels shows the interweaving of artistic traditions from Pictland, Northumbria, Rome and Byzantium. It bears many allusions to royal power and prestige, playing with imperial imagery. On the main panel the massive image of the biblical King David dominates the whole, rending the jaws of a lion (recalling 1 Samuel 17: 34–6); but the biblical figure is dressed in the garb of a Roman emperor and is wearing the imperial brooch, or *kaiserfibel*, at his throat. This image proclaims Unust both as divinely appointed ruler like David and as Roman *imperator* (like the Emperor Justinian depicted with a similar brooch in a sixth-century mosaic in San Vitale, Ravenna). In this carving the sword on David's thigh – or should we treat this carving as a portrait of Unust, and call it Unust's thigh? – has aroused some art-historical comment as being an oddity. But its position on the king's thigh is surely another expression of royal potency using biblical imagery. In Psalm 44, a poetic celebration of God-given royal power, the king is urged, 'O mighty one, gird your sword upon your thigh.' The sword on the king's thigh on the sarcophagus can therefore be seen as an expression of the biblical ideology of divinely ordained kingship, an ideology that Adomnán and the Iona community had long been at pains to 'sell' to Pictish kings. Indeed, Adomnán records that it was by singing precisely this psalm, Psalm 44, that Columba terrified the Pictish king, Bruide, when the local court magicians were trying to silence him (VC i, 37). One might wonder if Psalm 44 had become a kind of royal anthem in Pictland. And in a context like this, when regnal succession was moving towards containment within a single patrilineal descent (the rule of Unust's descendants for most of the period from 729 to 839 represented a new pattern of dynastic continuity in Pictland), Psalm 44 would also provide divine backing for such a development: 'Sons shall be yours in place of your fathers; you will make them rulers over all the land.'

The kingdom of the Picts extended its overlordship during the eighth and early ninth centuries, having the upper hand for at least part of the time in relation to British and Northumbrian power, and completely dominating the Gaelic west. But it also absorbed cultural influences from those territories, together with powerful individuals and kindreds. So though Gaelic-speakers in the west were regarded as living in *Pictavia* in the political sense, many of the *Picti* in the east were becoming linguistically and culturally Gaelic. What would Bruide and Nechtan, sons of a Gaelic royal dynasty but kings of the Picts in the later seventh and early eighth centuries, have made of the question, 'Are you a Gael or a Pict?' Perhaps they would have challenged the assumption underlying the question on the grounds that it confused genealogy, language and political power. And such a confusion underlies many of our own difficulties concerning key events in ninth-century history, in particular. the rise to power of Cinaed mac Ailpín (popularly Kenneth MacAlpine), and the emergence of *Alba* and *Scotia* as the names of the kingdom formerly imagined as Pictland, ruled by his descendants. These processes involved a transformation of Pictland, the understanding of which continues to challenge the historian, and which we will now explore.

WAYS OF READING

First we must acknowledge that we are faced with serious difficulties in seeking to give an account of this transformation. In comparison with the quantity and quality of historical sources that we have used for the seventh and early eighth centuries, when we explore the late eighth and ninth centuries we enter something of an information desert. And even more alarmingly, the information that we do have is not by and large from contemporary witnesses, but from later writers whose writings are shaped by the demands of their own circumstances a century or more after the events they purport to describe, and by the literary traditions in which they operated. The most important single source is one found in a fourteenth-century manuscript in the Bibliothèque nationale in Paris, the 'Poppleton Manuscript'. In its pages we find texts first composed long before the manuscript was made, giving accounts of kings and their reign lengths, their ancestry, the events that took place in their reigns and the territories they ruled. These documents have exercised a great influence over the way historians have imagined the ninth century, but they have sometimes been used a little naively. We are particularly interested in two of these texts: a Pictish king-list and the text that follows it in the manuscript, generally known as the *Chronicle of the Kings of Alba* (hereafter CKA, though it is sometimes known by other names such as the *Scottish Chronicle* or the *Chronicle of the Kings of Scotland*). Although they have some integrity of their own as they stand in the manuscript, these two are themselves actually composite texts, woven together from several strands of material, and have gone through various stages of writing and re-writing. We will return to this aspect of CKA in due course, but for now it will suffice to remind ourselves of the complex nature of the material and the care needed in reading it.

The Pictish king-list contains the supposed names of dozens of kings of the Picts. Some of the later ones can be identified with kings who appear in other contemporary or near-contemporary sources, but with respect to the earlier ones we are generally at a loss to make any connection between the name and any person known to us from elsewhere. Although the text is composed in Latin, the spelling of the personal names in the original core of the Pictish king-list suggests that it originates in a Pictish-language context: it has Pictish *Bredei* rather than the Gaelic spelling of the name *Bruide*; Pictish *Onust* and *Urgust* rather than Gaelic *Óengus* and *Fergus*. It contains a foundation legend for the monastery of Abernethy, which strongly suggests that part of its creation took place in that Pictish mon-astery, probably in the ninth century. The legend says that the monastery was founded by a Pictish king, but it is worth noting that it also gives a decidedly Gaelic slant to Abernethy's origins: it is dedicated to the Irish St Brigid, it was co-founded by an Irish nun, Darlugdach, and the king himself is said to have been in exile in Ireland just before founding it.

At some point (probably in the mid-ninth century) new mate-rial was added to the beginning of the Pictish-language section. It begins with a foundation legend for the kingdom of the Picts.

> Cruidne son of Cinge was the father of the Picts living in this island. He reigned for one hundred years and had seven sons. These are their names. Fib, Fidach, Floclaid, Fortrenn, Got, Ce, Circinn. Circin reigned for sixty years; Fidaich for forty; Fortrenn for seventy; Floclaid for thirty; Got for twelve; Ce for fifteen; Fibaid for twenty-four.

This passage is followed by the names and reign lengths of a further six kings, and then a series of 'thirty Brudes'. We will turn to the Brude section shortly, but for the present we will look at the material on Cruithne and his seven sons. First, we note that this passage is a Latin version of an earlier Gaelic poem which survives in supplementary material in the *Lebor Bretnach*, in one of whose manuscripts the poem reads:

> *Morfeiser do Chruithne claind*
> *Raindset Albain i seacht raind.*
> *Cait Ce Cirig cetach clann,*
> *Fib Fidach Fotla Fortreand.*
> > *Et is e ainm cach fir dib fil for a fearand, ut Fib, Ce,*
> *Cait et rel.*

> Seven of Cruithne's children
> divided Alba into seven parts:
> Cait, Ce, Cirig, children with hundreds;
> Fib, Fidach, Fotla, Fortriu.
> > And the name of each man of them is on his territory,
> such as Fib, Ce, Cait and the rest.

There are several interesting things to note about these two versions of the Pictish foundation legend. The first is that the spelling of the personal names clearly shows a Gaelic origin, not only in the Gaelic verse but also in the Latin prose version. The name of the founder, Cruithne, is simply the old Gaelic word for 'Pict'; *Cruidne filius Cinge pater Pictorum* simply means 'Pict son of Champion, father of the Picts'. There are also four names beginning in F, which would typically have initial U in Pictish spelling. Alba, the territory they divided, is the Gaelic word for Britain and subsequently for Pictland (we will return to this shift in meaning in due course).

The note at the end of the poem states that each of the seven sons gave his name to a territory that formed part of Pictland or Alba. Some of these we can identify: *Fib* is Fife, *Fotla* is a shortened form of *Athfhotla*, the name which survives as modern Atholl. *Fortriu* is the name of what was probably the most powerful northern Pictish kingdom (*Fortrenn* in genitive), whose kingship had at some times been synonymous with the over-kingship of all the Picts. *Cait* is the far north – Sutherland (which is *Cataibh* in modern Gaelic, a dative plural form of the name) and Caithness (a Norse name, *Katanes*, meaning 'promontory of the Cat-folk'). *Cirig* or *Circinn* is the name for the Mearns in medieval Gaelic texts. One can understand why a Scottish historian might fall on such a story with a glad cry: here we have a window onto the political structure of ninth-century Pictland!

Alas, there is something rather artificial about this list of kings. The names of the sons and their territories fall into two groups on two lines; all the first group begin with C- and all the second group with F-. This makes for satisfying alliteration from a poetic point of view, but its artificiality obscures the identities of the territories that the ninth-century poet had in mind. *Fidach*, for example, is not now identifiable – if it ever was. The name means simply 'woody', which hardly narrows it down in ninth-century Scotland. The names also fit suspiciously well to the rhythmic scheme of the poem, which has seven syllables in each line – metrics may have been more important here

than precise recording of political territories. It is probably a
mistake, therefore, to seek to identify each of these territories
with ancient territorial units within a 'greater Pictland'.

There may be a further artificiality about this story of
Cruithne and his sons. These men constitute a nation-founding
community of eight, which may be an echo of a long tradition of
narrating the foundation of a people or nation in terms of eight
founders. Craig Haggart has noted the occurrence elsewhere
of a 'company of eight' founding a kingdom. In the *Historia
Brittonum* the island of Britain is described as being taken by
someone called Damhoctor 'whose descendants remain there
to this day'. The British author has misunderstood the term
in his source, however, as Damhoctor is not a personal name
but an Old Gaelic phrase, *dám ochtair*, meaning a 'company
of eight persons'. Another founding eightsome appears in the
Lebor Gabála Érenn, or 'book of the conquests of Ireland',
whose earliest version dates to the eleventh century, though
later versions followed. This work begins with some biblical
history as background, including an Irish version of the story
of Noah's Flood. It describes Noah, his wife, his three sons and
their three wives as a *muintir ochtair*, 'a company of eight'. And
after the Flood, of course, this company of eight emerges from
the ark and occupies and repopulates the entire world, for 'the
Flood drowned the seed of Adam except for Noe and his three
sons, Sem, Ham, Iafeth, and their four wives Coba, Olla, Oliva
and Olivana'. This suggests that the Cruithne legend about a
company of eight occupying and populating land may have a
biblical model. There may be other echoes of Noah's world-
founding eightsome in other sections of *Lebor Gabála Érenn*.
When Partholon and his family take Ireland in a subsequent
wave 'eight persons (*ochtar*) were their number' – he, his three
sons and their four wives, corresponding exactly to the makeup
of Noah's *ochtar*. And in the final wave of invaders it is again an
eightsome who occupy Ireland:

Ocht meic Golaim na ngáire
darb ainm Mílid Easpaine

ro sleachtadar míli mag
ca tír as a táncadar?

The eight sons of Golam of the laughings,
whose name was Mil of Spain,
they cleared a thousand plains:
what was the land from which they came?

The notion that the legend of Noah-plus-seven may have helped to shape our text is perhaps reinforced by the fact that the Cruithne-plus-seven story in *Lebor Bretnach* is followed by a passage tracing Cruithne's ancestry back to Japheth son of Noah. Given this tradition of the founding *ochtar*, perhaps we should see in Cruithne and his seven sons not a reflection of Pictish political geography, but a kind of Gaelic–Pictish recapitulation of a biblical theme.

What we do hear in the story of Cruithne and his seven sons is a claim that Pictland is – or should be – a single united territory, albeit one containing subdivisions, stretching from Caithness in the north to Fife in the south. It is significant that this story is told in a Gaelic milieu, because by the mid-ninth century Gaelic-speakers occupied positions of power in Pictland. In the legend of Cruithne they sought to assert the antiquity of Pictland, and to relate it to a paradigm whose origins lay in the great and authoritative story of Noah in the book of Genesis, validating their definition of the country and legitimating their power: this is what the occupation of land and the creation of a people ought to look like.

We may now turn to another part of the Pictish king-list. The story of Cruithne and his seven sons is followed by the names of six other kings, and then a whole list of people apparently called 'Brude':

Brude Bont, after whom thirty Brudes ruled Ireland and Britain for a period of one hundred fifty years. He ruled for 48 years, that is Brude Pant. Brude Urpant. Brude Leo, Brude U[r]leo, Brude Gant, Brude Urgant, Brude Gnith, Brude Urgnith . . .

So the list continues until 'Brude Mund, Brude Urmund', the last being the twenty-eighth in the sequence, not the thirtieth as

the opening passage stated. Let us look at the use of Brude and
the claim that there were thirty rulers of this name. First, we
may doubt that there really were thirty kings in succession, all
named Brude. One possible explanation for this sequence is that
an earlier version of the list stated that there were thirty kings
between Brude Bont and *Bridei filius Mailcon*, and that a later
scribe misunderstood it as saying that there were thirty kings
called Brude, and so created a list of them and inserted them
here.

But there is another interesting aspect of the list of *brudes*. It
is possible that at some point in the text's development *brude*
was understood not as a name but as a title, so that this was
seen as a list of *brudes* called Pant, Urpant, Leo, Urleo and so
on. That is not to deny that Brude or Bruide in Gaelic, Bridei or
Bredei in Pictish, was also a personal name. But in this context,
where all the kings have other personal names as well, *brude*
looks much more like a title. If *brude* was being used as a title
here, what did it mean to the scribe who transmitted this aspect
of the text? We should bear in mind that the text as we have it
now is the work of a Gaelic scribe working with material, possibly of Pictish origin, that he may not have fully understood.
So we might look for a Pictish word, perhaps meaning 'king' or
'ruler' or something of that sort, which a Gaelic-speaking scribe
rendered instead as a personal name, Brude, which was already
familiar to him. One such word that might suggest itself is a
hypothetical Pictish word for 'judge', a word cognate with Old
Welsh *brawt*, 'judgement' (cf. Welsh *brawdwr*, 'judge'; there is
an also Old Gaelic cognate of this word in *brithem*, 'judge'). If
the term *brude* in our list represents a Gaelic-speaking scribe's
misunderstanding of a Pictish term, we might hypothesise a
Pictish word meaning 'judge' as the origin of the 'thirty Brudes'.
The Picts would not be the only ones to regard some rulers as
judges in the early Middle Ages. In *Y Gododdin* we come across
Uruei described as *ut Eidyn*, or 'ruler of Edinburgh'. The word
ut, here translated as 'ruler', is actually a loan-word into Old
British from Latin *iudex*, 'judge'.

If the list of *brudes* in the king-list was originally a Pictish list of rulers who were seen as 'judges', might this shed light on political theorising in Pictland? It might tempt us to suggest that rulers had some kind of judicial role, deciding the outcome of legal disputes. More likely, I would suggest, is that *brude* is an echo of the biblical story of the arrival of the tribes of Israel in their 'promised land'. Joshua led them across the Jordan and got them to swear to obey God (Joshua 24:26ff.). Having thus established a new 'state', though not yet a kingdom, Israel suffered great troubles, so the Lord established a sequence of judges (*iudices*) to deliver them from the hands of their enemies (Judges 2:16). But a repeated refrain occurs thereafter: 'In those days there was no king in Israel, and everyone did what was right in his own eyes.' Finally, the people demanded a king, and Samuel, the last judge, acceded to their demand (1 Samuel 8). This biblical pattern – the establishment of a nation, its rule by judges, and its final acquisition of kings – could be seen as the model for the sequence of *brudes* understood as 'judges' in the Pictish king-list. It constructs an origin legend for Pictland using the reigns of thirty 'judges' as a conscious echo of the biblical narrative.

Interestingly, the *Lebor Bretnach* story of the foundation of Pictland makes precisely this connection to the Bible story. Noting that the *brudes* ruled Scotland for 150 years, 'as is found in the books of the Picts', it adds that 'Alba was without a king all that time until the time Gud, the first king, took all of Alba by negotiation or by force.' The statement that the nation was without a king is surely a reference to the repeated refrain in the period of the biblical judges, 'there was no king in Israel', clearly suggesting that the author of the *Lebor Bretnach* list saw the *brudes* as Pictish rulers comparable to the judges of Israel. And it is worth observing in this context that some of the manuscripts of the shorter Pictish king-lists mention that Cruithne himself was a *iudex clemens*, 'a merciful judge', which may be another attempt to locate Pictland within a biblical schema of rule by judges.

If we remove all the *brude* forms from the king-list, we are still left with a puzzle. In this list the names form pairs, each pair consisting of a name followed by that name with the prefix *Ur-* added to it: 'Pant, Urpant, Leo, Urleo, Gant, Urgant, Gnith, Urgnith . . .' and so on. To explain this strange pattern we may look at similar occurrences in other king-lists and genealogies. The section on Gwynedd in the Welsh Genealogies in Harleian MS. 3859, for example, offers a striking parallel:

> *Ouen map Higuel map Catell . . . map Cein map Guorcein map Doli map Guordoli map Dumn map Gurdumn map Amguoloyt . . .*

In this sequence *Guor* seems to be the British cognate of *Ur* in the Pictish king-list, and seems to function in the same way in a sequence of names: a name is followed by the same name repeated with a prefix. Now, if we remove the occurrences of *map*, 'son of', from this section we are left with a section reading: *Cein Guorcein Doli Guordoli Dumn Gurdumn Amguoloyt . . .* The word *guor* (modern Welsh *ar*) seems to mean 'on, on top of', a cognate of Old Gaelic *for* 'on, upon, in succession to, after'. This would allow us to propose that our list of *brude* names was the result of a genealogist incorporating an earlier Pictish king-list, without understanding it, which read:

A
after A, B
after B, C
after C, D . . .

This would offer a satisfactory explanation of the strange pairings of names and the prefixed forms found in both Pictish and Welsh texts. If this suggestion is right, it would also add the word *ur*, 'on' (and perhaps also 'after') to what little we know of the Pictish language.

The foregoing discussion reminds us that the texts we rely on for an understanding of ninth-century Scotland are not only few and far between, but are problematic and must be read in ways that allow for several forms of confusion and distortion. These include at the very least:

(i) A surviving text can be composed of several distinct strands, written at different times and in different languages, spliced together at various points in the process of its creation. It is not always easy to say which parts were added when.

(ii) Medieval writers were not primarily concerned to represent the past accurately, but to create a 'useable past', one that served their present-day agenda.

(iii) Their writing – much like our own – reflected their own theological, cultural and political perspectives, and depended on biblical and classical models.

(iv) Later medieval writers sometimes simply misread, misunderstood and mis-copied the earlier sources they incorporated into their work.

We will bear this in mind as we look at the material that has traditionally been exploited to explain the later ninth-century history of Scotland.

WHAT HAPPENED TO PICTLAND?

By the end of the ninth century, most contemporary Latin writers ceased referring to a people called *Picti*, or to a country called *Pictavia*, and Gaelic chroniclers no longer referred to *Cruithne* 'Picts', or *Cruithentúath* 'Pictfolk, Pictland'. A new terminology appeared: the people became *Albanaich* in Gaelic or *Scotti* in Latin, named after a territory now called *Alba* or *Scotia*.

There is a conventional narrative, broadly accepted until recently, which talks of the 'union of the Picts and Scots' or even the conquest of the Picts by the Scots. It says that after the disastrous defeat of the Picts of Fortriu in AU 839, a king of Dál Riata called Cináed mac Ailpín exploited the weakness of the Picts and conquered their kingdom. Under his powerful rule the two distinct kingdoms of the Scots (Dál Riata) and the Picts were united in a Gaelic kingdom that would become known as *Alba* or *Scotia*, whence Scotland in English. The story has recommended itself to generations of readers for various reasons, one of them being that it might explain the disappearance of the

Pictish language and the eventual dominance of Gaelic in much of what had once been Pictland. However, the disappearance of the Pictish language may be explained by the much longer process of Gaelicisation that we have already discussed, which makes the idea of a 'Gaelic conquest' unnecessary.

Another factor that has encouraged people to accept the conventional story is a passage in CKA which states that Cinaed mac Ailpín was 'the first [king] of the Scots' and:

> He ruled this Pictland happily for sixteen years. Now Pictland (*Pictauia*) was so-called from the Picts (*Picti*) whom, as we have said, Cinaed wiped out. For God deigned to estrange them and render them dead to their own inheritance, because they not only spurned the Lord's Mass and precept, but also refused to be equal to others in the law of justice. He indeed, two years before he came to Pictland, had taken over the rule of Dál Riata.

Clearly, this passage supports the traditional idea of a conquest of Pictland by a king of Dál Riata. But we should remind ourselves that Dál Riata had been more or less continually subject to the kings of Picts since the mid-eighth century. The near-complete disappearance of Dál Riatan kings from the record suggests a kingdom in a state of collapse, and such a collapse can only have been accelerated by the continued dominance of Pictland to its east, and the ferocious assaults of Norsemen from the north and west. The picture of this collapsing kingdom suddenly rising up in the 840s and conquering Pictland is not a compelling one.

Second, we must remember that the core text of CKA began life as a king-list (a list of rulers and their reign lengths) in the late tenth century. We know this because the place where the reign length of Cinaed son of Máel Coluim (AD 971–95) should have been entered is left blank: *Cinadius filius Maelcolaim regnauit . . . an[nis]*. The scribe left it blank because Cinaed was still reigning, and so his reign length was unknown. During the century-and-a-half of its development up to this point it began with an original chronicle of kings' names and reign lengths, together with records of events that took place during their

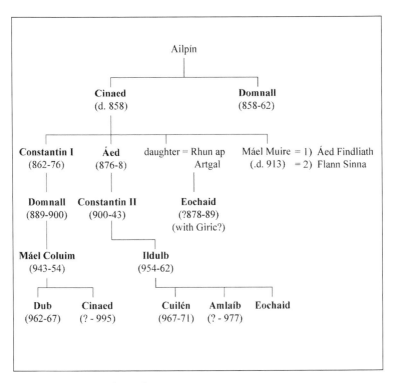

```
                              Ailpín
                                |
          ┌─────────────────────┴─────────────────────┐
        Cinaed                                      Domnall
        (d. 858)                                    (858-62)
           |
   ┌───────┼────────────┬──────────────────────────┐
Constantin I  Áed   daughter = Rhun ap    Máel Muire = 1) Áed Findliath
(862-76)     (876-8)            Artgal     (.d. 913)  = 2) Flann Sinna
   |            |                  |
Domnall   Constantin II        Eochaid
(889-900)  (900-43)           (?878-89)
   |                          (with Giric?)
   |          └──────┐
Máel Coluim        Ildulb
(943-54)          (954-62)
   |                 └────┐
┌──┴────┐         ┌───────┼────────┐
Dub    Cinaed   Cuilén  Amlaíb   Eochaid
(962-67) (? - 995) (967-71) (? - 977)
```

'Reges Scotorum' *after Ailpin*

reigns. Some of these apparently came from a chronicle kept in a Pictish church, perhaps Dunkeld, and are more or less contemporary with the events they record. Other stories were later spliced into this material, including the story of Cinaed mac Ailpín's destruction of the wicked Picts because of their sins. This is a much later theological gloss on what by this time had become a popular narrative about the creation of the *regnum Scottorum*, the Kingdom of the Scots.

By the time the core text of CKA was created in the later tenth century, Cinaed mac Ailpín, his brother Domnall and nine of Cinaed's direct descendants had enjoyed almost complete dominance of the regnal succession (see genealogical table). We say 'almost complete' because the reign of Eochaid (878–89), son of Rhun and grandson of Cinaed, is recorded by CKA as having been compromised by the role of Girig, his *alumnus* and *ordinator*. There may have been some power-sharing between Eochaid and Girig at this point, but the identity and kinship of Girig is in doubt. It may be that *alumnus* is a scribal error for *auunculus*, 'uncle', in which case Girig was a member of the same family as Eochaid, perhaps a son of Domnall mac Ailpín. In any case, from the 830s until the reign of Cinaed son of Máel Coluim one dynasty's dominance allowed tenth-century writers to project back into their past the known fact of their present identity, which was by now thoroughly Gaelic, to create a legend of the 'founding ancestor' of their kingdom. That is why they can call Cinaed 'the first [king] of Scots', *primus Scottorum*. But there is no reason to think that Cinaed mac Ailpín would have thought of himself as the first king of Scots, or as king of Scots at all. Indeed, on his death in 858 he is called *rex Pictorum*, 'king of the Picts' by the *Annals of Ulster*. And during his reign, in what is probably a contemporary record rather than a later insertion in CKA, his territory is referred to as *Pictauia*. The same is true of Cinaed's successors *Domnall . . . rex Pictorum, Custantin rex Pictorum and Aedh . . . rex Pictorum*, who died, respectively, in AU 862, AU 876 and AU 878. They were not seen by the contemporary annalists as rulers of a Gaelic kingdom or 'of Scots'. They were 'kings of the Picts'.

It is not until AU 900 that Cinaed's successors are called anything other than kings of the Picts by the annalists. In this year, Domnall son of Constantin, Cinaed's grandson, is referred to in his death notice as *rí Alban*, 'king of Alba'. The terminology for the kingdom has changed, but not because of any conquest or change of dynasty. On the contrary, the descendants of Cinaed mac Ailpín remain firmly in control and will continue to rule for some time. But these rulers and the scholars or scribes who record significant events during their reigns had begun to use a new name for the same kingdom. The kingdom of the Picts had not disappeared; it had not been conquered and wiped out by a Gaelic-speaking kingdom. But it had been re-imagined by its own Gaelicising rulers and elites who had created for themselves a new narrative accounting for the origins of their power, stressing the kingdom's identity in a new way, stressing a Gaelic dimension to their identity.

It may be that Cinaed mac Ailpín had Gaelic ancestry, or he may have been of a Pictish family, or both. The contemporary evidence does not allow us to say, and the later evidence is unreliable because it is conditioned by the reconceiving of *Pictauia* as *Alba*, and by the emerging Gaelic self-consciousness during the decades following his death. He may or may not have ruled Dál Riata before acquiring the kingship of *Pictauia*. The passage in CKA that tells us he did is not a reliable witness. But even if he did, he might have done so as the scion of a Pictish family whose power extended over the Gaelic west, rather than as a member of a native family of Dál Riata. Of course, even if Cinaed had royal Pictish ancestry he may well also have spoken Gaelic, having to wield power in what was a culturally and linguistically hybrid Gaelic–Pictish kingdom.

In respect of Cinaed's possible Dál Riatan origin, there is an interesting detail in Cinaed's entry in CKA: 'In the seventh year of his reign he brought the relics of St Columba to the church which he had built.' This is one of those contemporary chronicles in CKA's king-list, and the church in question seems to be the monastery and later cathedral of Dunkeld, which would enjoy a close association with kings of Pictland–Alba for several centuries. This was the great church of Atholl, the name of a territory that was still a kingdom when the death of 'Talorgan son of Drostan, king of Atholl (*rex Athfoitle*)' was recorded in AU 739. The name Atholl appears in the record in various guises, but it appears to represent Gaelic *ath-Fhotla*, or 'new Ireland', implying that there was sufficient Gaelic settlement in the area by the early eighth century for it to be perceived as an 'Irish' or Gaelic territory. This might be confirmed by the dedications of early Iona saints in Atholl and upper Tayside: Columba himself at Dunkeld and Moulin, and a number of dedications to Adomnán (Glen Lyon, Ardeonaig, Dull) and Bishop Céti of Iona (Fortingall, Kenmore, Logierait). If Atholl was an early Gaelic enclave in the highlands of southwestern Pictland, these dedications to Iona saints suggest that the Gaelic settlers brought their saintly devotions with them. We might then ask why Cinaed chose to identify Dunkeld as his royal church and to move some relics of St Columba there, as he did in about AD 849. Was it the action of a man with close connections to a Dál Riatan dynasty, as later genealogists claimed, who sought to bring his own family's patron saints into his newly acquired Pictish kingdom? Or was it the action of a Pictish ruler who sought to appropriate the spiritual power of Columba and Iona by absorbing these relics into his own Pictish domain? Or was it simply a measure to ensure that, even though Iona was now under the control of Scandinavian settlers, Columba's relics would still provide protection to his devotees in Pictland?

The traditional narrative of Cinaed mac Ailpín as a potentate of Dál Riata who somehow managed to conquer Pictland does not hold water. The earliest text suggesting that the rulers of Alba were descended from rulers of Dál Riata is found in the *Míniugud Senchasa fher nAlban* – a tenth-century text, albeit one containing some earlier material. And Cinaed's descent from the most high status of Dál Riata kindreds, the Cenél nGabráin, is not attested anywhere until the tenth-century genealogy of the kings of Alba attached to an earlier text, *Cethri Prímchenéla Alban* ('the four chief kindreds of Alba'), in the reign of Constantin son of Cuilén (995–7). Such texts were put together in the tenth century to satisfy late tenth-century needs. They are not evidence of the ancestry of a Pictish ruler in the earlier ninth century.

REBRANDING PICTAVIA

Recent scholarship, especially the work of Dauvit Broun, has transformed our understanding of the so-called 'union of Picts and Scots'. It has also interrogated the evidence for the creation of a new identity. As we have noted, around AD 900 the kingdom formerly known as *Pictavia*, 'Pictland', began to be described in new terms which reflect the increasingly Gaelic-speaking identity of the kingdom. The Latin names *Scotia* and *Scotti* originate in Latin names for Ireland and its inhabitants, but from at least the eighth century *Scotia* was also used to refer to the parts of Scotland where Gaelic (the language of the Irish) was spoken. Thus, Bede could refer to Iona as lying in *Scotia*. There was therefore already a certain eastward slippage of the term's reference as early as the 730s, at least in the English perspective. It is interesting in this context to note what seems to be a contrasting point of view in Adomnán's writings: when Columba left Ireland to go to Scotland and Iona, he was going from *Scotia* to *Britannia*, suggesting that Adomnán did not naturally think of Scottish Dál Riata as part of *Scotia*, even though he regarded himself and his neighbours as *Scotti Brittanniae*, 'the Gaels of Britain' (VC ii, 46). As the Gaelic language spread further east, the adoption of *Scotia* as a new Latin name for Pictland around AD 900 reflects the triumph of that language – though not, as we have seen, the triumph of a Gaelic kingdom over a Pictish one. The same perspective appears in Anglo-Saxon sources, which begin to refer to the country as *Scotland*, and its inhabitants no longer as *Peohtas*, 'Picts', but as *Scottas*.

The triumph of the Gaelic language over Pictish, and of Gaelic culture and laws over some earlier Pictish traditions, is clear enough. And this would be sufficient to explain the change in the name of the country and its people to *Scotia* and *Scotti* in Latin (e.g., in CKA), and to *Scotland* and *Scottas* in Anglo-Saxon sources. Ironically, however, in the triumphant Gaelic language, the former *Pictavia* was given a name that stressed not its Gaelic character but its British origin. The new Gaelic name for the former Pictland was *Alba*, which had formerly been the Gaelic name for the island of Britain as a whole. The new name stressed the kingdom's Britishness, its non-Gaelic origin, while doing so in the Gaelic language. This is a re-branding of some subtlety. It is also one that plays creatively on the Picts' own way of conceiving and representing themselves.

It seems that the Picts' own word for themselves in earlier centuries, in their own language, had stressed their Britishness. In British the word *Pryden* or *Prydyn* was used to refer to the Picts or Pictland, and the Picts probably had a very similar word for themselves in their own language. This word is very similar to the Old British word for the island of Britain, *Prydain*. In Old Welsh sources these two words for 'Britain' and 'Pictland' are regularly confused – which will surprise no one – and both words have their origin in the earlier (pre-Roman) Celtic word for the whole island of Britain, *Priteni* or *Pritani* (clearly the origin also of Latin *Britannia*).

This raises a most interesting question: why did the Picts think that they were particularly 'British', as distinct from the Welsh or the Strathclyde Britons, and could therefore claim the use of *Pryden* for themselves? It may be that the Picts stressed their Britishness to highlight the fact that unlike the Britons further south they had never been part of the Roman Empire. They were therefore the 'true British'. They may have recognised that their language had not undergone the Latinisation that had affected the southern British during and after the Roman occupation of Britannia. The differences between British and Pictish had been significant enough in the 730s for Bede to identify them as two distinct languages, in spite of their presumed common origin. The Picts may also have been encouraged to use a term meaning 'Britain' of themselves by the fact that most of Britannia to the south of them now spoke Anglo-Saxon rather than British.

The Old Gaelic word for Pictland and for the Pictish people as a whole was *Cruithentúath*, which compounded the Gaelic word *Cruithne*, 'a Pict', with the word for a 'tribe' or 'people', *túath*. But *Cruithne* had originally meant simply 'British'; it was the Gaelic (Q-Celtic) cognate of the P-Celtic *Pritani/*Priteni*. With Gaelic *Cruithne*, therefore, the same narrowing of reference had taken place, from 'British' to 'Pictish', distinguishing the Picts from the rest of the island of Britain in terms of their Britishness – just as the Picts had done with their name for themselves. This change in the meaning of *Cruithne* among Gaelic-speakers probably reflected the shift in meaning of *Pryden* etc. that the Picts themselves had adopted.

The same change in meaning from 'Britain' to 'Pictland' also took place with the Gaelic name *Alba*, which Cinaed's dynasty finally gave to their kingdom. *Alba* originally referred to the whole island of Britain, but during the ninth century contemporary writers in Gaelic began to use *Alba* to refer in particular to the kingdom formerly known as **Pryden* to its inhabitants, and as *Cruithentúath* to the Gaels. Just as the Picts had hijacked a word for 'Britain' to refer to themselves, so the new Gaelic elite of the kingdom were hijacking the Gaelic word for 'Britain', *Alba*, making the same identification of Pictland with the 'true Brits'. In other words, the re-naming of *Pryden* as *Alba* (and in Latin as *Albania*) did not represent a rejection of the notion of Pictland, but a new assertion of its distinctive identity and its ancient British roots, using new Gaelic terminology.

We naturally try to imagine the political and cultural circumstances in which such a re-branding made sense. One possible factor is that it may have been particularly urgent for the rulers of Pictland to re-assert its 'British' identity just as the Pictish language was disappearing. By re-naming the kingdom in Gaelic in this way, the new rulers could give the new language a central place in the nation's identity, while at the same time insisting on the kingdom's solidly British roots and its unshakeable continuity with the past. Did the adoption of *Alba* imply an argument in something like this form: 'The Pictish language is disappearing, but the kingdom of the Picts remains'?

There is a feature of Scottish place-name history that may provide an insight into this period of transformation. There was a Pictish word **pett* which referred to a certain type of land-holding or farming settlement. The word survives in hundreds of Scottish place names in the form Pit-X. One important aspect of *pett*-names is their distribution. Apart from a tiny handful, they all lie in the territory that was once Pictland, which sometimes encourages people to think of them as 'Pictish place names'. But there is a second interesting feature of these *pett*-names: most of them have a second element from the Gaelic lexicon. Pitlochry contains Gaelic *luachair*, 'rush, rushy place, marsh'; Pittenweem contains Gaelic *uamh*, 'cave'; Pitcorthie contains Gaelic *coirthe*, 'standing stone'. In other words, these are Gaelic place names, not Pictish, coined by Gaelic-speakers using a term they had borrowed from Pictish and used, almost entirely in Pictland, presumably in a period when both Gaelic and Pictish were being spoken there. *Pett must have been part of the Pictish vocabulary relating to land management – matters of local lordship, tribute or render from tenants and subjects, and so on. The fact that the term *pett was absorbed into Gaelic in Pictland strongly suggests that there was a continuity of these economic and political practices from the Pictish period, but a continuity of practice accompanied by linguistic change. The process could almost be seen as a kind of 'icon' representing the wider pattern of continuity and change which saw Pictland turning into *Alba*.

CONCEIVING A NATION

The re-naming of Pictland as *Alba* involved not only an insistence on continuity with its ancient past, but also a degree of re-imagining or re-conceiving of identity. The Gaelicisation of the kingdom encouraged historians some generations later to offer genealogies of earlier rulers of Pictland and Alba which gave them roots in Gaelic-speaking Dál Riata, and beyond that in Ireland. But other forces were at play in the conception of Alba. We have already mentioned in this chapter the impact of Viking raids in the north and west of Scotland where Norsemen laid waste and then took political and military control of swathes of territory. But eastern Scotland, the core territory of Pictland, was not immune to such attacks. The *Annals of Ulster* and CKA refer to many Scandinavian attacks on Pictland during the ninth century. And we should probably assume that the attacks that are mentioned represent only some instances of what must have been a long and sustained campaign. The great battle of AU 839 was probably the single most significant event:

> A battle of the heathens against the men of Fortriu in which Uuen son of Unust, and Bran son of Unust, and Aed son of Boanta fell, and others almost innumerable fell.

One of the consequences of this battle in Fortriu in northern Pictland, the heartland of some of the most powerful rulers, was the collapse of the powerful dynasty of Unust son of Uurgust, which had probably ruled Pictland for most of the century from

AD 729. As a result, rulers in southern Pictish territories were able to assert themselves militarily and politically as the new rulers of Pictland. This may be the best explanation for the rise of Cinaed mac Ailpín. With his church at Dunkeld and his palace at Forteviot, his rule brought a southward shift in Pictland's centre of gravity. But southern Pictland was far from safe. Viking attacks are recorded here, too, in the heartland of Cinaed's territory. During his own reign (842–58) CKA records that the Scandinavians (*Danari*) 'laid waste *Pictauia* as far as Clunie and Dunkeld'. In the same period also 'the Britons burned Dunblane' – perhaps taking advantage of some weakening of Cinaed's kingdom in the face of Scandinavian attacks, though such 'weakening' did not prevent him from invading *Saxonia* six times, once as far south as Melrose (now in Scotland but then deep in English territory). It is worth recalling that it was during this Scandinavian pressure on Cinaed's kingdom that the *Annals of St Bertin* recorded that 'the Northmen took possession of the surrounding islands [of the *Scotti*] and remained there since no one resisted'. Cinaed evidently had enough of a challenge to defend his territory in Pictland proper; it would have been madness to have tried to hold on to the western islands too.

Norse pressure continued in the 860s during the reign of Cinaed's son, Constantin (862–76). Early in his reign CKA records, probably from a contemporary chronicle: 'Amlaíb with his people laid waste *Pictauia* and he dwelt there from 1st January until the feast of St Patrick (17 March).' This is a short reference to what must have been a formidable assault by the rulers of Scandinavian Dublin, two and a half months of violence and destruction. This is no mere hit-and-run attack in the old Viking piratical way, but a determined attempt to bring Pictland into subjection. And in AU 866, 'Amlaíb and Auisle went with the foreigners of Ireland and Britain (Alba) to Fortriu, and they plundered the whole of Pictland (*Cruthentuaith*) and took away hostages from them.' These hostages were supposed to guarantee the future docility of Constantin and his kingdom – the payment of tribute and probably the guarantee of Pictish military support when called for, as such subjection required.

We have already noted the huge siege of Clyde Rock by Amlaíb and Ímar in AU 870, its destruction, and the transportation of 200 ships full of captives back to Dublin in the following year. These captives comprised 'Angles, Britons and Picts', a fact which again points to sustained raiding in Pictish territory and the capturing of Pictish people in considerable numbers. During Constantin's reign CKA also records that 'Amlaíb was killed while taking tribute' (the text's *centum* is an error for *censum*, the tribute taken from a conquered people). CKA states that this was in the third year of Constantin's reign (863 or 864), but this is clearly wrong for Amlaíb continues to appear in the annals for some years afterwards, in AU 869 and in the siege of Clyde Rock in AU 870–871. The phrase *tercio anno* in CKA may be an error for *decimo tercio anno*, 'the thirteenth year', which would give a date of 874 or 875 for Amlaíb's tribute-raising in Pictland and his death there. All this was warfare of a type long-familiar to Gaels and Picts: the attacks and destruction, the seizure of hostages, the enforcement of tribute were all part of the 'normal' violence of Insular politics by which one kingdom brought another into subjection. And from the point of view of the Dublin Norse, this was a far more effective way of obtaining wealth and power in the long term than running around raiding monasteries and coastal settlements.

A new force was to threaten the Picts at about this time, however. CKA reports 'a little later . . . a battle in Dollar between *Danarii* and *Scotti* . . . and the Norsemen (*Normanni*) stayed a whole year in *Pictauia*'. Part of this passage about the reign of Constantin is garbled, but it suggests that invaders penetrated Pictland as far as Atholl (*Achochlam*). The reference probably represents the same event as that reported by the *Anglo-Saxon Chronicle* for AD 874:

> In this year the host went from Repton, and Halfdan went with part of the host to Northumbria and took winter quarters on the river Tyne; and the host overran that land, and made frequent raids against Picts and against the Strathclyde Britons.

'The host' here is 'the great heathen army' already referred to, moving north from Northumbria under the leadership of Hálfdan. One of their 'frequent raids' against the Picts must be the one referred to in AU 875: 'A battle of the Picts against the Dark Foreigners (*Dubghallu*), and a great slaughter of the Picts was made'. In the same year, in the following entry, AU records the death of Oistín son of Amlaíb, king of the Dublin Norsemen, 'by the treachery by Albann'. The name Albann here is Hálfdan. Unfortunately, the text does not make it clear whether Hálfdan killed Oistín in northern Britain while he was raiding the Picts and Britons – in which case we must assume that Oistín had been there at the same time pursuing his father's policy of trying to hold both Britons and Picts in subjection – or in Amlaíb's and Oistín's home territory of Dublin. Constantin himself was slain the following year, possibly at Inverdovat (NO419276) on the north coast of Fife, and probably by Hálfdan's Norsemen as some later medieval king-lists suggest, though this is not indicated by CKA or the *Annals of Ulster*.

The impact of the Dublin Norse and of Hálfdan's great army from the south probably brought Pictland close to collapse during the 870s. Such was the danger that in AU 878 'the shrine of Colum Cille and his other relics arrived in Ireland, in flight from the foreigners'. As these relics were normally kept at Dunkeld, we may assume that Pictish rulers feared that Atholl itself would be not only attacked but utterly overwhelmed. It is about this time that some confusion in regnal succession appears in the record of CKA. After the death of Constantin in AD 877, CKA states that Áed ruled for one year and was slain in *Nrurím* or *Uturím* – now unidentifiable – and then Eochaid ruled for eleven years, 'though some say that Giric ruled', suggesting a disputed succession. According to the same source, both Giric and Eochaid were expelled from the kingdom, and perhaps a degree of stability returned with the accession of Domnall son of Constantin (889–900). Although 'the Norsemen laid waste Pictland' during his reign, according to CKA, there was 'a battle *inuisibsolian* between *Danarii* and *Scotti*, and the *Scotti* had the victory', though later it seems from a slightly damaged passage in CKA that Domnall was slain by the 'heathens' at the Pictish fort of Dunnottar.

By the time Constantin son of Áed came to rule in AD 900, the rulers of Pictland, later Alba, had managed for over a century to prevent the long-term Norse domination of their core territories. One reason for their success must have been the achievement of the descendants of Cinaed mac Ailpín in welding together a single and perhaps increasingly centralised kingdom under the rule of a single dynasty. The subdivisions of Pictland, formerly sub-kingdoms or *prouinciae* in Bede's view, were becoming more firmly knitted into a single state. The successors of minor kings lost their royal status, becoming *mormaers*, regional rulers under a single Pictish king. Thus, in CKA, in material that probably originates in ninth-century Abernethy, Nechtan is called *rex omnium prouinciarum Pictorum*, 'king of all the provinces of the Picts'. Furthermore, as elsewhere in Europe, kingship was increasingly understood in terms of territorial authority, rather than authority over a people, thus making distinctions between Pict, Gael, Norse, Angle or Briton less significant.

This process of consolidation must have had legal and constitutional aspects which are largely unrecorded, but we do get a glimpse of one in the reign of Domnall son of Ailpín (858–62) when CKA states that 'the Gaels (*Goedeli*) made the rights and laws of the reign of Áed mac Echdach with their king at Forteviot', the Pictish royal palace in Strathearn. Áed mac Echdach had been king of Dál Riata a century earlier, and had fought against Cinaed, king of the Picts, in AU 768, presumably attempting to break free of Pictish overlordship. It seems that he failed, but he was still king of Dál Riata when he died in AU 778, and it is likely that his rule was allowed to continue because he made some kind of legal submission to Pictish overlordship. What CKA is describing in the ninth century, when 'the rights and laws of the reign of Áed mac Echdach' were made 'by the Gaels with their king', is a renewal of the treaty of submission by the rulers of Dál Riata (or what was left of it after the Viking seizure of much of its territory) to the rulers of the Picts.

Other accounts of legal reform can be found in the reign of

Giric (878–89) who, according to a later king-list, 'first gave freedom to the Scottish church, which had been in servitude until that time following the custom and use of the Picts'. It is possible that the earlier Pictish Church had been more directly under the control of secular rulers, while the Church in the Gaelic-speaking tradition had enjoyed more independence. An example of such secular control of the Church may perhaps be seen in the actions of Nechtan mac Derile over the Easter-dating dispute in the early eighth century. Bede describes Nechtan ordering all the Pictish churches to change their practice, taking on himself a role that some bishops might have thought was properly theirs. But perhaps we should understand Giric's later reform not simply as the triumph of Gaelic over Pictish constitutional thinking so much as an example of the new thinking about church–state relations that was taking place more widely in western societies. One of the ideas that interested the Céli Dé movement had been the question of the *sóerad*, or 'freeing', of a church. If a church fulfilled its duties of sacramental celebration of baptism and Eucharist, if it prayed as it should for the living and the dead, if it supported scholarship, then it was entitled to a certain status. If it lacked these things, then its independence lapsed, and it lost its proper character as a free (*sóer*) church, and could perhaps be taken over by a secular lord and lose revenues too. A similar concern to define the proper relationship between church authority and royal power appears in Gaelic legal texts, in the *Collectio Canonum Hibernensis*, and in Carolingian church councils.

It is therefore striking that kings of Pictland and Alba during this period adopted the name Constantine (it appears in the records in various forms as Constantin, Custantin, Castantin), for this was the name of the first Christian Roman emperor. As churchmen of the ninth century reflected on church–state relations, they used the memory of the first Christian Roman emperor, Constantine, as a paradigm for the proper behaviour of a ruler in church affairs. The Irish scholar Sedulius Scottus worked in the schools of Carolingian Francia from the 840s until at least 860. His work *De rectoribus Christianis* ('on

Christian rulers') uses Constantine as a guiding figure. The ruler is to 'do those things which are pleasing to God' – to rule with justice and mercy, to have wise friends and advisers, to avoid pride and vainglory, and to support the church, complying with the 'wholesome admonitions and corrections of the bishops'. Allowing himself to be guided in these ways by the bishops – for he is a Christian and a member of their flock – his rule will be blessed by God and his people will enjoy peace and prosperity. Sedulius also tells the ruler to summon regular decision-making synods of Church leaders:

> For a holy council of bishops is the precious crown of a religious ruler. In this the most famous emperor, Constantine the Great, rejoicing in the Lord, gloried. He assembled the holiest men from almost all the peoples under heaven to whom the Gospel of Christ had been preached . . . for the discussion of the Catholic faith in one body, the Council of Nicaea

The ruler, however, is not to interfere with the formulation of holy teaching, for that is the prerogative of the clergy. Pictish and then Scottish kings must have kept an eye on such develop ments of political–ecclesiastical thinking. Their interest in the name 'Constantine' echoes the ideological use of the Roman emperor's memory in the Frankish world, where Charlemagne and his successors presented themselves as Constantine's heirs. And in the year 906, CKA records:

> In the sixth year [of his reign] King Constantin and Bishop Cellach, on the Hill of Faith (*colle credulitatis*) beside the royal *civitas* of Scone, vowed to keep the laws and the disciplines of the faith and the laws of the churches and of the Gospels, *pariter cum Scottis*. And from that day this hill has deserved its name, that is 'the Hill of Faith'.

The adverbial phrase '*pariter cum Scottis*' is something of a puzzle. It may modify the verb *custodire*, 'to keep', and so would mean that the kingdom of Alba would keep the laws and disciplines 'in the same way as the Gaels', and this is how it has generally been understood. But there are other ways of reading it. The word *pariter* can mean 'together', and if the phrase modifies the verb *deuouerunt*, 'they vowed', it would mean that Constantin and Cellach swore their oath 'together with the *Scotti*' – as the people of Alba/Scotia were now termed. An alternative understanding would be that *pariter* is being used in the sense of 'in the same way as', and so implies that the actual rite of oath-swearing was carried out in conformity with a 'Scottish' or 'Gaelic' fashion in some way we cannot now discern.

Whatever the precise meaning of *'pariter cum Scottis'*, it is inconceivable that Constantin and Cellach were acting alone. This act must have been the climax of a church synod at which the bishops, clergy and monks of Scotia had gathered under royal patronage, at the royal *civitas* of Scone. On the 'Hill of Faith' in 906, Constantin of Alba was fulfilling the duty of a Christian ruler, following the example of his Roman imperial namesake.

We can see the forty-three-year reign of Constantin as putting the seal on the re-branded kingdom. It was during his reign that the kingdom and its people are first referred to in Anglo-Saxon as *Scotland* and *Scottas*. He seems to have enjoyed a stable rule over a kingdom that stretched from the Forth in the south, northwards beyond the Mounth into Fortriu. It was bounded on the west by the mountains of Drumalban. It is unlikely that he enjoyed much power over Dál Riata, much of the west of Scotland now being under the control of Norsemen. Having beaten off attacks from the Dublin Norse, Alba was probably now gaining the benefits of some form of collaboration with them, allowing them trading opportunities. It may be that Constantin married his daughter to Amlaíb son of Gothfrith, king of Dublin. Certainly, there was an alliance in AD 937 when Constantin joined Amlaíb and Owain king of Strathclyde in an attack on England. While it was a military disaster for Constantin (probably part of the reason he had to resign and enter a monastery in AD 943), it reflected a new rapprochement between Alba and Dublin. Perhaps political negotiation and commercial relations became more profitable than warfare. The appearance of hog-back stones in Alba from the following century or so indicates that Norsemen – merchants as much as warriors – were finding a role for themselves in Alba, with the consent of its rulers, along the trading routes of rivers and coastal waters where these hog-backs are found, as well as in Strathclyde. Other alliances may be indicated by the fact that Constantin's aunt, Máel Muire daughter of Cinaed, was married to two Irish high kings: Áed Findliath (d. AU 879) and his successor Flann Sinna (d. AU 916).

By the time Constantin retired into monastic life at St Andrews the Pictish language had probably disappeared from much of his kingdom. The Gaelic-speakers in Pictland–Alba had long had the edge in military and political power, and probably in scholarship and administration, too. The Pictish symbols, which during the preceding three or four centuries had been carved on stones all over Pictland – clearly important, though their meaning and function are still unknown to us – disappeared from the repertoire of public monuments. The kingdom of the Picts had survived, but had been transformed both in name and in character. Alba, known to its southern neighbours as Scotland, formed the embryo that would expand in coming centuries to dominate and then absorb the British and Anglo-Saxon territories to the south and the Norse territories to the west and north, all of which would eventually become part of medieval Scotland, and of the modern nation.

Bibliography

There is no substitute for returning – again and again – *ad fontes*, to the original sources for the understanding of our history. These include documents in Gaelic, British, Anglo-Saxon, Old Norse and Latin. They also include place names and surviving inscriptions on stone, which are essentially 'micro-documents' of their period. The following selection offers some essential reading. Publications of primary sources are marked with an asterisk. Many of these primary sources (sometimes in the editions cited below) can also be found online. Abbreviations used for references to such primary sources in this book include:

AU *Annals of Ulster*; see Mac Airt and MacNiocaill (1983). (NB: events recorded in the *Annals of Ulster* for our period are usually dated one year earlier than they should be. References to AU in the present book give the corrected year.)

CCH *Collectio Canonum Hibernensis*; see Wasserschleben (1885).

HE Bede, *Ecclesiastical History*; see Colgrave and Mynors (1991); McClure and Collins (1994).

VC Adomnán, *Life of Columba*; see Anderson and Anderson (1991); Sharpe (1995).

VSC Bede, *Life of St Cuthbert*; see Webb and Farmer (1965).

A handful of books should be highlighted as of fundamental importance to the study of our period. Two fine works in the *New Edinburgh History of Scotland* are James Fraser's *From Caledonia to Pictland: Scotland to 795* (Edinburgh, 2009) and Alex Woolf's *From Pictland to Alba: 789–1070* (Edinburgh, 2007). Two works by Thomas Charles-Edwards should also be regarded as indispensable: *Early Christian Ireland* (Cambridge, 2000) and *Wales and the Britons* (Oxford, 2013).

The following list includes monographs, articles and some edited collections that contain several chapters which represent recent scholarship in a field.

Aitchison, N., *Forteviot: A Pictish and Scottish Royal Centre* (Stroud, 2006).

*Anderson, Marjorie O., *Kings and Kingship in Early Scotland* (Edinburgh, 1973).

*Anderson, A. O. and M. O Anderson (eds), *Adomnán's Life of Columba* (Oxford, 1991).

Ballin Smith, B., S. Taylor and G. Williams (eds), *West Over Sea: Studies in Scandinavian Sea-Borne Expansion and Settlement Before 1300* (Leiden and Boston, MA, 2007).

Bannerman, J., *Studies in the History of Dál Riata* (Edinburgh, 1974).

Bannerman, J., 'The Scottish takeover of Pictland and the relics of Columba', *Innes Review*, 48 (1997): 27–44.

Breeze, D. J., *Roman Scotland: Frontier Country*, 2nd edn (London, 2006).

Breeze, D. J., *The Antonine Wall* (Edinburgh, 2006).

*Bieler, L. (ed.), *The Irish Penitentials* (Dublin, 1975).

*Bieler, L., *The Patrician Texts in the Book of Armagh* (Dublin, 1979).

*Binchy, D. A. (ed.), 'Bretha Crólige', *Ériu*, 12 (1938): 1–77.

*Binchy, D. A. (ed.), *Críth Gablach* (Dublin, 1941).

Broun, D., 'The origin of Scottish identity in its European context', in D. Crawford (ed.), *Scotland in Dark Age Europe* (St Andrews, 1994), pp. 21–31.

Broun, D., 'Dunkeld and the origin of Scottish identity', *Innes Review*, 48 (1997): 112–24.

Broun, D., 'Pictish kings 761–839: Integration with Dál Riata or separate development', in Sally Foster (ed.), *The St Andrews Sarcophagus: A Pictish Masterpiece and its International Connections* (Dublin, 1998), pp. 71–83.

Broun, D., '*Alba*: Pictish homeland or Irish offshoot?' in P. O'Neill (ed.), *Exile and Homecoming* (Sydney, 2005), pp. 234–75.

Broun, D. and T. O. Clancy (eds), *Spes Scotorum: Hope of Scots: Saint Columba, Iona and Scotland* (Edinburgh, 1999).

Brown, P., *The Cult of the Saints: Its Rise and Function in Latin Christianity* (Chicago, 1981).

Campbell, E., *Saints and Sea-Kings: The First Kingdom of the Scots* (Edinburgh, 1999).

Campbell, E., 'Were the Scots Irish?' *Antiquity*, 75 (2001): 285–92.

Carver, M., *Portmahomack: Monastery of the Picts* (Edinburgh, 2008).

*Carey, J., *King of Mysteries: Early Irish Religious Writings* (Dublin, 1998).

*Cary, E. (ed.), *Dio's Roman History*, vol. IX (London and Cambridge, MA, 1927).

Charles-Edwards, T. M. (ed.), *After Rome* (Oxford, 2003).

Charles-Edwards, T. M., 'Celtic kings: "priestly vegetables"?' *Early Medieval Studies in Memory of Patrick Wormald* (Aldershot, 2009), pp. 65–79.

Clancy, J., *The Earliest Welsh Poetry* (London, 1970).

*Clancy, T. O. (ed.), *The Triumph Tree: Scotland's Earliest Poetry, 550–1350* (Edinburgh, 1998).

Clancy, T. O., 'Iona in the kingdom of the Picts: a note', *Innes Review*, 55(1) (2004): 73–6.

Clancy, T. O., 'Philosopher-king: Nechtan mac Der-Ilei', *Scottish Historical Review*, 83 (2004): 125–49.

Clancy, T. O., 'The Gall-Ghàidheil and Galloway', *Journal of Scottish Name Studies*, 2 (2008): 19–50.

Clancy, T. O., 'Gaelic in Scotland: advent and expansion', *Proceedings of the British Academy*, 167 (2010): 349–92.

Clancy, T. O., 'The kingdoms of the north: poetry, places, politics', in Alex Woolf (ed.), *Beyond the Gododdin: Dark Age Scotland in Medieval Wales* (St Andrews, 2013), pp. 153–75.

*Clancy, T. O. and G. Márkus, *Iona: The Earliest Poetry of a Celtic Monastery* (Edinburgh, 1995).

Clarke, D., 'Reading the multiple lives of Pictish symbol stones', *Medieval Archaeology*, 51 (2007): 19–39.

Clarke, D., A. Blackwell and M. Goldberg, *Early Medieval Scotland: Individuals, Communities and Ideas* (Edinburgh, 2013).

*Colgrave, B. (ed.), *The Life of Bishop Wilfrid by Eddius Stephanus* (Cambridge, 1927).

Collins, R., 'Soldiers to warriors: renegotiating the Roman frontier in the fifth century', in F. Hunter and K. Painter (eds), *Late Roman Silver: The Traprain Treasure in Context* (Edinburgh, 2013), pp. 29–43

*Colgrave, B. and R. A. B. Mynors (eds), *Bede's Ecclesiastical History* (Oxford, 1991).

Crawford, B., *Scandinavian Scotland* (Leicester, 1987).

Creighton, J., *Coins and Power in Late Iron Age Britain* (Cambridge, 2000).

Dark, K. R., 'A sub-Roman re-defence of Hadrian's Wall?' *Britannia*, 23 (1992): 111–20.

Davies, J. R., *The Cult of St Constantine* (Glasgow, 2010).

Davies, W., *Wales in the Early Middle Ages* (Leicester, 1982).

Driscoll, S. T., *Alba: The Gaelic Kingdom of Scotland*, AD 800–1124 (Edinburgh, 2002).

Driscoll, S. T., *Govan, from Cradle to Grave* (Govan, 2004).

Driscoll, S. T., J. Geddes and M. Hall (eds), *Pictish Progress: New Studies on Northern Britain in the Early Middle Ages* (Leiden and Boston, MA, 2011).

Dumville, D. N., 'The Chronicle of the Kings of Alba', in S. Taylor (ed.), *Kings, Clerics and Chronicles in Scotland, 500–1297* (Dublin, 2000), pp. 73–86.

Dumville, D. N., 'Ireland and north Britain in the earlier Middle Ages: contexts for *Míniugud senchasa fher nAlban*', in C. Ó Baoill and N. R. McGuire (eds), *Rannsachadh na Gàidhlig 2000* (Aberdeen, 2002), pp. 185–211.

Dumville, D. N., 'Cethri Prímchenéla Dáil Riata', *Scottish Gaelic Studies*, 20 (2006): 170–91.

Dumville, D. N. et al., *Saint Patrick*, A.D. 493–1993 (Woodbridge, 1993).

Edmonds, F. and P. Russell (eds), *Tome: Studies in Medieval Celtic History and Law in Honour of Thomas Charles-Edwards* (Woodbridge, 2011).

Etchingham, C., *Viking Raids on Irish Churches in the Ninth Century* (Maynooth, 1996).

Etchingham, C., *Church Organisation in Ireland*, AD 650 to 1000 (Kildare, 1999).

Evans, N., 'Ideology, literacy and matriliny: approaches to medieval texts on the Pictish past', in S. T. J. Driscoll, J. Geddes and M. Hall (eds), *Pictish Progress: New Studies on Northern Britain in the Early Middle Ages* (Leiden and Boston, MA, 2011), pp. 45–65.

Fleming, R., *Britain after Rome: the Fall and Rise, 400–1070* (London, 2010).

Farr, C., *The Book of Kells, its Function and Audience* (London and Toronto, 1997).

Follett, W., *Céli Dé in Ireland: Monastic Writing and Identity in the Early Middle Ages* (Woodbridge, 2006).

Forsyth, K., *Language in Pictland: The Case against 'non-Indo-European Pictish'* (Utrecht, 1997).

Forsyth, K., '*Hic Memoria Perpetua*: the inscribed stones of sub-Roman southern Scotland', in S. M. Foster and M. Cross (eds), *Able Minds and Practised Hands: Scotland's Early Medieval Sculpture in the Twenty-First Century*, Society for Medieval Archaeology Monograph Series (Leeds, 2005), pp. 113–34.

Foster, S., *Picts, Gaels and Scots* (London, 1996).

Foster, S. (ed.), *The St Andrews Sarcophagus: A Pictish Masterpiece and its International Connections* (Dublin, 1998).

Fraser, I. (ed.), *The Pictish Symbol Stones of Scotland* (Edinburgh, 2008).

Fraser, J. E., 'Adomnán, Cumméne Ailbe, and the Picts', *Peritia*, 17/18 (2003/4): 183–98.

Fraser, J. E., 'The Iona Chronicle, the descendants of Áedán mac Gabráin and the "Principal kindreds of Dál Riata"', *Northern Studies*, 38 (2004): 77–96.

Fraser, J. E., 'Strangers on the Clyde: Cenél Comgaill, Clyde Rock and the bishops of Kingarth', *Innes Review*, 56 (2005): 102–20.

Fraser, J. E., 'Picts in the west in the 670s? Some thoughts on AU 673.3 and AU 676.3', *Journal of Scottish Name Studies*, 1 (2007), 144–8.

Fraser, J. E., 'From ancient Scythia to *The Problem of the Picts*: thoughts on the quest for Pictish origins', in S. T. J. Driscoll, J. Geddes and M. Hall (eds), *Pictish Progress: New Studies on Northern Britain in the Early Middle Ages* (Leiden and Boston, MA, 2011), pp. 15–43.

Geary, P., *The Myth of Nations: The Medieval Origins of Europe* (Princeton, NJ, 2002).

Green, M. A., *Dying for the Gods: Human Sacrifice in Iron Age and Roman Europe* (Stroud, 2001).

Haggart, C., 'The *Céli Dé* and the early medieval Irish church: a reassessment', *Studia Hibernica*, 34 (2007): 17–62.

Halsall, G. (ed.), *Violence and Society in the Early Medieval West* (Woodbridge, 1998).

Halsall, G., *Barbarian Migrations and the Roman West, 376–568* (Cambridge, 2007).

Halsall, G., *Worlds of Arthur: Facts and Fictions of the Dark Ages* (Oxford, 2013).

Henderson, G. and I. Henderson, *The Art of the Picts: Sculpture and Metalwork in Early Medieval Scotland* (London, 2004).

Henry, D. (ed.), *The Worm, the Germ and the Thorn: Pictish and Related Studies Presented to Isabel Henderson* (Balgavies, 1999).

Herbert, M., *Iona, Kells and Derry: The History and Hagiography of the Monastic Familia of Columba* (Oxford, 1988).

*Hood, A., *St Patrick, his Writings and Muirchú's Life* (London, 1978).

Hudson, B. T., 'Kings and Church in early Scotland', *Scottish Historical Review*, 73 (1994): 145–70.

Hudson, B. T., *Viking Pirates and Christian Princes: Dynasty and Empire in the North Atlantic* (New York, 2005).

Hunter, F., *Beyond the Edge of the Empire: Caledonians, Picts and Romans* (Rosemarkie, 2007).

James, A. G., 'Dating Brittonic place-names in southern Scotland and Cumbria', *Journal of Scottish Name Studies*, 5 (2011): 57–114.

James, E., 'Burial and status in the early medieval West', *Transactions of the Royal Historical Society*, 39 (1989): 23–40.

Jennings, A., 'Iona and the Vikings: survival and continuity', *Northern Studies*, 33 (1998): 37–54.

Jennings, A., 'Norse place-names of Kintyre', in J. Adams and K. Holman (eds), *Scandinavia and Europe 800–1350* (Turnhout, 2004), pp. 109–19.

Jennings, A. and A. Kruse, 'One coast – three peoples: names and ethnicity in the Scottish west during the early Viking period', in Alex Woolf (ed.), *Scandinavian Scotland: Twenty Years After* (St Andrews, 2009), pp. 75–102.

Jones, H. R. (1996), 'A consideration of Pictish names', available at: http://heatherrosejones.com/names/pictish.

Kelly, F., *Early Irish Farming* (Dublin, 1997).

Kelly, F., *A Guide to Early Irish Law* (Dublin, 1998).

Koch, J., *The* Gododdin *of Aneirin: text and context from Dark-Age North Britain* (Cardiff and Andover, MA, 1997).

Koch, J., 'The place of Y *Gododdin* in the history of Scotland', in *Celtic Connections: Proceedings of the Tenth International Congress of Celtic Studies*, vol. 1 (East Linton, 1999), pp. 199–210.

Koch, J., 'Waiting for Gododdin: thoughts on Taliesin and Iudic Hael, Catraeth and unripe time in Celtic studies', in A. Woolf (ed.), *Beyond the Gododdin* (St Andrews, 2013), pp. 177–204.

Kyle, D. G, *Spectacles of Death in Ancient Rome* (London, 1998).

Lane, A. and E. Campbell, *Dunadd: An Early Dalriadic Capital* (Oxford, 2000).

Lowe, C., *Angels, Fools and Tyrants: Britons and Anglo-Saxons in Southern Scotland* (Edinburgh, 1999).

*Mac Airt, S. and G. MacNiocaill (eds), *The Annals of Ulster to* AD *1131* (Dublin, 1983).

*McClure, J. and R. Collins (eds), *Bede: The Ecclesiastical History of the English People* (Oxford, 1994).

McCone, K., *Pagan Past and Christian Present* (Maynooth, 1990).

McManus, D., *A Guide to Ogam* (Maynooth, 1991)

McNeill, P. G. B. and H. L. MacQueen (eds), *Atlas of Scottish History to 1707* (Edinburgh 1996).

Macquarrie, A., 'The kings of Strathclyde, *c.* 400–1018', in A. Grant and K. Stringer (eds), *Medieval Scotland: Crown, Lordship and Community* (Edinburgh, 1993), pp. 1–19.

Mann, J. C., 'A history of the Antonine Wall: a reappraisal', *Proceedings of the Society of Antiquaries of Scotland*, 118 (1988): 131–7.

*Márkus, G., *Adomnán's Law of the Innocents – Cáin Adomnáin: A Seventh-century Law for the Protection of Non-combatants* (Kilmartin, 2008).

Márkus, G., 'Dewars and relics in Scotland: some clarifications and questions', *Innes Review*, 60 (2009): 95–144.

Márkus, G., 'From *Goill* to *Gall-Ghàidheil*: place-names and Scandinavian settlement in Bute', in A. Ritchie (ed.), *Historic Bute: Land and People* (Edinburgh, 2012), pp. 1–16.

Márkus, G., *The Place-Names of Bute* (Donington, 2012).

*Meehan, D. (ed.), *Adamnan's De Locis Sanctis* (Dublin, 1983).

Ó Carragáin, É. and T. Ó Carragáin, 'Singing in the rain in Hinba: archaeology and liturgical fictions, ancient and modern', in E. Mullins and D. Scully (eds), *Listen, O Isles, unto me: Studies in Medieval Word and Image in Honour of Jennifer O'Reilly* (Cork, 2011), pp. 204–18.

Ó Corráin, D., 'The Vikings in Scotland and Ireland in the ninth century', *Peritia*, 12 (1998): 296–339.

Ó Corráin, D., L. Breatnach and A. Breen, 'The laws of the Irish', *Peritia*, 3 (1984): 382–438.

*Ogilvie, R. M. and J. Richmond (eds), *Cornelii Taciti: De Vita Agricolae* (Oxford, 1967).

Overbey, K. E., *Sacral Geographies: Saints, Shrines and Territory in Medieval Ireland* (Turnhout, 2012).

Parsons, D., 'Sabrina in the thorns: place-names as evidence for British and Latin in Roman Britain', *Transactions of the Philological Society*, 109 (2011): 113–37.

Petts, D., *Christianity in Roman Britain* (Stroud, 2003).

Petts, D., *Pagan and Christian: Religious Change in Early Medieval Europe* (London, 2011).

Petts, D. and S. Turner, eds, *Early Medieval Northumbria* (Turnhout, 2011).

Proudfoot, E., 'The Hallow Hill and the origins of Christianity in eastern Scotland', in B. Crawford (ed.), *Conversion and Christianity in the North Sea World* (St Andrews, 1998), pp. 57–73.

*Reeves, W., *The Culdees of the British Islands as they Appear in History with an Appendix of Evidences* (Dublin, 1864, repr. Felinfach, 1994).

Rivet, A. L. F. and C. Smith, *The Place-Names of Roman Britain* (London, 1979).

Rhys, G., 'Approaching the Pictish language: historiography, early evidence and the question of Pritenic', unpublished thesis, University of Glasgow, 2015.

*Rolfe, J. C. (ed.), *Ammiannus Marcellinus, Res Gestae*, vol. III (London and Cambridge, MA, 1972).

Ross, A., *Pagan Celtic Britain: Studies in Iconography and Tradition* (London and New York, 1967).

Salway, P., *A History of Roman Britain* (Oxford, 1997).

Scheidel, W., 'The Roman slave supply', *Princeton/Stanford Working Papers in Classics*, (2007), available at: http://www.princeton.edu/~pswpc/pdfs/scheidel/050704.pdf.

Sellar, W. D. H., 'Celtic law and Scots law: survival and integration', *Scottish Studies*, 29 (1989): 1–28.

*Sharpe, R., *Adomnán of Iona: Life of St Columba* (London, 1995).

Sims-Williams, P., *The Celtic Inscriptions of Britain: Phonology and Chronology c. 400–1200* (London, 2003).

Smith, J., *Europe after Rome: A New Cultural History, 500–1000* (Oxford, 2005).

Smyth, A. P., *Warlords and Holy Men* (Edinburgh, 1984).

Stacey, R. C., *The Road to Judgement: From Custom to Court in Medieval Ireland and Wales* (Philadelphia, PA, 1994).

Stacey, R. C., *Dark Speech: The Performance of Law in Early Ireland* (Philadelphia, PA, 2007).

Stancliffe, C., *Bede and the Britons*, Whithorn Lecture (Whithorn, 2007).

*Stokes, W., *Félire Óengusso Céli Dé: the Martyrology of Oengus the Culdee* (London, 1905, repr.1984).

Swift, C., *Ogam Stones and the Earliest Irish Christians* (Maynooth, 1997).

Taylor, S., with G. Márkus, *The Place-Names of Fife*, 5 vols (Donington, 2006–12).

Veitch, K., 'The Columban Church in northern Britain, 664–717: a reassessment', *Proceedings of the Society of Antiquaries of Scotland*, 127 (1997): 627–47.

Veitch, K., 'The alliance between church and state in early medieval Alba', *Albion: A Quarterly Journal Concerned with British Studies*, 30 (1998): 193–220.

Walker, G. S. M. (ed.), *Sancti Columbani Opera* (Dublin, 1970).

*Wasserschleben, H. (ed.), *Die irische Kanonensammlung* (Leipzig, 1885).

Watson, W. J., *The History of the Celtic Place-Names of Scotland* (Edinburgh, 1926).

*Webb, J. F. and D. H. Farmer (eds), *The Age of Bede* (London, 1965).

*Winterbottom, M. (ed.), *Gildas: the Ruin of Britain and Other Documents* (London, 1978).

Wood, S., *The Proprietary Church in the Medieval West* (Oxford, 2006).

Wooding, J. M., R. Aist, T. O. Clancy and T. O'Loughlin (eds), *Adomnán of Iona: Theologian, Lawmaker, Peacemaker* (Dublin, 2010).

Woolf, A., 'Pictish matriliny reconsidered', *Innes Review*, 49 (1998): 147–67.

Woolf, A., 'Dun Nechtain, Fortriu and the geography of the Picts', *Scottish Historical Review*, 85 (2006): 182–201.

Woolf, A., 'Apartheid and economics in Anglo-Saxon England', in N. J. Higham (ed.), *The Britons in Anglo-Saxon England* (Woodbridge, 2007), pp. 115–29.

Woolf, A., *From Pictland to Alba, 789–1070* (Edinburgh, 2007).

Woolliscroft, D. J. and B. Hoffmann, *Rome's First Frontier: The Flavian Occupation of Northern Scotland* (Stroud, 2006).

USEFUL WEBSITES

CANMORE is a website of Historic Environment Scotland, offering access to a database of Scottish archaeology, available at: www.canmore.org.uk.

CELT (Corpus of Electronic Texts) at University College Cork offers original texts and translations of many important (mostly Irish) literary sources, available at:: www.ucc.ie/celt/index.html.

The 'Celtic Inscribed Stones Project' offers an online record of all the non-*ogham* carved stones in Celtic-speaking areas (Ireland,

Scotland, Wales, Brittany, Domnonia and the Isle of Man), available at: www.ucl.ac.uk/archaeology/cisp/database.

The Database of Scottish Hagiotoponyms records all Scottish place names that refer to a saint, available at: www.saintsplaces.gla.ac.uk.

Index